The False Claims Act and Government Contracts

The Intersection of Federal Government Contracts, Administrative Law, and Civil Fraud

SECOND EDITION

Christine Couvillon and Shelley R. Slade
EDITORS

AMERICAN BAR ASSOCIATION
Public Contract Law Section

Cover design by Amanda Fry/ABA Design

Printed in the United States of America.

27 26 25 24 23   5 4 3 2 1

A catalog record for this book is available from the Library of Congress.

TABLE OF CONTENTS

CHAPTER 2

CHAPTER 3

CHAPTER 9
Liability 113

CHAPTER 10

CHAPTER 11

CHAPTER 13

EDITORS AND CONTRIBUTORS

Editors

Christine Couvillon, Senior Attorney, IBM

Shelley R. Slade, Vogel, Slade & Goldstein

Contributors

Stephen D. Altman, Altman Dispute Resolution Services

Edward V. Arnold, Seyfarth Shaw

Suzanne Boehm, Perkins Coie

Renée Brooker, Tycko & Zavareei,

Alexander O. Canizares, Perkins Coie

Elizabeth J. Cappiello, Miller & Chevalier

David F. Dowd, Potomac Law Group

Cameron Edlefsen, Mayer Brown

Julia Fox, Perkins Coie

Laurence Freedman, Mintz

Terra Fulham, Covington & Burling

Leila George-Wheeler, Holland & Knight

Sara Gerber, Blank Rome

Susan Gouinlock, Wilbanks & Gouinlock

Lynne Halbrooks, Nichols Liu

Brian A. Hill, Miller & Chevalier

Amy C. Hoang, Seyfarth Shaw

Robert Huffman, Covington & Burling

Luke Levasseur, Mayer Brown

Marcia G. Madsen, Mayer Brown

Hamsa Mahendranathan, Constantine Cannon
Kevin J. Maynard, Wiley Rein
Dave Nadler, Blank Rome
Adam Proujansky, Blank Rome
Kara M. Sacilotto, Wiley Rein
Jennifer Short, Blank Rome
Elizabeth Soltan, Constantine Cannon
Mark B. Sweet, Wiley Rein
Rob Vogel, Vogel, Slade & Goldstein
Michael Wagner, Covington & Burling

EDITORS' INTRODUCTION

CHRISTINE COUVILLON AND SHELLEY SLADE[1]

The Civil False Claims Act, 31 U.S.C. § 3729 *et seq.*, ("FCA") was enacted in 1863 to address the submission of fraudulent claims for payment by unethical government contractors during the Civil War. Notably, the original FCA contained a qui tam provision, modeled on similar laws dating back to medieval England,[2] allowing private citizens, known as "relators," to file suit on behalf of the United States and receive a portion of the recovery as an award for their efforts. In 1986, Congress substantively amended the FCA to strengthen its liability provisions, bolster the government's investigative tools, and increase the protections and incentives for relators. After more than 100 years in which the FCA was infrequently used, the FCA became the government's primary civil enforcement weapon for combating fraud, waste, and abuse of federal funds. The FCA was substantively amended again in 2009 and 2010 to further strengthen its efficacy.

Today, the FCA is the United States' principal civil tool in its anti-fraud efforts. Litigation under the FCA that involves government contracts is a complicated dance involving the Department of Justice (DOJ), contracting agencies, contractors, and, frequently, relators who have availed themselves of the qui tam provisions of the FCA. In 2021, the government and relators collectively recovered more than $5.6 billion under the FCA.[3] While the overwhelming majority of these dollars are attributable to health care cases, more than $150 million was recovered in procurement fraud matters involving falsified pricing data, noncompliant goods and services, kickbacks, and other violations.

In this book, the authors explore the relationship between federal procurement and the FCA. The chapters describe the regulated nature of government contracting and the players in the policy and enforcement communities who regulate and

---

1. Christine Couvillon is Senior Attorney at IBM. Shelley R. Slade is a partner at Vogel, Slade & Goldstein. Ms. Couvillon and Ms. Slade acknowledge the substantial and valuable assistance of Sam Gould, a paralegal at Vogel, Slade & Goldstein, with all aspects of the editing process.

2. Charles Doyle, writing for the Congressional Research Service, *Qui Tam: The False Claims Act and Related Federal Statutes* (Apr. 26, 2021), https://sgp.fas.org/crs/misc/R40785.pdf.

3. https://www.justice.gov/opa/pr/justice-department-s-false-claims-act-settlements-and-judgments-exceed-56-billion-fiscal-year. U.S. DOJ included in its $5.6 billion figure a $2.8 billion allowed, unsubordinated, general unsecured bankruptcy claim agreed to by Purdue Pharma.

police government contracts. They also detail the complex processes for initiating, litigating, and resolving FCA actions, and how those processes interact with the equally complex processes of performing and closing out government contracts. In addition, they identify the substantive requirements and evolving evidentiary challenges of litigating an FCA case in a government contracts context. Finally, they highlight the various types of procurement fraud schemes that can create liability under the FCA and emerging enforcement trends. The authors intend this volume to serve as a desk book that can be used as a first stop for any inside, outside, government, or relator's counsel who face issues at the intersection of the FCA and federal government contracting.

CHAPTER 1

Varieties of Misconduct Risking FCA Liability

CHRISTINE COUVILLON AND SHELLEY R. SLADE[1]

I. Introduction

This chapter flags for the reader the key categories of government contractor and grantee misconduct that create a risk of False Claims Act (FCA) liability, summarizing some of the most pivotal legal authorities and noting press releases reflecting government enforcement priorities. This chapter is not meant to be an exhaustive collection of all categories of misconduct giving rise to FCA liability nor a collection of all relevant authorities. It is also not intended to provide detailed legal analysis of the theories of liability applicable to each category of misconduct; other chapters of this book address liability, defenses, and damages. Rather, this chapter is intended as a starting point for more in-depth research focused on the particulars of your case.

II. Bid Rigging

Bid rigging in government contracts involves potential bidders colluding to increase the ultimate price to the purchaser by, for example, (1) agreeing that one or more parties will refrain from bidding; (2) conspiring for one or more parties to submit non-winning bids; or (3) fixing bid prices artificially high, with the end result being that the government is denied the benefit of a truly competitive bidding process. Bid rigging is illegal under section 1 of the Sherman Antitrust Act, 5 U.S.C. In addition, the Procurement Integrity Act, 41 U.S.C. §§ 2101–2107, and its implementing rules prohibit contractors from soliciting or receiving nonpublic

1. Christine Couvillon is Senior Attorney at IBM. Shelley R. Slade is a partner at Vogel, Slade & Goldstein.

source selection or bid information before the award of the federal contract to which the information relates.[2] For the past 60 years, the courts have consistently ruled that FCA liability can arise from bid rigging under a fraudulent inducement theory of liability.[3] The seminal FCA bid-rigging case was *United States ex rel. Marcus v. Hess*.[4] In *Marcus*, the Supreme Court found the defendants liable under the FCA for having rigged their bids to provide electrical services for Public Works Authority (PWA) projects, ruling:

> The government's money would never have been placed in the joint fund for payment to respondents had its agents known the bids were collusive. By their conduct, the respondents thus caused the government to pay claims of the local sponsors in order that they might in turn pay respondents under contracts found to have been executed as the result of the fraudulent bidding. This fraud did not spend itself with the execution of the contract. Its taint entered into every swollen estimate which was the basic cause for payment of every dollar paid by the P.W.A. into the joint fund for the benefit of respondents. The initial fraudulent action and every step thereafter taken, pressed ever to the ultimate goal—payment of government money to persons who had caused it to be defrauded.[5]

The government remains committed to unearthing and prosecuting bid rigging in procurements. On November 5, 2019, the U.S. Department of Justice (DOJ) announced the formation of the Procurement Collusion Strike Force, a cross-agency initiative focusing "on deterring, detecting, investigating and prosecuting antitrust crimes, such as bid-rigging conspiracies and related fraudulent schemes, which undermine competition in government procurement, grant and program funding."[6] Evidencing this focus on the prosecution of bid rigging, in May 2022,

---

2. 41 U.S.C. § 2102(c); FAR 3-104-3(b); DFARS 203.1.

3. *See, e.g.*, Kellogg Brown & Root Servs., Inc. v. United States, 99 Fed. Cl. 488, 511 (2011) ("Fraud-in-the-inducement cases include claims involving collusive bidding, bid-rigging; contracts obtained due to false information, fraudulent pricing or inflated cost estimates; or false representations about the ability to perform"), *aff'd*, 728 F.3d 1348 (Fed. Cir. 2013); United States *ex rel.* Barko v. Halliburton Co., 241 F. Supp. 3d 37, 52 (D.D.C.), *aff'd*, 709 F. App'x 23 (D.C. Cir. 2017); United States *ex rel.* Blaum v. Triad Isotopes, Inc., 104 F. Supp. 3d 901, 913–15 (N.D. Ill. 2015); United States *ex rel.* McGee v. IBM Corp., 81 F. Supp. 3d 643, 663 (N.D. Ill. 2015); Miller v. Holzmann, 563 F. Supp. 2d 54, 78 (D.D.C. 2008), *aff'd in part, vacated in part, remanded sub nom.* United States *ex rel.* Miller v. Bill Harbert Int'l Constr., Inc., 608 F.3d 871 (D.C. Cir. 2010); United States v. Inc. Vill. of Island Park, 888 F. Supp. 419, 439 (E.D.N.Y. 1998); United States v. CFW Constr. Co., 649 F. Supp. 616, 618 (D.S.C. 1986); *see also* United States v. Dynamics Rsch. Corp., No. CIVA 03CV11965-NG, 2008 WL 886035, at *11 (D. Mass. Mar. 31, 2008) ("a claim is false under the FCA where it is the direct product of secret self-dealing or collusion, as in the bid-rigging cases").

4. 317 U.S. 537 (1943).

5. *Id.* at 543–44.

6. U.S. DOJ, *Justice Department Announces Procurement Collusion Strike Force* (Nov. 5, 2019), https://www.justice.gov/opa/pr/justice-department-announces-procurement-collusion-strike-force-coordinated-national-response.

DOJ announced that seven South Korean companies had agreed to pay $3.1 million to resolve FCA allegations that they engaged in big rigging in connection with U.S. Army Corps of Engineers contracts for construction and engineering services at U.S. military bases in South Korea.[7]

III. "Pay-to-Play"

A. Anti-Kickback Laws

The Federal Acquisition Regulation (FAR) implements the requirements of the federal Anti-Kickback Act (AKA)[8]—a law that prohibits kickbacks in public contracting—and incorporates these regulatory anti-kickback requirements in government contracts exceeding $150,000 in value.[9] The few cases to address the issue have held that kickbacks by government contractors and subcontractors can lead not only to AKA liability but also to FCA liability.[10] In June 2022, Kellogg Brown & Root Services, Inc. and three affiliates (KBR) paid $13.67 million to resolve qui tam allegations that they engaged in bid rigging and kickbacks in connection with KBR's subcontracts under a prime contract to provide logistics support for the U.S. Army in Iraq.[11]

A separate law, the federal, health care Anti-Kickback Statute (AKS),[12] penalizes kickbacks associated with goods and services paid for by Medicare, Medicaid,

7. U.S. DOJ, *Seven South Korean Companies Agree to Pay Approximately $3.1 Million to Settle Civil False Claims Act Allegations for Bid Rigging on U.S. Department of Defense Contracts* (May 18, 2022), https://www.justice.gov/opa/pr/seven-south-korean-companies-agree-pay-approximately-31-million-settle-civil-false-claims-act. Bid-rigging allegations were also resolved in the settlements announced in these recent DOJ press releases: U.S. DOJ, *KBR Defendants Agree to Settle Kickback and False Claims Allegations* (June 14, 2022), https://www.justice.gov/opa/pr/kbr-defendants-agree-settle-kickback-and-false-claims-allegations; U.S. DOJ, *Quantadyn Corporation and Owner Settle False Claims Act Allegations of Bribery to Obtain Government Contracts for Simulators* (Sept. 15, 2020), https://www.justice.gov/opa/pr/quantadyn-corporation-and-owner-settle-false-claims-act-allegations-bribery-obtain-government.

8. 41 U.S.C. §§ 8701 *et seq.*

9. *See* 48 C.F.R. § 52.203-7 (prohibits "[p]roviding or attempting to provide or offering to provide any kickback" or "[s]oliciting, accepting, or attempting to accept any kickback" in connection with any federal government contract or subcontract. It further proscribes "including, directly or indirectly, the amount of any kickback in the contract price charged by a prime Contractor to the United States."); 48 C.F.R. § 43.502-3.

10. *See, e.g.*, United States v. Kellogg Brown & Root Servs. Inc., No. 4:06-CV-04024, 2021 WL 2766396, at *2 (S.D. Tex. June 3, 2021) (permitting FCA claims based on AKA violations to proceed to trial); Morse Diesel Int'l, Inc. v. United States, 79 Fed. Cl. 116 (2007); United States *ex rel.* Campbell v. KIC Dev., LLC, No. EP-18-CV-193-KC, 2019 WL 6884485, at *8 *et seq.* (W.D. Tex. Dec. 10, 2019); United States v. Merck-Medco Managed Care, L.L.C., 336 F. Supp. 2d 430, 448–49 (E.D. Pa. 2004).

11. U.S. DOJ, *KBR Defendants Agree to Settle Kickback, supra* note 7.

12. 42 U.S.C. § 1320a-7b(b).

TRICARE, and other federal health care programs, as well as certain state health care programs.[13] In 2010, the Affordable Care Act (ACA)[14] amended the AKS to impose civil liability under the FCA when health care providers bill the government for "items or services resulting from" a violation of the AKS. Both before and after the ACA, courts frequently have allowed FCA cases based on AKS violations to proceed.[15]

B. The Stark Law

Violations of the Physician Self-Referral Law[16] may also create FCA liability.[17] Commonly referred to as the "Stark law" in recognition of Congressman Pete Stark's introduction of the original bill, this law prohibits physicians, with certain exceptions, from referring Medicare and Medicaid patients to receive certain, specified health care services from entities with which the physician or an immediate family member has a financial relationship. It also prohibits a person from billing Medicare or Medicaid for goods or services resulting from referrals prohibited by the

---

13. The law excludes the Federal Employees Health Benefits Plan from the definition of "federal health care program."

14. Patient Protection and Affordable Care Act, Pub. L. No. 111-148, 124 Stat. 119 (2010); *see* 42 U.S.C. § 1320a-b(g).

15. *See, e.g.*, United States *ex rel.* Travis v. Gilead Scis., Inc., No. CV 17-1183, 2022 WL 991382, at *8 (E.D. Pa. Apr. 1, 2022) ("A claim that is induced by bribery in violation of the AKS is inherently false or fraudulent for the purposes of applying the FCA."); United States *ex rel.* Bilotta v. Novartis Pharms. Corp., 50 F. Supp. 3d 497, 514–17 (S.D.N.Y. 2014); United States *ex rel.* Westmoreland v. Amgen, Inc., 812 F. Supp. 2d 39, 54 (D. Mass. 2011) (collecting cases and noting that "courts, without exception, agree that compliance with the Anti-Kickback Statute is a precondition of Medicare payment, such that liability under the False Claims Act can be predicated on a violation of the Anti-Kickback Statute"); United States *ex rel.* Pogue v. Diabetes Treatment Ctrs. of Am., 565 F. Supp. 2d 153, 159 (D.D.C. 2008) (noting that to hold that compliance with the Anti-Kickback Statute is not a precondition of Medicare payment would result in the government funding illegal kickbacks); United States *ex rel.* Bidani v. Lewis, 264 F. Supp. 2d 612, 616 (N.D. Ill. 2003) (holding that to reimburse a claimant "for supplies purchased illegally only because the claimant had the luck of not being caught and convicted in the first place . . . would put the government in the position of funding illegal kickbacks after the fact").

16. 42 U.S.C. §§ 1395nn and 1396b. Implementing regulations are found at 42 U.S.C. §§ 411.350–.389.

17. *See, e.g.*, United States *ex rel.* Thompson v. Columbia/HCA Healthcare Corp., 125 F.3d 899, 902–03 (5th Cir. 1997); United States *ex rel.* Bruno v. Schaeffer, 328 F. Supp. 3d 550, 557 (M.D. La. 2018); United States *ex rel.* Riedel v. Bos. Heart Diagnostics Corp., 332 F. Supp. 3d 48, 69–70 (D.D.C. 2018); United States *ex rel.* Bartlett v. Ashcroft, 39 F. Supp. 3d 656, 673 (W.D. Pa. 2014); Barker *ex rel.* United States v. Columbus Reg'l Healthcare Sys., Inc., 977 F. Supp. 2d 1341, 1344 (M.D. Ga. 2013); United States *ex rel.* Pogue v. Diabetes Treatment Ctrs. of Am., 565 F. Supp. 2d at 159 ("Legion other cases have held violations of . . . Stark can be pursued under the FCA, since they would influence the Government's decision of whether to reimburse Medicare claims.").

law. As one court has noted, "[i]n the healthcare context, two laws that often serve as FCA predicates are the AKS and Stark."[18]

C. Bribery and Gratuities Offered or Paid to Federal Officials

Federal law proscribes offering or paying bribes or gratuities to government employees and others acting on behalf of the federal government.[19] In addition, a federal statute specifically prohibits the use of appropriated, taxpayer funds to bribe public officials.[20] Government procurement contracts typically include FAR provisions that reflect these mandates,[21] along with a provision requiring contractors to take steps to prevent and disclose such payments.[22]

Violations of anti-bribery laws can serve as the basis for an FCA violation, at least where the bribes caused the government to enter into a contract that it otherwise would not have entered into or to pay out more than it would have otherwise.[23] For example, in September 2020, DOJ announced that QuantaDyn had agreed to enter a guilty plea and pay more than $37 million to resolve criminal and civil liability arising from the company's payment of bribes to a U.S. Air Force contracting officer in exchange for his agreement to provide QuantaDyn with sensitive procurement information regarding contracts for training simulators.[24]

IV. False Representations as to Cost and Pricing

A. In Support of a Claim

As a general matter, when a contractor knowingly submits false cost or pricing data to the government in support of a claim and the government determines the amount to pay the contractor based on this data, the contractor can face liability under the FCA. In such circumstances, the contractor's representations as to

18. United States *ex rel.* Parikh v. Citizens Med. Ctr., 977 F. Supp. 2d 654, 662 (S.D. Tex. 2013), *aff'd sub nom.* United States *ex rel.* Parikh v. Brown, 762 F.3d 461 (5th Cir. 2014), *opinion withdrawn and superseded on reh'g*, 587 F. App'x 123 (5th Cir. 2014), *withdrawn from bound volume* (Oct. 1, 2014), *and aff'd sub nom.* United States *ex rel.* Parikh v. Brown, 587 F. App'x 123 (5th Cir. 2014).

19. *See* 18 U.S.C. § 201.

20. *See* 31 U.S.C. § 1352.

21. *See, e.g.*, 48 C.F.R §§ 52.203-3 (Gratuities) and 52-203.12 (Limitation on Payments to Influence Certain Federal Transactions).

22. FAR 52.203-13, the "Contractor Code of Business Ethics and Conduct." 48 C.F.R. § 52.203-13.

23. *See, e.g.*, United States *ex rel.* Marsteller v. Tilton, 556 F. Supp. 3d 1291, 1306–07 (N.D. Ala. 2021); Campbell v. KIC, 2019 WL 6884485; United States *ex rel.* Reeves v. Mercer Transp. Co., Inc., 253 F. Supp. 3d 1242, 1253–54 (M.D. Ga. 2017) (citing Kellogg Brown & Root Servs., Inc. v. United States, 99 Fed. Cl. 488, 513 (2011), *aff'd*, 728 F.3d 1348 (Fed. Cir. 2013) and United States v. Shaw, 725 F. Supp. 896, 900 (S.D. Miss. 1989)).

24. U.S. DOJ, *Quantadyn Corporation and Owner Settle*, *supra* note 7.

costs and pricing go to the "essence of the bargain" between the contractor and the government and are necessarily material to the government's payment decisions.[25] Multiple courts have held that misrepresentations as to costs or pricing submitted in support of claims are material to and result in false claims.[26]

B. During Contract Negotiations

A person subject to the Truth in Negotiations Act (TINA)[27] or other requirements to disclose cost or pricing data during contract negotiations can face FCA liability if they knowingly misrepresent or omit material cost or pricing information and the government is thereby induced to enter into a contract to which it otherwise might not have agreed.[28] Similarly, those who are subject to Multiple Award Schedule

25. *See* 31 U.S.C. § 3729(a)(1)(B) (imposing liability on anyone who "knowingly makes, uses, or causes to be made or used, a false record or statement *material* to a false or fraudulent claim") (emphasis added); Universal Health Servs., Inc. v. United States *ex rel.* Escobar, 579 U.S. 176, 193 n.5 (2016) (citing Junius Constr. Co. v. Cohen, 257 N.Y. 393, 400, 178 N.E. 672, 674 (1931) ("a misrepresentation is material if it 'went to the very essence of the bargain'")).

26. *See, e.g.*, United States *ex rel.* Grubea v. Rosicki, Rosicki & Assocs., P.C., 318 F. Supp. 3d 680, 701 (S.D.N.Y. 2018) (misrepresentations by loan servicers concerning necessary and reasonable foreclosure expenses); United States v. Pub. Warehousing Co. K.S.C., No. 1:05-CV-2968-TWT, 2017 WL 1021745, at *6–*7 (N.D. Ga. Mar. 16, 2017) (overcharges and failure to pass on discounts by contractor supplying food and other subsistence items to U.S. military in the Middle East); United States v. DynCorp Int'l, LLC, 253 F. Supp. 3d 89, 101–02 (D.D.C. 2017) (misrepresentations of reasonable and necessary costs by Department of State contractor providing lodging, security and transportation to Iraqi civilian police force); *see also* United States *ex rel.* Garbe v. Kmart Corp., 824 F.3d 632, 639 (7th Cir. 2016) (overstatements of "usual and customary charges" of prescription drugs when seeking Medicare and Medicaid reimbursement); Mass. v. Mylan Labs., 608 F. Supp. 2d 127, 156 (D. Mass. 2008) (misrepresentations by pharmaceutical manufacturers of average wholesale price to the state of Massachusetts supporting claims under Massachusetts state false claims law)); United States *ex rel.* Costa v. Baker & Taylor, Inc., No. C-95-1825-VRW, 1998 WL 230979, at *9 (N.D. Cal. Mar. 20, 1998) (violations of "most favored customer" clause by book distributor selling books to libraries funded with federal grant money).

27. 10 U.S.C. § 2306a.

28. *See, e.g.*, USN4U, LLC v. Wolf Creek Fed. Servs, Inc., 34 F.4th 507 (6th Cir. 2022) (inflated cost estimates in bid to NASA for facilities maintenance contract); Marsteller v. Tilton, 880 F.3d 1302, 1314–15 (11th Cir. 2018) (incomplete TINA-required pricing data); Hooper v. Lockheed Martin Corp., 688 F.3d 1037, 1049 (9th Cir. 2012) (fraudulent underbidding); United States v. United Techs. Corp., 626 F.3d 313, 319–20 (6th Cir. 2010), *as amended* (Jan. 24, 2011) (false statements as to derivation of TINA-required cost estimates); United States *ex rel.* Campbell v. KIC Dev., LLC, No. EP-18-CV-193-KC, 2019 WL 6884485, at *12 (W.D. Tex. Dec. 10, 2019) (inflated costs and misstated profit structure in bid documents submitted to U.S. Army Corps of Engineers); United States *ex rel.* Woodlee v. Sci. Applications Int'l Corp., No. SA-02-CA-028-WWJ, 2005 WL 729684, at *2–*3 (W.D. Tex. Feb. 4, 2005) (omission of material information concerning derivation of TINA-required cost data). *Cf.* United States *ex rel.* Watkins v. KBR, Inc., 106 F. Supp. 3d 946, 957 (C.D. Ill. 2015) (finding no FCA liability based on any TINA violations prior to contract award because, inter alia, "there is

(MAS) requirements[29] to disclose commercial pricing practices during contract negotiations and over the life of the contract can face FCA liability if they knowingly misrepresent their commercial pricing and thereby fraudulently induce the government to award them a contract or continue paying the contractual price.[30]

When the government is fraudulently induced to award a contract or to continue with contractual pricing based on misrepresentations of the contractor's costs or pricing, every claim under the fraudulently obtained contract or pricing structure will be deemed a false claim regardless of whether the claim contains an express false statement.[31]

V. Nonconforming Products and Services

If a contractor knowingly violates "core" requirements of a government contract and bills for specific products or services that don't meet contract specifications, the contractor faces potential FCA liability.[32] This is the case regardless of whether the contractor *expressly* certified compliance with the violated contractual requirement. Implicit misrepresentations of compliance are actionable.[33]

---

no allegation here that the LOGCAP III or any of its Task Orders were procured by fraud such that invoices for payment under them are tainted").

29. The MAS program is authorized under title III of the Federal Property and Administrative Services Act of 1949, 41 U.S.C. §§ 251 *et seq.*, and title 40, 40 U.S.C. § 501. Implementing regulations are found within the FAR, 48 C.F.R. §§ 8.401 *et seq.* The General Services Administration administers the MAS program.

30. *See, e.g.*, United States *ex rel.* Morsell v. Symantec Corp., 471 F. Supp. 3d 257, 303 (D.D.C. 2020) (inaccurate and incomplete MAS-required information both pre-contract award and during the course of the contract); United States *ex rel.* Shemesh v. CA, Inc., 89 F. Supp. 3d 36, 51 (D.D.C. 2015) (inaccurate and incomplete MAS-required information on Commercial Sales Practices form); United States *ex rel.* Frascella v. Oracle Corp., 751 F. Supp. 2d 842, 855–56 (E.D. Va. 2010) (failure to accurately disclose commercial pricing as required by price reduction clause).

31. This "fraud-in-the-inducement" theory of FCA liability is based on a line of judicial decisions holding that liability attaches to each claim submitted to the government under a contract obtained through false statements or fraudulent conduct, regardless of whether the claims themselves contain false statements. *See* United States *ex rel.* Marcus v. Hess, 317 U.S. 537, 543–44 (1943); Veridyne Corp. v. United States, 758 F.3d 1371, 1379–80 (Fed. Cir. 2014); United States *ex rel.* Hendow v. Univ. of Phoenix, 461 F.3d 1166, 1173 (9th Cir. 2006); Harrison v. Westinghouse Savannah River Co., 176 F.3d 776, 787–88 (4th Cir. 1999) (surveying the case law on fraud-in-the-inducement FCA liability); S. Rep. No. 99–345, at *9 (1986), 1986 U.S.C.C.A.N. 5266, 5274 ("each and every claim submitted under a contract, loan guarantee, or other agreement which was originally obtained by means of false statements or other corrupt or fraudulent conduct, or in violation of any statute or applicable regulation, constitutes a false claim").

32. United States v. Triple Canopy, Inc., 857 F.3d 174, 178 (4th Cir. 2017) (claims for services of armed guards who had failed required marksmanship requirements).

33. Universal Health Servs., Inc. v. United States *ex rel.* Escobar, 579 U.S. 176, 188 (2016) ("half-truths—representations that state the truth only so far as it goes, while omitting critical qualifying information—can be actionable misrepresentations").

Under long-standing precedent, such conduct also risks FCA liability regardless of whether the delivered goods perform at a level comparable to the promised goods or the delivered services are of the same quality as the promised services. As the Fifth Circuit has explained:

> [T]he mere fact that the item supplied under contract is as good as the one contracted for does not relieve defendants of liability if it can be shown that they attempted to deceive the government agency.[34]

VI. Violations of Contractual Requirements Other Than Product Specifications

A contractor risks FCA liability if they knowingly violate a contractual requirement that is *material* to the deal between the contractor and the government regardless of whether the contractual violation relates to the price, nature, or quality of the delivered good or service. This is true for requirements that are incorporated by reference in the contract, by, for example, citation of a FAR provision or other regulation, as well as requirements that are expressly spelled out.

However, if a contractor's violations are not obviously related to important elements of the contract, an FCA case premised on such violations can be more tenuous. Questions about the materiality of compliance with the regulation to the government's decision to pay may feature prominently in these cases. Courts often observe that the FCA is not intended to punish noncompliance with every regulation.[35] Indeed, some courts, often disagreeing with other courts, have ruled that contractual provisions that one might expect to provide a basis for FCA liability—for instance, OSHA regulations,[36] Title IX or education law violations,[37] and

34. United States v. Aerodex, Inc., 469 F.2d 1003, 1007 (5th Cir. 1972) (substitution and mislabeling of different aircraft engine bearings than those ordered by the U.S. Navy). *See also* United States *ex rel.* Campie v. Gilead Sciences, Inc., 862 F.3d 890, 900 (9th Cir. 2017) (failure to comply with FDA rules in selling antiretroviral drugs); United States *ex rel.* Compton v. Midwest Specialties, Inc., 142 F.3d 296, 304 (6th Cir. 1998) (failure to conduct required quality assurance testing on jeep brake shoes).

35. *E.g.*, *Escobar*, 579 U.S. at 194 ("The materiality standard is demanding. The False Claims Act is not 'an all-purpose antifraud statute,' or a vehicle for punishing garden-variety breaches of contract or regulatory violations.").

36. United States and State of Tex. *ex rel.* Simms v. Austin Radiological Ass'n., No. A-10-CV-914-LY, 2012 WL 12850250, at *7 (W.D. Tex. Aug. 29, 2012) (finding whistleblower actions "with respect to a potential OSHA violation . . . are not protected conduct under the False Claims Act, as health-code violations could not lead to a viable false claim").

37. United States *ex rel.* Hopper v. Anton, 91 F.3d 1261, 1266–67 (9th Cir. 1996) (finding no viable cause of action under the FCA for false statements related to California's receipt of federal special education funding). One case indicates that title IX and the FCA may combine to create a viable theory of liability under the right circumstances. In *Christian Employers Alliance v. U.S. Equal Opportunity Comm'n*, No. 1:21-cv-195, 2022 WL 1573689 (D.N.D. May 16, 2022), an organization of

International Traffic in Arms Regulation (ITAR) violations[38]—are not a viable basis for an FCA action.

A. Domestic Sourcing Requirements

With certain exceptions,[39] the Buy American Act (BAA)[40] and the Trade Agreements Act (TAA)[41] collectively require that, whenever the contract amount is above a micro-threshold (typically $10,000), goods sold to the government for public use in the United States must be sourced either domestically or from certain designated countries with which the United States has trade agreements. In addition, the Berry Act imposes unique domestic sourcing requirements on DOD procurements of specialty metals, food, clothing, tents, certain fabrics and fibers, hand or measuring tools, stainless steel flatware, and dinnerware; and a number of other domestic content requirements apply in specific circumstances.[42] A contractor who knowingly violates domestic content provisions in its contract with the government can face FCA liability.[43]

---

religious employers and universities sued in opposition to the Biden administration's reinstatement of a 2016 rule defining discrimination on the basis of sex to include refusal to pay for gender transition care within their healthcare plans. The rule made no exceptions for religious organizations beyond RFRA. The Court granted the preliminary injunction, finding that under the rule, Plaintiffs must either violate "sincerely held religious beliefs or face monetary losses, fines, and even civil liabilities" and debarment as discriminatory institutions under title IX and the FCA. *Id.* at *6–8.

38. United States *ex rel.* McGrath v. Microsemi Corp., 140 F. Supp. 3d 885, 902 (D. Ariz. 2015), *aff'd*, 690 F. App'x 551 (9th Cir. 2017) ("Turning to the narrower issue of whether compliance with ITAR is a condition of payment, the Court finds that it is not.").

39. Exceptions include when the head of the procuring agency determines sourcing from the United States or the designated countries would be contrary to the public interest or involve an unreasonable cost, or that insufficient supplies are available from domestic and designated-country sources.

40. 41 U.S.C. §§ 8302 *et seq.*, which provides, in pertinent part:

> Only unmanufactured articles, materials, and supplies that have been mined or produced in the United States, and only manufactured articles, materials, and supplies that have been manufactured in the United States substantially all from articles, materials, or supplies mined, produced, or manufactured in the United States, shall be acquired for public use unless the head of the Federal agency concerned determines their acquisition to be inconsistent with the public interest, their cost to be unreasonable, or that the articles, materials, or supplies of the class or kind to be used, or the articles, materials, or supplies from which they are manufactured, are not mined, produced, or manufactured in the United States in sufficient and reasonably available commercial quantities and of a satisfactory quality.

41 U.S.C.A. § 8302(a).

41. 19 U.S.C. §§ 2501 *et seq.*

42. *See* 10 U.S.C. §§ 1862–1863.

43. *See, e.g.*, United States v. Rule Indus., Inc., 878 F.2d 535 (1st Cir. 1989); United States *ex rel.* Medina v. Stryker Orthopaedics, No. CV 16-2583, 2022 WL 522788 (D.N.J. Feb. 22, 2022); United

B. Cybersecurity Rules

DOJ's cybersecurity fraud initiative, the rapidly evolving landscape of government agency cybersecurity rules, and the meteoric explosion of new hacking methods and innovative cybersecurity technologies to counter these threats pose a serious risk to government contractors who fail to stay on top of requirements. In November 2021, DOJ indicated that it considers compliance with cybersecurity rules of paramount importance, announcing a Civil Cybersecurity Initiative that will use the FCA to pursue government contractors who have committed cybersecurity fraud.[44] This FCA initiative is focused on the following types of misconduct if committed "knowingly" and involving "material" breaches of standards:

- The failure to comply with statutory, regulatory, or contractual cybersecurity standards governing the procurement of information technology products or services;
- Misrepresentations of cybersecurity practices regardless of whether the procurement is for IT products or services; and,
- Failure to timely report a suspected breach of cybersecurity requirements.

In March 2022, DOJ announced the first cybersecurity fraud settlement reached since it launched this initiative. To resolve qui tam allegations[45] that Comprehensive Health Services, LLC, among other things, violated contractual requirements to disclose to the State Department and Air Force that it had not kept patient records exclusively on secure electronic medical records systems at government-run health care facilities in Iraq and Afghanistan, the company agreed to pay $930,000.[46] Several months later, a second such settlement followed with Aerojet Rocketdyne, a supplier of propulsion and power systems for space vehicles, on the

---

States *ex rel.* Kress v. Masonry Sols. Int'l, Inc., No. CIV.A. 12-2380, 2015 WL 3604760, at *4 (E.D. La. June 8, 2015); United States *ex rel.* Scott v. Actus Lend Lease, No. CV0807940RGKSSX, 2011 WL 13177635, at *4 (C.D. Cal. Apr. 22, 2011).

44. U.S. DOJ, *Deputy Attorney General Lisa O. Monaco Announces New Civil Cyber-Fraud Initiative* (Oct. 6, 2021), https://www.justice.gov/opa/pr/deputy-attorney-general-lisa-o-monaco-announces-new-civil-cyber-fraud-initiative.

45. *See* United States *ex rel.* Lawler v. Comprehensive Health Servs., Inc. et al., Case No. 20-cv-698, Dkt. 1, Complaint (E.D.N.Y. May 10, 2019), and United States *ex rel.* Watkins et al. v. CHS Middle East, LLC, Case No. 17-cv-4319, Dkt. 1, Complaint (E.D.N.Y. July 21, 2017).

46. U.S. DOJ, *Medical Services Contractor pays $930,000 to Settle False Claims Act Allegations Relating to Medical Service Contracts at State Department and Air Force Facilities in Iraq and Afghanistan* (Mar. 8, 2022), https://www.justice.gov/opa/pr/medical-services-contractor-pays-930000-settle-false-claims-act-allegations-relating-medical.

second day of trial agreeing to pay $9 million to resolve qui tam allegations that it misrepresented its compliance with contractual cybersecurity requirements.[47]

In ruling on whether violations of a particular cybersecurity requirement give rise to FCA liability, the key questions for the courts likely will be the clarity of the standard, the magnitude of the risk, any actual harm resulting from the violation, and the materiality of compliance to the government's decision on payment. One of the few courts to date to address legal issues in a cybersecurity FCA case held that the materiality of the cybersecurity standard could not be decided as a matter of law, but rather was a question for the jury.[48]

C. Environmental Rules

Contractors have been found liable for implicit false claims when they bill for goods or services made or provided in violation of contractual, environmental provisions deemed material to government payment.[49]

D. Conflict of Interest Rules

FCA liability can arise from both express and implicit false certifications of compliance with organizational conflict of interest (OCI) rules imposed by FAR subpart 9.5 and incorporated in many government contracts.

---

47. U.S. DOJ, *Aerojet Rocketdyne Agrees to Pay $9 Million to Resolve False Claims Act Allegations of Cybersecurity Violations in Federal Government Contracts* (July 8, 2022), https://www.justice.gov/opa/pr/aerojet-rocketdyne-agrees-pay-9-million-resolve-false-claims-act-allegations-cybersecurity.

48. *See* United States *ex rel.* Markus v. Aerojet Rocketdyne Holdings, Inc., No. 2:15-CV-02245 WBS AC, 2022 WL 297093, at *7 (E.D. Cal. Feb. 1, 2022).

49. *See, e.g.*, Shaw v. AAA Eng'g & Drafting, Inc., 213 F.3d 519, 531 (10th Cir. 2000) (because defendant "was being paid not only for photography services but also for environmental compliance, its false implied certification of compliance with the contract's silver recovery requirement gives rise to liability under the FCA"); United States *ex rel.* Holder v. Special Devices, Inc., 296 F. Supp. 2d 1167, 1176 (C.D. Cal. 2003) ("Defendant SDI may be liable under the FCA for failure to comply with federal [environmental and health and safety] regulations, whether or not affirmative certification of compliance was required."); Pickens v. Kanawha River Towing, 916 F. Supp. 702, 708 (S.D. Ohio 1996) (denying motion to dismiss reverse false claims count alleging violations of contractual Clean Water Act provisions by tugboat operators hired to repair river dam and lock); United States *ex rel.* Fallon v. Accudyne Corp., 880 F. Supp. 636, 638 (W.D. Wis. 1995) (denying motion to dismiss qui tam alleging that "the contracts expressly required compliance with environmental regulations and that defendant knowingly failed to comply with such regulations and falsely certified that it had so complied in order to induce payments under the contracts"); United States *ex rel.* Stevens v. McGinnis, Inc., No. C-1-93-442, 1994 WL 799421, at *7 (S.D. Ohio Oct. 26, 1994) ("Violations of the reporting requirements of the Clean Water Act which arguably are misrepresentations to the Government give rise to liability under 31 U.S.C. § 3729(a)(7) of the False Claims Act.").

Thus, in *United States ex rel. Harrison v. Westinghouse Savannah River Co.*,[50] the court of appeals affirmed a district court ruling that an express certification of OCI compliance was material to the government's award, noting that the winning subcontractor "would have been disqualified from bidding on the subcontract had it not provided a no-OCI certification," and the false certification had "undermined the integrity of the procurement system," because the certification ensures that "all government contracts are bid fairly."[51]

And, in *United States v. Science Applications International Corp.* (SAIC),[52] the D.C. Circuit upheld the jury verdict finding SAIC liable under the FCA for violations of OCI contractual requirements despite the lack of an express certification, ruling that compliance with the OCI provision was material to payment because "[n]umerous witness[es] from both the NRC [Nuclear Regulatory Commission] and SAIC testified that the [organizational conflict of interest] obligations in SAIC's contracts with the NRC were important to the overall purpose of the contract."[53] Accordingly, per the court, SAIC's claims could give rise to liability under the FCA, because they implicitly and inaccurately certified compliance with this material requirement.[54]

E. Service Contract Act and Davis-Bacon Minimum Wage Requirements

Courts generally have permitted FCA cases alleging violations of the McNamara-O'Hara Service Contract Act of 1965,[55] 41 U.S.C. §§ 351 *et seq.*, or the Davis-Bacon Act of 1931,[56] 40 U.S.C. §§ 3141–3148, to proceed into litigation.[57] Moreover, two

50. 352 F.3d 908 (4th Cir. 2003).

51. *Id.* at 916.

52. 626 F.3d 1257 (D.C. Cir. 2010).

53. *Id.* at 1271.

54. *Id.* at 1267–71.

55. The McNamara-O'Hara Service Contract Act of 1965 requires government prime contractors and subcontractors to pay service employees minimum wages and benefits. For contracts in excess of $2,500, wages and benefits must be no less than the locally prevailing wages and benefits, as determined by the Department of Labor (DOL), or those set in a predecessor contractor's collective bargaining agreement. The act also requires contractors to pay at least the federal minimum wage for contracts at or below $2,500 in value, and to pay overtime to some employees for contracts greater than $100,000.

56. The Davis-Bacon Act of 1931 requires contractors and subcontractors on federally funded or assisted public construction contracts in excess of $2,000 to pay laborers and mechanics the locally prevailing wage and benefits, as defined by the DOL.

57. *See, e.g.*, United States *ex rel.* Plumbers & Steamfitters Local Union No. 38 v. C.W. Roen Const. Co., 183 F.3d 1088, 1092 (9th Cir. 1999) ("We have no doubt . . . that a false certification that workers have been paid at the legally required wage rate may give rise to liability under the FCA"); United States *ex rel.* Sutton v. Double Day Off. Servs., Inc., 121 F.3d 531, 534 (9th Cir. 1997) ("Because Sutton's qui tam claim under the FCA is based on different actions and for different damages than

courts of appeals have expressly ruled that payroll certifications made to show Davis-Bacon Act compliance are material to government payment.[58]

VII. Customs Duties and Tariffs

Those who knowingly evade customs duties or tariffs or conspire to do so risk liability under the FCA's so-called "reverse false claims provision," 31 U.S.C. § 3729(a)(1)(G), or the FCA's conspiracy provision, 31 U.S.C. § 3729(a)(1)(C).[59] In such circumstances, the person "need not have made any express statement to the Government to give rise to reverse false claims liability"; the knowing avoidance of the duties or tariffs alone is sufficient.[60] Moreover, a person may be liable even when the obligation to pay a customs duty arises only after and because of the person's false statement on customs forms, because Congress broadly defined the

---

a claim under the SCA [Service Contract Act] would be, his suit is not barred by the SCA's bar on private rights of action"); United States *ex rel.* Int'l Bd. of Elec. Workers Loc. Union No. 98 v. Fairfield Co., 438 F. Supp. 3d 348, 398 (E.D. Pa. 2020) (finding liability under FCA based on false certification of Davis-Bacon compliance), *aff'd*, 5 F.4th 315 (3d Cir. 2021); United States *ex rel.* Sheet Metal Workers Int'l Ass'n, Loc. Union No. 20 v. Horning Invs., LLC, No. 1:12-CV-00830-JMS, 2013 WL 5503327, at *5–*6 (S.D. Ind. Oct. 1, 2013) (rejecting argument that DOL has primary jurisdiction over claims, finding FCA violations alleged with particularity and denying defendants' motion to dismiss); United States *ex rel.* Head v. Kane Co., 798 F. Supp. 2d 186 (D.D.C. 2011) (finding plaintiffs adequately alleged fraudulent inducement, false certification, and materiality, and denying motions to dismiss); United States *ex rel.* Rueter v. Sparks, 939 F. Supp. 636, 638 (C.D. Ill. 1996), *aff'd sub nom.* United States *ex rel.* Ruetter v. Sparks, 111 F.3d 133 (7th Cir. 1997) (court permitted action to proceed to bench trial but dismisses case due to lack of requisite scienter); United States v. Greenberg, 237 F. Supp. 439, 440–41, 443 (S.D.N.Y. 1965) (finding FCA liability where "the wages certified to in these reports were higher than the wages actually paid"); *but see* United States *ex rel.* Windsor v. DynCorp, Inc., 895 F. Supp. 844, 850–52 (E.D. Va. 1995) (finding contractor's failure to provide weekly payroll reports as required under Davis-Bacon was not a basis for an FCA claim, because the statute required the DOL to make a determination on whether worker classification was compliant).

58. *See* United States *ex rel.* Int'l Bd. of Elec. Workers Loc. Union No. 98 v. Fairfield Co., 5 F.4th 315, 342–47 (3d Cir. 2021) (compliance with Davis-Bacon Act goes to the "essence of the bargain"); United States *ex rel.* Wall v. Circle C Constr., L.L.C., 697 F.3d 345, 357 (6th Cir. 2012). *Cf.* United States *ex rel.* Sorenson v. Wadsworth Bros. Constr. Co., Inc., No. 21-4005, 2022 WL 4112781, at *6–*7 (10th Cir. Sept. 9, 2022) (affirming district court's finding that relator's complaint, which failed to specify the amount of the underpayments or how DOL handles false certifications of Davis Bacon Act compliance, did not adequately plead the materiality of the DBA violations to the government's decision to pay the defendant for work under a federal contract, but noting "[t]his court need not make any grand pronouncements about the general materiality of Davis-Bacon violations to resolve Sorenson's appeal").

59. *See, e.g.*, United States *ex rel.* Customs Fraud Investigations, LLC v. Victaulic Co., 839 F.3d 242, 252–56 (3d Cir. 2016); United States *ex rel.* Univ. Loft Co. v. Blue Furniture Solutions, LLC, No. 1:15-CV-588-LY, 2018 WL 4494999, at *4–*5 (W.D. Tex. Sept. 18, 2018); S. Rep. 111-10, 14 and 24, n.10, 2009 U.S.C.C.A.N. 430, 441, and 444, n.10 (citing both import tariffs and customs duties as examples of "obligations" covered by the reverse false claims provision).

60. *Victaulic*, 839 F.3d at 255.

term "obligation" in the reverse false claims provision to encompass even those obligations that are not "fixed" at the time of a person's false statement.[61]

VIII. Foreign Military Sales

A defense contractor can face FCA liability for misconduct in connection with a sale under the DOD's Foreign Military Sales (FMS) Program or FMS Financing (FMF) Program,[62] such as misrepresenting in its FMS contract with the United States an intention to comply with certain laws or contractual provisions,[63] supplying false cost and pricing data in negotiating prices with the government,[64] or falsely certifying on an invoice to the United States its compliance with the foreign government's contractual provisions.[65] The government has pursued and settled FCA cases involving FMS or FMF contracts based on Foreign Corrupt Practices Act violations, diversion of U.S. funds to unauthorized uses, and violations of requirements that goods and services be sourced domestically.[66]

The courts that have considered the issue agree that FCA violations in connection with an FMS contract can give rise to damages suffered by the government, notwithstanding the foreign government's reimbursement of the United States' expenditures.[67]

---

61. *See* 31 U.S.C. § 3729 (b)(3)); *see also* S. Rep. 111-10, 24, n.10; 2009 U.S.C.C.A.N. 430, 444, n.10 (citing "customs duties" arising after the mismarking of country of origin as encompassed by the term "obligation," and indicating legislative intent to correct *American Textile Manufacturers Institute, Inc. v. The Limited, Inc.*, 190 F.3d 729 (6th Cir. 1999).

62. The FMS and FMSF programs are authorized under the Arms Export Control Act, 22 U.S.C. §§ 2751 *et seq.*, and administered by the Defense Security Cooperation Agency of the DOD.

63. *See* Marsteller for Use & Benefit of United States v. Tilton, 880 F.3d 1302, 1314 (11th Cir. 2018) (FAR provision requiring disclosure of violations of anti-bribery, kickback, and gratuity laws).

64. *See Tilton*, 880 F.3d 1302; *see also* United States *ex rel.* Campbell v. Lockheed Martin Corp., 282 F. Supp. 2d 1324 (M.D. Fla. 2003).

65. *See* United States *ex rel.* Yannacopoulos v. Gen. Dynamics, 652 F.3d 818, 824 (7th Cir. 2011) (domestic sourcing requirements).

66. *See, e.g.*, UPI, *GE Pleads Guilty in Israeli Defense Fraud Case* (July 22, 1992), https://www.upi.com/Archives/1992/07/22/GE-pleads-guilty-in-Israeli-defense-fraud-case/2107711777600/; USAO Southern District of California, *Tungsten Heavy Powder of San Diego Agrees to Pay $5.6 Million to Settle False Claims Act Allegations* (Apr. 29, 2021), https://www.justice.gov/usao-sdca/pr/tungsten-heavy-powder-san-diego-agrees-pay-56-million-settle-false-claims-act; U.S. DOJ, *ABS Development Corporation Agrees to Pay $2.8 Million to Settle False Claims Act Allegations and to Waive Administrative Claims* (Nov. 13, 2019), https://www.justice.gov/opa/pr/abs-development-corporation-agrees-pay-28-million-settle-false-claims-act-allegations-and; U.S. DOJ, *Texas Aircraft Maintenance Firm Pays U.S. Nearly $1.4 Million to Settle Civil Dispute* (Feb. 18, 2000), https://www.justice.gov/archive/opa/pr/2000/February/073civ.htm.

67. *See* United States *ex rel.* Marsteller v. MD Helicopters, Inc., No. 5:13-CV-00830-AKK, 2021 WL 4409093, at *6 (N.D. Ala. Sept. 27, 2021); Campbell v. Lockheed Martin, 282 F. Supp. 2d at 1341–42; United States *ex rel.* Hayes v. CMC Elecs., Inc., 297 F. Supp. 2d 734 (D.N.J. 2003).

IX. Small, Disadvantaged Business Programs

The Small Business Administration's (SBA) "Section 8(a) Program" provides set-aside and sole-source government contracts to small businesses owned and controlled by members of socially or economically disadvantaged groups, such as African Americans and Native American tribes. The SBA has a similar priority program for service-disabled veteran-owned small businesses (the SDVOSB program). Fraud in these programs appears to be rampant: a Department of Veterans Affairs (VA) 2012 audit found that 76 percent of the VOSB and SDVOSB contract recipients that were reviewed in the audit were ineligible for the program and/or the contract award, potentially resulting in $2.5 billion awarded to ineligible businesses; a DOD audit of just 29 contractors found that the agency wrongfully awarded $827.8 million to ineligible SDVOSBs; and a recent SBA audit found that 90 percent of the contracts set aside for Women Owned Small Businesses (WOSBs) were awarded to potentially ineligible companies.

Misrepresentations as to eligibility for these contracts can give rise to FCA liability under a fraud-in-the-inducement theory or an implied falsity theory, with the courts generally agreeing that such misrepresentations can be material to the government's decisions on payment.[68] Representative of the general trend in the courts is a recent Second Circuit ruling in a case involving a company that allegedly used a veteran-owned small business as a "front" to receive SBA contracts for which it was not eligible:

> In fraudulent inducement cases, the government's "payment decision" under *Escobar* encompasses both its decision to award a contract and its ultimate decision to pay under that contract. . . .
>
> . . .
>
> [The government's] allegations lead to a reasonable inference that, in general, the government does not award contracts to companies that it knows not to have complied with SDVOSB requirements. This suggests that defendants' misrepresentations were material to the government's decision to enter the contract in the first instance."[69]

---

68. Indeed, the Small Business Act expressly provides that:

> [A]ny small business concern that is determined by the Administrator to have misrepresented the status of that concern as a small business concern owned and controlled by women for purposes of this subsection, shall be subject to—
>
> (i) section 1001 of Title 18; and
>
> (ii) sections 3729 through 3733 of Title 31.

15 U.S.C.A. § 637 (m)(5)(C).

69. United States v. Strock, 982 F.3d 51, 64 (2d Cir. 2020). *Accord* Veridyne Corp. v. United States, 758 F.3d 1371, 1380 (Fed. Cir. 2014) (because the SBA contract "was obtained by fraud, each invoice

And, more recently, the Ninth Circuit ruled that a plaintiff sufficiently alleged the falsity and materiality elements of the FCA when they alleged that (1) the government conditioned a contract award for the supply and distribution of radiopharmaceutical products to the VA on the contractor's status as an SDVOSB; and (2) defendants, who were not service-disabled veterans, concealed from the government that they would be performing the majority of the work and that the SDVOSBs awarded the contract would perform only nominal work under the contracts.[70] The court held that the complaint sufficiently alleged FCA violations under either the theory of fraud in the inducement or implied false certification.[71]

Moreover, when a person obtains section 8(a) or SDVOSB status through fraud and deceit and then uses this unearned status to obtain government contracts, the SBA presumes the government's loss to be the full amount paid out under the contracts.[72] Two federal district courts have applied this SBA presumption-of-loss rule in fraud cases.[73]

---

submitted pursuant to that contract was tainted by that fraud"); Ab-Tech Constr., Inc. v. United States, 31 Fed. Cl. 429, 434 (1994), *aff'd sub nom.* Ab-Tech Constr. v. United States, 57 F.3d 1084 (Fed. Cir. 1995) (Ab Tech's "payment vouchers represented an implied certification by Ab–Tech of its continuing adherence to the requirements for participation in the 8(a) program"). *See also* United States *ex rel.* Gogineni v. Fargo Pac. Inc., No. CV 17-00096, 2020 WL 1958627 (D. Guam Apr. 23, 2020) (allegations of material omissions relating to joint venture status with person ineligible for section 8(a) program adequately allege false claims); United States *ex rel.* Lardner v. Smith & Nephew Inc., No. 217CV02013JPMEGB, 2018 WL 7050835, at *5 (W.D. Tenn. Sept. 17, 2018) ("a company that goes through the process of following the requirements to obtain small business contracts should know that the government would attach importance to the accuracy of information provided"); LW Constr. of Charleston, LLC v. United States, 139 Fed. Cl. 254, 291 (2018) (materiality adequately alleged where, inter alia, the agency's solicitation made clear that, "but for [Defendant's] representation that it was a SDVOSB, the VA would not have considered Defendant's proposal for the award of the . . . contract"); United States *ex. rel.* Scollick v. Narula, 215 F. Supp. 3d 26, 43 (D.D.C. 2016) (allegations suffice to state FCA claim where defendant allegedly fraudulently obtained SDVOSB set-aside contracts by misrepresenting ownership and control by service-disabled veteran); United States *ex rel.* Head v. Kane Co., 798 F. Supp. 2d 186, 198 (D.D.C. 2011) (allegations of false certifications to the SBA that a small minority-owned business would perform the contractual work adequately allege false claims). *But see* United States *ex rel.* Guzder v. MKM Engineers Inc., No. CV H-05-895, 2009 WL 10697670 (Mar. 3, 2009), at *9 ("Here, Guzder has not shown that 'certification' of compliance with the SBA requirements was, in fact, a condition of the government's obligation to pay for work performed under the contracts"), *report and recommendation adopted sub nom.* United States v. MKM Engineers Inc., No. CV H-05-895, 2009 WL 10697686 (S.D. Tex. Mar. 30, 2009), *and amended*, No. CV H-05-895, 2009 WL 10697658 (S.D. Tex. May 1, 2009), *report and recommendation adopted sub nom.* United States v. MKM Engineers Inc., No. CV H-05-895, 2009 WL 10697687 (S.D. Tex. June 25, 2009) (S.D. Tex. Mar. 3, 2009) (magistrate opinion).

70. United States *ex rel.* UPPI LLC v. Cardinal Health, Inc., No. 21-35905, 2022 WL 3594081 (9th Cir. Aug. 23, 2022).

71. *Id.* at *2.

72. *See* 15 U.S.C. § 632(w)(1); 13 C.F.R. § 121.108(a).

73. *See* United States *ex rel.* Savage v. Washington Closure Hanford LLC, No. 2:10-CV-05051-SMJ, 2017 WL 3667709, at *3–*4 (E.D. Wash. Aug. 24, 2017) (applying rule to calculation of damages in

X. Grants and Cooperative Agreements

The government contracts with private companies to acquire goods and services not only for its own uses, such as missiles for the Air Force or computers for government agency personnel, but also for use by segments of the public, such as the scientific community or users of bridges and highways.[74] The 1977 Federal Grant and Cooperative Agreement Act (FGCAA)[75] requires government agencies (and pass-through entities) to disburse funds using a grant agreement rather than a contract when the principal purpose of the instrument is not to acquire a good or service but rather to transfer a thing of value to a state or local government or other recipient to "carry out a public purpose of support."[76] The FGCAA requires agencies to use a cooperative agreement when the principal purpose is the same as a grant but substantial coordination between the executive agency and the recipient of the federal funds is anticipated.[77] False claims made in connection with these grants and cooperative agreements can also give rise to FCA liability.

Federal grants and cooperative agreements are governed by federal statutes, regulations, and contracts; and, when the federal funding passes through a state or municipality or is supplemented with state or municipal funding, they will also be governed by state or municipal requirements. FCA cases involving grants or cooperative agreements historically have focused on (1) false statements in applications for research funding; (2) misuse of funding in violation of regulatory or contractual requirements; (3) violation of conflict of interest provisions; (4) violation of match requirements; and (5) failure to report and refund program income.

A. False Statements on Applications for Research Grants

If an application for a research grant misrepresents the identity or qualifications of key personnel, the other resources funding the project, or other data relevant to the research, the grant recipient may be liable under the FCA. The first such case successfully pursued by the government after the 1986 FCA amendments was *United States ex rel. Condie v. Board of Regents of the University of California, et al.*,[78] in which the relator alleged that the defendant universities—the University

FCA action alleging defendant knowingly misrepresented small business and women-owned business status of subcontractors); United States v. Singh, 195 F. Supp. 3d 25, 29–31 (D.D.C. 2016) (applying rule in criminal prosecution).

74. In recent years, the federal government has distributed more than $600 billion of grant and cooperative agreement funding each year. *See* U.S. Gov't Accountability Office, *Federal Grants to State and Local Governments*, https://www.gao.gov/federal-grants-state-and-local-governments#t=0 (last visited June 2, 2023).

75. 31 U.S.C. §§ 6301 *et seq.*

76. *Id.* § 6304(1).

77. *Id.* § 6305(2).

78. No. C89-3550-FMS, 1993 WL 740185 (N.D. Cal. Sept. 7, 1993).

of California and the University of Utah—had falsified research data on their application for a $1.2 million National Institutes of Health (NIH) grant. In order to obtain the federal funding, a researcher affiliated with both universities allegedly lied about his findings as to the causes of immune system suppression after burn injury. The government intervened in the action in 1990 and, in 1994, after several years of litigation, resolved the case for a total of $1.575 million, with each of the universities paying a share. A number of other cases involving false statements to obtain government-funded research grants have followed on the heels of *Condie*, with many of these cases surviving motions to dismiss and leading to settlements or judgments.[79]

B. Misuse of Grant or Cooperative Agreement Funds

Grants and cooperative agreements are usually awarded for specific purposes, and the recipient's use of grant or cooperative agreement funds for an unauthorized purpose can create liability under the FCA. For example, in 2012, the Second Circuit upheld a jury verdict finding Cornell University and a Cornell professor of psychiatry liable under the FCA for using NIH grant funding intended for research into the neuropsychology of HIV/AIDS for clinical work and research unrelated to HIV/AIDS.[80] Importantly, the damages for misuse of such funds may be the entire amount paid to the recipient.[81]

79. *See, e.g.*, United States *ex rel.* Resnick v. Weill Med. Coll. of Cornell Univ., No. 04 Civ. 3088(WHP), 2010 WL 476707, at *2 *et seq.* (S.D.N.Y. Jan. 21, 2010) (denying defendant's motion to dismiss FCA claims based on university submitting false data on NIH grants applications—relabeling data on experiments involving renal cells to falsely state the experiments involved prostrate cells—and using NIH and DOD grant funding in ways other than disclosed to NIH and DOD, changing designated personnel and uses of funds); United States *ex rel.* Longhi v. Lithium Power Techs., Inc., 513 F. Supp. 2d 866 (S.D. Tex. 2007) (denying defendant summary judgment on claims it violated FCA by falsifying data on corporate status, hiring of personnel, construction of laboratory and other research facilities, and purported cooperative arrangements with other laboratories, in applications for U.S. Army research funding); United States *ex rel.* Kozhuhk v. Constellation Technology Corp., 64 F. Supp. 2d 1239 (M.D. Fla. 1999) (denying motion to dismiss claims alleging defendant fraudulently induced Air Force to award research grants to study mercuric iodide for military uses by disclosing misleading summary of relevant scientific literature).

80. United States *ex rel.* Feldman v. van Gorp & Cornell Univ. Med. Coll., 697 F.3d 78 (2d Cir. 2012); *see also Resnick*, 2010 WL 476707; United States *ex rel.* Boerrigter v. Beth Israel Deaconess Med. Ctr, No. 97-11858 (D. Ma. 1999), reported in 17 False Claims Act & Qui Tam Q. Rev. 31 (July 1999) ($920,000 settlement of qui tam allegations that defendant medical center used NIH grant intended for the study of gene mutations in mice for unauthorized purposes after scientist who had applied for the grant left the country).

81. United States *ex rel.* Feldman v. van Gorp, 697 F.3d 78, 88–90 (2d Cir. 2012) ("when a third-party successfully uses a false claim regarding how a grant will be used in order to obtain the grant,

C. Violation of Conflict of Interest Rules

As do contracts, grants and cooperative agreements generally contain provisions aimed at preventing conflicts of interest. Violating these provisions can expose the recipient of federal funding to potential FCA liability.[82] For example, in 2004, a federal district court granted summary judgment for the United States on claims that a Harvard University professor and the director of a Harvard-affiliated international development program violated the FCA by ignoring conflict of interest provisions in a U.S. Agency for International Development (USAID) cooperation agreement calling for Harvard University to help USAID facilitate Russia's transition to capitalism.[83] The agreement expressly prohibited those working on the project from investing in Russia, but the Harvard professor and the director of the international development program nonetheless invested in the Russian securities market and oil industry. The case, which also included breach of contract claims, was eventually settled, with Harvard paying $26.5 million and the individuals each paying between $1 million and $2 million.[84]

D. Matching Contributions

Grants and cooperative agreements often require the recipient to contribute (or acquire) additional funds or supplement the activity with noncash contributions (i.e., in-kind contributions). These so-called "matching" requirements may be self-imposed by the recipient, who makes such representations in a grant application, or may be specifically required at the outset by the federal agency, which would not move forward with federal funding without additional cash or noncash contributions. Misrepresentations regarding matching cash or in-kind contributions can

---

the government has entirely lost its opportunity to award the grant money to a recipient who would have used the money as the government intended. . . . [T]he government bargained for something qualitatively, but not quantifiably, different from what it received"); *see also* United States *ex rel.* Bauchwitz v. Holloman, 671 F. Supp. 2d 674, 688 (E.D. Pa. 2009) ("In the federal grant context, the government suffers harm at the time the false application is made. . . . When it awards a grant to the applicant on the basis of the false representations, it excludes other applicants, thus losing the benefits of their contributions. At the same time, it commits public monies to an undeserving applicant at the expense of the public.").

82. *See, e.g.*, United States *ex rel.* Cantekin v. Univ. of Pittsburgh, 192 F.3d 402 (3d Cir. 1999) (reversing district court grant of summary judgment for defendant on claims that defendant violated the FCA by knowingly failing to disclose conflict of interest arising from several million dollars in pharmaceutical company funding on applications for NIH grants to evaluate medications).

83. United States v. President & Fellows of Harvard Coll., 323 F. Supp. 2d 151 (D. Mass. 2004).

84. Zachary M. Seward, *Harvard to Pay $26.5 Million in HIID Settlement*, Harv. Crimson (July 29, 2005), https://www.thecrimson.com/article/2005/7/29/harvard-to-pay-265-million-in/.

create FCA liability when they induce the agency to award or proceed with a grant or cooperative agreement.[85]

E. Program Income

Another unique feature of grants or cooperative agreements is their potential to generate "program income."[86] Generally, the recipient of the federal funding must report the program income to the funding agency and then either (1) return the program income to the agency, which may be accomplished by the agency reducing the amount of the grant or cooperative agreement by a corresponding amount; or (2) with approval of the agency, reinvest the income into the program or use it to meet any cost share or match requirement.[87]

The failure to report program income and/or return or utilize such income correctly can create substantial FCA exposure. For example, in 1998, the University of Minnesota paid $32 million to resolve claims in an intervened qui tam action alleging, inter alia, that the university failed to disclose program income earned on NIH-funded development of antilymphocyte globulin (ALG), an immune-system suppressing medication used by patients after organ transplants.[88] According to the DOJ press release announcing the settlement, the "University's ALG program built a manufacturing operation that sold the drug to more than 200 institutions internationally earning more than $80 million. Because ALG's study and production was partially funded with NIH grant money, the University was required to, but did not, report its ALG income to NIH so that NIH could adjust the grant amount according to the University's other income sources."[89] Prior to the settlement, the federal district court, "[o]ver the course of nearly two years of litigation . . . issued a number of decisions establishing that the University would be required to forfeit profits earned on the illegal drug sales and pay the United States for mischarging federally funded grants."[90]

---

85. *See, e.g.*, United States *ex rel.* Schell v. Bluebird Media, LLC, No. 12-CV-04019, 2013 WL 3288005 (W.D. Mo. June 28, 2013) (denying motion to dismiss qui tam claims based on false statements on availability of matching funds in application for $45 million grant from the American Reinvestment Recovery Act Broadband Technology Opportunities Program).

86. "Program income means gross income earned by the non-Federal entity that is directly generated by a supported activity or earned as a result of the Federal award during the period of performance." 2 C.F.R. § 200.1.

87. *Id.* § 200.307(e).

88. U.S. DOJ, *University of Minnesota Pays $32 Million to Settle Allegations of Selling an Unlicensed Drug and Mishandling NIH Grant Funds* (Nov. 17, 1998), https://www.justice.gov/archive/opa/pr/1998/November/549civ.htm.

89. *Id.*

90. *Id.*, referencing decisions in United States *ex rel.* Zissler v. Regents of the Univ. of Minnesota, No. 3-95-168 (D. Minn.).

CHAPTER 2

Government Contracts: A Regulated Business Relationship

MARCIA MADSEN AND CAMERON EDLEFSEN[1]

I. Role of the Contracting Officers

A. The Authority to Negotiate and Make Decisions about Government Contracts Lies with the Contracting Officer

It is a fundamental principle of government contracting that the government can only be bound by a contract or contract modification if it is approved by a contracting officer (CO) who has actual authority to bind the government.[2] COs, therefore, play a central role in government contracting because they are charged with negotiating with contractors and making decisions obligating the taxpayer funds.[3]

The Federal Acquisition Regulation (FAR) confers on COs broad authority over government contracts. "Contracting officers have authority to enter into, administer, or terminate contracts and make related determinations and findings. Contracting officers may bind the Government only to the extent of the authority delegated to them."[4] In exercising this power, COs are charged with "ensur[ing]

1. Marcia Madsen is a partner at Mayer Brown, where she chairs the firm's Government Contracts practice and co-chairs its National Security practice. Cameron Edlefsen is of-counsel at Mayer Brown.

2. Wilber Nat'l Bank v. United States, 294 U.S. 120 (1935); *see also* Federal Crop Ins. Corp. v. Merrill, 332 U.S. 380, 384 (1947) (holding that the doctrine of apparent authority does not apply to the government); Hawkins & Powers Aviation, Inc. v. United States, 46 Fed. Cl. 238, 246 (2000) (assistant director of Forest Service lacked authority to modify aircraft contract); Schism v. United States, 316 F.3d 1259, 1276–77 (Fed. Cir. 2002) (military recruiters lacked the authority to bind the government to promises of free lifetime medical care).

3. *See* FAR 1.601(a) ("Contracts may be entered into and signed on behalf of the Government *only by contracting officers*" [emphasis added]).

4. FAR 1.602-1.

that all requirements of law, executive orders, regulations, and all other applicable procedures, including clearances and approvals, have been met."[5]

In exercising these responsibilities, the FAR confers on COs considerable latitude to exercise judgment to act in the interest of the United States at every stage of the procurement process:

> Contracting officers are responsible for ensuring performance of all necessary actions for effective contracting, ensuring compliance with the terms of the contract, and safeguarding the interests of the United States in its contractual relationships. In order to perform these responsibilities, *contracting officers should be allowed wide latitude to exercise business judgment.*[6]

Thus, at the outset, the CO determines how to structure a procurement, based on the needs of the agency. During the competition phase of an agency procurement, the CO is responsible for the evaluation of bids and proposals. Over the course of performance, the CO administers the contract by evaluating the contractor's performance, determining whether the contractor is complying with applicable contractual and legal requirements, and authorizing payment to the contractor. If necessary, the CO has the power to change, amend, and adjust the contract (formally and informally, if warranted by changing requirements, circumstances, budgets, or other agency needs), as well as to withhold or make partial payment (if performance issues exist). At the conclusion of the contract, the CO is responsible for ending the relationship with the contractor—when performance is complete (if all goes well) or by terminating the contract for cause (i.e., nonperformance) or convenience (if due to changing circumstances, the agency no longer needs the product or service being procured). Upon completion or termination, the CO has the authority to commence a new procurement.

To be sure, COs have a duty to ensure that "all the requirements of law . . . have been met" and do not have the power to disregard the law.[7] Likewise, COs do not have the power to waive statutory or regulatory requirements, absent some statutory grant to exercise such discretion. For instance, although an agency "may waive" the application of the FAR's organizational conflict of interest (OCI) rules or procedures if it determines that their application "would not be in the Government's interest," such a waiver cannot be made unilaterally by a CO.[8] Nonetheless,

5. *Id.*; *see also* FAR 1.602-2 (listing some of the responsibilities of COs).

6. FAR 1.602-2 (emphasis added).

7. FAR 1.602-1; *see also* Fluor Enterprises, Inc. v. United States, 64 Fed. Cl. 461, 492 (2005) ("Failure to follow the applicable rules negates the agent's authority to enter into a contract binding on the government.") (quotations omitted).

8. FAR 9.503; *see, e.g.*, Filtration Dev. Co., LLC v. United States, 63 Fed. Cl. 418, 420 (2005) (upholding a rare example of an agency waiver); *see also* M-R-S Mfg. Co. v. United States, 492 F.2d 835, 841 (1974) (a statutory duty "cannot be waived by a Government agent").

within the gray areas of the law, contracting officers have considerable discretion to determine whether to accept the contractor's performance and to determine whether a contractor is complying with applicable contractual and legal requirements. Thus, although a CO cannot disregard legal requirements, the CO has considerable discretion in determining whether the contractor complied with them in the first place.

The CO's authority and discretion to make business and legal judgments on behalf of the government has practical consequences for False Claims Act (FCA) litigation, especially in light of the *Escobar* decision. Although DOJ has exclusive authority to litigate and settle claims on behalf of government agencies,[9] its freedom of action to adopt a particular argument in litigation is defined and constrained by the actions taken by COs.

B. Contracting Officers May Delegate Many Procurement and Contract Management Responsibilities

The government has created an enormous framework of large agencies with substantial responsibilities to assist with the regulation, management, administration, and oversight of federal contracts. Within government contracting offices, much of the day-to-day management of contract performance is handled by program personnel, such as the CO's representative. In fact, one of the CO's formal responsibilities is to:

> [d]esignate and authorize, in writing and in accordance with agency procedures, a contracting officer's representative (COR) on all contracts and orders other than those that are firm-fixed price, and for firm-fixed-price contracts and orders as appropriate, unless the contracting officer retains and executes the COR duties.[10]

Additionally, pursuant to FAR subpart 42.2, the CO has the authority to delegate certain contract administration responsibilities to designated administrative contracting officers (ACOs, also referred to as contract administration officers, or CAOs), who are, in effect, subordinate COs.

> As provided in agency procedures, contracting officers may delegate contract administration or specialized support services, either through interagency agreements or by direct request to the cognizant CAO listed in the Federal Directory of Contract Administration Services Components.[11]

---

9. *See* 28 U.S.C. § 516.
10. FAR 1.602-2(d).
11. FAR 42.202(a).

Only the procuring CO is authorized to negotiate and award a contract, authorize changes, and grant or deny requests for equitable adjustments. Nonetheless, COs have the option to delegate numerous (82, to be precise) administrative tasks to ACOs.[12] In fact, in most agencies, COs are actually required to delegate the following four specialized administrative responsibilities to ACOs: (1) negotiating forward pricing rate agreements, (2) establishing indirect cost rates and billing rates, (3) evaluating the adequacy of the contractor's disclosure statements and compliance with cost accounting standards, and (4) determining the adequacy of the contractor's accounting system.[13]

ACOs are not located at the procurement office but operate out of a separate contract administration office. In the case of the Department of Defense (DOD), ACOs operate out of the Defense Contract Management Agency (DCMA) and the Defense Contract Audit Agency (DCAA).

1. Role of DCMA: Contract Management

The administration of DOD contracts is centralized within DCMA, which was established in March 2000 as an independent defense agency under the direction of the Under Secretary of Defense for Acquisition, Technology and Logistics. As a result of DOD restructuring its acquisition, technology, and logistics functions in 2018, DCMA now reports to the Under Secretary of Acquisition and Sustainment.

The creation of DCMA was the product of a decades-long effort to streamline the management of defense contracts and to control costs. DCMA is organized into various directorates and commands, including the Headquarters Directorates, Cost and Pricing Regional Command, Western Regional Command, Eastern Regional Command, Central Regional Command, Special Programs Command, International Command, and Aircraft Integrated Maintenance Operations (AIMO) Command.[14] DCMA currently manages approximately 249,000 active contracts, which have a total face value of $4.96 trillion, of which $2.2 trillion has been obligated.[15]

Although COs for non-DOD contracts have considerable discretion in delegating administrative duties to ACOs,[16] in the case of DOD contracts, COs are required to delegate contract administration to DCMA, except as provided under DOD's Defense Federal Acquisition Regulation Supplement (DFARS) 242.202.

---

12. *See* FAR 42.302.

13. *Id.*

14. *See* DCMA website, http://www.dcma.mil/Contact-Us/DCMAHQ/.

15. DCMA, Fiscal Year 2022 President's Budget 2 (May 2021), https://comptroller.defense.gov/Portals/45/Documents/defbudget/fy2022/budget_justification/pdfs/01_Operation_and_Maintenance/O_M_VOL_1_PART_1/DCMA_OP-5.pdf.

16. *See* FAR 42.302.

2. Role of DCAA: Contract Audits

The auditing of costs is a central aspect of contract administration. Generally speaking, government contractors in non-fixed-price contracts must comply with the accounting rules set forth in FAR part 31, which prohibits contractors from recovering costs unless they are able to establish that they are (1) allowable, (2) allocable to the contract, and (3) reasonable.[17] Certain contractors with substantial government cost-type contracts, in which contractors are paid on the basis of allowable costs, are also subject to a separate set of complex Cost Accounting Standards (CAS), as set forth under section 26 of the Office of Federal Procurement Policy Act Amendments of 1988.[18] The CAS apply in full only to contracts of $50 million or more (so-called "full" CAS coverage). In the case of contracts "over $2 million, but less than $50 million," only four of the 19 CAS standards apply.[19] Additionally, contractors that are subject to modified or full CAS coverage are required to bill their indirect costs at "forward pricing rates," rates that must be approved in advance by government auditors.

COs' responsibilities include overseeing the review and auditing of contracts—COs are required to "[r]equest and consider the advice of specialists in audit, law, engineering, information security, transportation, and other fields, as appropriate."[20] To ensure compliance with accounting requirements, government contractors are required to "make available records, which includes books, documents, accounting procedures and practices, and other data . . . to satisfy contract negotiation, administration, and audit requirements of the contracting agencies and the Comptroller General" for up to three years after final payment.[21] Government auditors, in turn, are required, upon the request of the CO, to "submit[] information and advice [to the CO] . . . as to the acceptability of the contractor's incurred and estimated costs," "review[] the financial and accounting aspects of the contractor's cost control systems," and "perform[] other analyses and reviews that require access to the contractor's financial and accounting records supporting proposed and incurred costs."[22] Upon completion of the audit, DCAA issues a report to the CO, who is required to "consider" it.[23]

17. FAR 31.201-2(d).
18. Pub. L. No. 100-679, 41 U.S.C. §§ 1501–1506 (formerly 41 U.S.C. § 422).
19. *See* FAR 30.201-4(b).
20. FAR 1.602-2(c).
21. FAR 4.703(a).
22. FAR 42.101(a).
23. FAR 1.602-2(c).

In the case of DOD contracts, this auditing function is performed by a specialized agency, the DCAA. DCAA also performs contract audit services and payment reviews for other federal agencies, as requested, on a fee-for-service basis.

DCAA is an independent defense agency under the purview of the Under Secretary of Defense (Comptroller)/Chief Financial Officer. DCAA was established in 1965 to centralize the auditing of DOD contracts, which had been previously performed separately by each U.S. military branch.[24] DCAA is currently headquartered in Fort Belvoir, Virginia, and is organized into three different geographical regional divisions. It also includes a field detachment group that handles contracts involving classified information. DCAA operates more than 300 field audit offices and suboffices around the world. DCAA is charged with a number of auditing responsibilities, such as assessing the accuracy and completeness of contractors' CAS disclosures and forward pricing rate proposals.[25]

In recent years, DCAA has been subject to substantial scrutiny with respect to the quality and timeliness of its audits. For example, a 2008 Government Accountability Office (GAO) report found that in three audits, senior DCAA management had agreed with a government contractor to limit the scope of audits and assigned inexperienced auditors. In one instance, DCAA management was found to have "threatened the senior auditor with personnel action if he did not delete [adverse] findings from the report and change the draft audit opinion to adequate."[26] GAO issued another report in 2009:

> GAO found audit quality problems at DCAA offices nationwide, including compromise of auditor independence, insufficient audit testing, and inadequate planning and supervision. . . . The [80 audits rescinded by DCAA] supported decisions on pricing and contract awards and impacted the planning and reliability of hundreds of other DCAA audits, representing billions of dollars in DOD expenditures.[27]

GAO concluded that "unless the overall problems with DCAA's culture and management environment that resulted in pervasive contract audit failures are resolved, billions of taxpayer dollars will continue to be at risk for fraud, waste, abuse, and mismanagement."[28]

---

24. *See* DCAA website, https://www.dcaa.mil/Media/Biographies/; GAO, DCAA Audits: Widespread Problems with Audit Quality Require Significant Reform (Report No. 09-468) 7–8 (2009) [hereinafter 2009 GAO Report], http://www.gao.gov/new.items/d09468.pdf.

25. *See, e.g.*, DFARS subpt. 215.4 (contract pricing).

26. GAO, Allegations That Certain Audits at Three Locations Did Not Meet Professional Standards Were Substantiated (Report No. 08-857) (July 2008), executive summary, http://www.govexec.com/pdfs/072308rb2.pdf.

27. 2009 GAO Report, *supra* note 24, executive summary.

28. *Id.* at 70.

More recently, DCAA has been subject to criticism for its lengthy backlogs, which "affect the ability of contractors to receive payment on current contracts or to submit bids on future contracts, as they may be deemed nonresponsive if their systems have not been approved."[29] In section 893 of the 2016 National Defense Authorization Act, Congress required that the DCAA "may not provide audit support for non-Defense Agencies unless the Secretary of Defense certifies that the backlog of incurred cost audits is less than 18 months of incurred cost inventory."[30]

Although these criticisms call the quality of DCAA's work into question, DCAA nonetheless plays a central role in overseeing contract costs and compliance of contractor business systems with regulatory requirements. DCAA advises the COs in pre-award audits and the ACOs in post-award audits.

II. Acquisition Policy Community

Procurement and acquisition policy and requirements are established by an extremely large network of statutory and regulatory bodies.

A. Role of Congress and Authorizing Committees

The modern federal procurement process for goods and services was founded primarily on two statutes: the Armed Services Procurement Act of 1947 (ASPA),[31] which governs the acquisition of goods and services by DOD, the National Aeronautics and Space Administration (NASA), and the Coast Guard; and the Federal Property and Administrative Services Act of 1949 (FPASA),[32] which established the General Services Administration (GSA) and governs the acquisition of goods and services by the civilian agencies. The ASPA and FPASA, in turn, have been amended by a number of other procurement statutes. For instance, the Competition in Contracting Act (CICA)[33] requires both the military and civilian agencies to seek "full and open competition through the use of competitive procedures" unless otherwise authorized by law. The Contract Disputes Act of 1978 (CDA)[34] waives sovereign immunity and creates a right to appeal final decisions by a contracting officer to an agency board of contract appeals or to the Court of Federal Claims. The Federal Acquisition Streamlining Act of 1994 (FASA)[35] promotes the

29. House Report 112-78, at 166 (2011).
30. National Defense Authorization Act for Fiscal Year 2016, Pub. L. No. 114-92, 129 Stat. 952 (2015).
31. Pub. L. No. 80-413.
32. Pub. L. No. 81-152.
33. Pub. L. No. 98-369 (1983).
34. Pub. L. No. 95-563.
35. Pub. L. No. 103-355.

acquisition of "commercial" products and services by reducing regulatory burdens for acquisition of commercial items and directing agencies to minimize the use of compulsory contract clauses for commercial items.

Each year the procurement laws are amended and updated through the mechanism of the annual National Defense Authorization Act (NDAA). Although this legislation is the province of the House and Senate Armed Services Committees, in practice, the procurement provisions are coordinated with the Senate Committee on Homeland Security and Governmental Affairs and the House Committee on Oversight and Government Reform. In the Fiscal Year 2022 NDAA, there are new procurement law provisions addressing a wide variety of issues, including the DOD's Other Transaction Authority, sourcing and supply chain security, and cybersecurity policies.

Aside from the general procurement laws just mentioned, Congress has passed a number of laws that affect a particular agency or area of concern. For instance, the National Aeronautics and Space Act,[36] the 1958 law that created NASA, authorizes the agency to enter into agreements with commercial businesses to fulfill the agency's mandate. These flexible "Space Act Agreements" (SAAs), most recently authorized under the National and Commercial Space Programs Act of 2010,[37] are not subject to FAR or GAO review.[38]

B. The Promulgation of the FAR and FAR Supplements

The initial version of the FAR was published in the Federal Register on September 19, 1983, by the Office of Federal Procurement Policy (OFPP), DOD, NASA, and the GSA. It took effect on October 1, 1984.[39] FAR replaced the separate Armed Services Procurement Regulation (ASPR) and Federal Procurement Regulation (FPR) and still contains many provisions that date back to previous regulations, particularly to the old ASPR. FAR was promulgated pursuant to the Office of Federal Procurement Policy Act Amendments of 1979,[40] which authorized the Administrator of the Office of Federal Procurement Policy (OFPP) to "issue policy directives . . . for the purpose of promoting the development and implementation of the uniform procurement system."[41] FAR implements the federal procurement statutes and related laws and has been amended regularly since its initial release.

36. Pub. L. No. 85-568.

37. Pub. L. No. 111-314.

38. For an overview of the operation of SAAs, *see* David S. Schuman, *Space Act Agreements: A Practitioner's Guide*, 34 J. Space L. 277, 280 (2008).

39. Establishing the Federal Acquisition Regulation, 48 Fed. Reg. 42102 (Sept. 19, 1983) (codified at 48 C.F.R. pt. 1).

40. Pub. L. No. 96-83.

41. Pub. L. No. 93-400.

Although these executive branch agencies promulgated FAR to unify and centralize federal procurement, FAR does afford agencies some flexibility to modify procurement regulations to fit their own unique needs. Thus, FAR 1.301(a)(1) allows the head of an agency to "issue or authorize the issuance of agency acquisition regulations that implement or supplement FAR and incorporate, together with FAR, agency policies, procedures, contract clauses, solicitation provisions, and forms that govern the contracting process or otherwise control the relationship between the agency, including any of its suborganizations, and contractors or prospective contractors."[42] Like FAR itself, these agency supplements must be published in the Federal Register in compliance with notice-and-comment rule-making procedures and must comply with the Paperwork Reduction Act and the Regulatory Flexibility Act.[43]

Like FAR itself, agency supplements are published in title 48 of the Code of Federal Regulations. Today there are 18 FAR supplements. One of the most prominent and frequently used agency supplements is DOD's DFARS, which is published in title 48, chapter 2, of the Code of Federal Regulations.

C. Office of Federal Procurement Policy

The OFPP is located within the Office of Management and Budget (OMB) and is part of the Executive Office of the President of the United States. OFPP was created pursuant to the Office of Federal Procurement Policy Act of 1974[44] "to provide overall direction for government-wide procurement policies, regulations and procedures and to promote economy, efficiency, and effectiveness in acquisition processes."[45]

As mentioned earlier, OFPP shared the responsibility for issuing the first version of the FAR in 1983. OFPP continues to play a prominent role in the maintenance and further development of the FAR. Notably, the OFPP Administrator serves as chair of the Federal Acquisition Regulatory Council (FAR Council), which as discussed next is charged with maintaining and updating the FAR. Moreover, if GSA, DOD, and NASA "are unable to agree on or fail to issue Government-wide regulations, procedures, and forms in a timely manner," the OFPP Administrator has the authority to act unilaterally.[46] The OFPP Administrator may also "deny the promulgation of or rescind any Government-wide regulation or final rule or

42. FAR 1.301(a).

43. FAR 1.301(b)–(c).

44. Pub. L. No. 93-400.

45. *See* OFPP website, https://www.whitehouse.gov/omb/management/office-federal-procurement-policy/.

46. 41 U.S.C. § 1121(d); *see also id.* § 1122 regarding the functions of the OFPP Administrator.

regulation of any executive agency relating to procurement if the Administrator determines that the rule or regulation is inconsistent with any policies, regulations, or procedures."[47]

D. Federal Acquisition Regulatory Council

Established under 41 U.S.C. § 1302, the FAR Council is charged with "manag[ing], coordinat[ing], control[ing], and monitor[ing] the maintenance of, issuance of, and changes in, the Federal Acquisition Regulation."[48] Members include the OFPP Administrator, the Secretary of Defense, the Administrator of NASA, and the Administrator of GSA.[49] The FAR Council formulates amendments to the FAR and issues proposed and final rules under the "notice-and-comment" procedures of the Administrative Procedure Act, 5 U.S.C. § 553. Typically, proposed rules are issued jointly by the Administrator of General Services, the Secretary of Defense, and the Administrator of National Aeronautics and Space.[50] However, the OFPP Administrator retains the seldom-exercised power to issue amendments unilaterally, as discussed earlier. Additionally, the FAR Council "provides the overall direction" to the Defense Acquisition Regulations Council (DAR Council) and Civilian Agency Acquisition Council (CAA Council), as discussed next.[51]

E. Defense Acquisition Regulations Council and Civilian Agency Acquisition Council

The DAR Council and CAA Council are charged with coordinating together to revise the FAR and issue amendments to the FAR.[52] The DAR Council is chaired by the representative of the Secretary of Defense.[53] Other members include "representatives of the military departments, the Defense Logistics Agency and the Defense Contract Management Agency."[54] The CAA Council is chaired by the representative

47. *Id.* § 1121(e).

48. *Id.* § 1303(d).

49. *Id.* § 1302(b).

50. *See id.* § 1303(a)(1) ("[T]he Administrator of General Services, the Secretary of Defense, and the Administrator of National Aeronautics and Space . . . shall jointly issue and maintain in accordance with subsection (d) a single Government-wide procurement regulation, to be known as the Federal Acquisition Regulation.").

51. Acquisition & Sustainment—Office of the Under Secretary of Defense, FAR Operating Guide 4 (2015), https://www.acq.osd.mil/dpap/dars/docs/far_dfars_guide/FAR_Operating_Guide_July_2015.pdf.

52. FAR 1.201-1.

53. FAR 1.201-1(c).

54. *Id.*

of the Administrator of General Services.[55] Other members include "one each representative from the (1) Departments of Agriculture, Commerce, Education, Energy, Health and Human Services, Homeland Security, Housing and Urban Development, Interior, Justice, Labor, State, Transportation, Treasury, and Veterans Affairs; and (2) Environmental Protection Agency, National Aeronautics and Space Administration, Social Security Administration, Small Business Administration, and U.S. Agency for International Development."[56]

These two councils are responsible for coordinating with each other and agreeing on all revisions, submitting proposed amendments for notice and comment, considering any comments, arranging for public meetings, preparing final revisions of FAR language, and submitting final revisions to the FAR Secretariat for publication in the Federal Register.[57]

III. The Unique Role of the Suspension and Debarment Official

As discussed in Chapter 12, to protect the integrity of the contracting process, agencies have the power of suspension and debarment and the officials designated to wield that power. These officials focus on the integrity of the contracting process and on the agency's mission. They are uniquely positioned to assess and address procurement regulatory infractions.

IV. Conclusion

There is a substantial body of law and an enormous federal bureaucracy devoted to careful, detailed management and control of federal government contracting. The relationship between these laws and agencies and the FCA is the focus of this handbook.

55. FAR 1.201-1(b).
56. *Id.*
57. FAR 1.201-1(e).

CHAPTER 3

The Enforcement Community

LYNNE HALBROOKS AND LEILA GEORGE-WHEELER[1]

This chapter details the role of the Inspectors General, U.S. Department of Justice (DOJ), and suspension and debarment officials (SDOs) charged with detecting, remedying, and addressing violations of the False Claims Act (FCA).

I. Inspectors General

There are currently 75 Offices of Inspectors General (OIGs) within the federal government whose duties include investigating fraud committed against their agency. They are independent offices within each federal agency designed to act objectively in promoting the economy and efficiency of the agency's programs while preventing fraud, waste, and abuse in its programs and operations.[2] The more than 14,000 employees of these offices accomplish this mission primarily by conducting audits and investigations.[3] Although other federal agencies also have jurisdiction to investigate violations of the FCA, such as the Federal Bureau of Investigation (FBI) and the Navy Criminal Investigative Service (NCIS), an OIG is usually involved.[4] OIGs investigate FCA matters in close coordination with DOJ attorneys as detailed later

1. Lynne Halbrooks is a partner at Nichols Liu. Leila George-Wheeler is a partner at Holland & Knight. The authors wish to acknowledge Timothy Taylor for his contribution to the original edition of this chapter.

2. Inspectors General Act of 1978, Pub. L. No. 95–452, § 2, Oct. 12, 1978, 92 Stat. 1101, 5 U.S.C. App. 3, as amended (hereinafter IG Act).

3. The number of civil fraud investigators in the Offices of Inspectors General is unknown, but the number of OIG employees has been cited as "over fourteen thousand." *See* CIGIE, Annual Report to the President and Congress Fiscal Year 2021 (2021).

4. For example, in its February 27, 2012, Financial Crimes Report to the Public (which reports 2010 and 2011 data), the FBI explains that as part of its national strategy to address health care fraud it pursues offenders "through parallel criminal and civil remedies." FBI, Financial Crimes Report to the Public (2012), at 17. *See* DoDI No. 5505.02 (Aug. 29, 2013) (the Defense Criminal Investigative Organizations "substantially share the responsibility of conducting fraud offense investigations affecting the Department of Defense").

in this chapter. The Council for Inspectors General for Integrity and Efficiency (CIGIE) is an umbrella organization for the Inspectors General (IG) community that coordinates but does not direct the work of the IGs.[5]

A. History and Purpose of the Federal Inspectors General

The system of Inspectors General began as part of a system to review Army troops and report deficiencies in their training or readiness to their commanders. The position of Inspector General of the Army was created by Congress on December 13, 1777.[6] But it was not until 1978 that civilian agencies began using IGs. In 1978, President Carter signed the IG Act, which established 12 federal IG offices, predominantly in cabinet-level agencies, with each office's IG appointed by the President.[7] Ten years later, Congress added additional IGs at 30 designated agencies, providing them essentially the same powers and duties as those appointed by the President, but allowing the head of the agency to appoint and remove them.[8]

Congress has merged and added IGs over the past four decades and, as of this writing, there are 75 IGs, including several in the legislative branch.[9] The IGs themselves are selected without regard to political affiliation and "solely on the basis of integrity and demonstrated ability in accounting, auditing, financial analysis, law, management analysis, public administration, or investigations."[10]

The IG Act created OIGs as independent and objective units:

> (1) to conduct and supervise audits and investigations relating to the programs and operations of the establishments[11] [set forth in the Act];
>
> (2) to provide leadership and coordination and recommend policies for activities designed to (A) to promote economy, efficiency, and effectiveness in the administration of, and (B) to prevent and detect fraud and abuse, in such programs and operations; and
>
> (3) to provide a means for keeping the head of the establishment and the Congress fully and currently informed about problems and deficiencies relating to

---

5. IG Act § 11.
6. An overview of the history of the U.S. Army Inspector General can be found at ig.army.mil/About/History/.
7. OIGs had been established before the IG Act within the Departments of Energy and Health and Human Resources.
8. *See* Inspector General Act Amendments of 1988, Pub. L. No. 100-504, 102 Stat. 2515 (1988).
9. An up-to-date list of OIGs is available on the CIGIE website at https://www.ignet.gov/content/inspectors-general-directory.
10. IG Act § 3(a).
11. The "establishments" are nearly all federal government agencies. *See id.* § 12(2).

the administration of such programs and operations and the necessity for and progress of corrective actions.[12]

"Independence" is the primary operating principle for IGs and the underpinning of the IG Act. The original IG Act in 1977 and its key amendments have focused on independence by specifically defining the IG relationship to its agency. The law requires the IG to "report to and be under the general supervision of the head of the establishment."[13] It also, except in very limited circumstances discussed later, ensures the IG is not prevented or prohibited from "initiating, carrying out, or completing any audit or investigation, or from issuing any subpoena during the course of any audit or investigation."[14] For instance, IGs must be granted access to agency records,[15] are required to have their own legal counsel independent from the agency,[16] and their annual budget submissions to Congress are managed independently by the head of the agency and the President.[17]

The IG Act also requires IGs to report to Congress. Each IG must keep the head of its agency and Congress "fully and currently informed" concerning "fraud and other serious problems and abuses."[18] This requirement can create a tension for IGs who are asked for information by Congress about a pending investigation, because IGs are also required to keep current investigations confidential. These tensions may be exacerbated by the FCA's requirement that the courts seal qui tam complaints during the period in which the United States is investigating the relator's allegations and deciding whether to intervene in the lawsuit.

B. The Role of Inspectors General in FCA Investigations

In 2021, the OIGs' investigative work resulted in 1,058 successful civil actions,[19] defined by the OIGs as actions "resolved through legal or legal-related actions other than criminal prosecution, including civil judgments, settlements, agreements or settlements in cases governed by the Program Fraud Civil Remedies Act or other agency-specific civil litigation authority, including civil monetary penalties."[20]

---

12. *Id.* § 2.

13. *Id.* § (3)(a) (which provides that the head of an establishment may delegate one level down) and § 8G(d) (which does not allow even that delegation).

14. *Id.*

15. *Id.* § 6.

16. *Id.* §§ 3(g); 8(G)(g)(4)(a).

17. *Id.* § 6(f) (requiring the IG to transmit a budget with certain elements to the head of the agency and the President to include the IG's proposal in his submission to Congress).

18. *Id.* § 4(a)(5).

19. CIGIE, Annual Report to the President and Congress Fiscal Year 2021 (2021), at I.

20. *Id.* at 25.

Published statistics do not identify the percent related to the FCA, but that is the most common civil fraud enforcement tool. These actions contributed to the nearly $12 billion of investigative receivables and recoveries attributed to OIGs' civil and criminal investigations.[21]

1. IG Act: Duties and Responsibilities Relating to Investigations

The IG Act provides little direction on how an OIG should be organized and, as a result, the structure of the offices varies across the federal government. The law requires, however, that each OIG have an Assistant Inspector General for Auditing and an Assistant Inspector General for Investigations (AIGI).[22] The AIGI is responsible under the IG Act for "supervising the performance of investigative activities relating to . . . [the IG's agency's] programs and operations."[23] The investigation components within OIGs vary from just a few investigators in a small office to hundreds of special agents in the largest.[24] If an agency uses an authority outside the OIG to play a role in the conduct of investigations, the IG Act still gives the IG the responsibility to conduct, supervise, and coordinate those investigations.[25]

OIGs conduct investigations in accordance with a set of standards established by the IG community, the Quality Standards for Investigation (QSI).[26] These are also the standards the IGs use to assess the sufficiency of their own investigative operations through periodic peer reviews. Despite not being particularly detailed or rigorous, the QSI do help ensure that investigations across IG offices are managed consistently and conducted according to the same general and qualitative standards. They may also provide defense counsel some assistance when trying to assess whether an investigation has been compromised by an agent's lack of qualifications or independence.

The IG Act requires OIGs to refer potential criminal violations to DOJ:

> In carrying out the duties and responsibilities established under this Act, each Inspector General shall report expeditiously to the Attorney General whenever

21. *Id.* at 1.

22. IG Act. § 3(d)(1).

23. *Id.* § 3(d)(1)(B). In some OIGs these individuals have other titles, such as Deputy Inspector General for Investigations.

24. One of the largest OIG offices, HHS OIG reports that it had 629 full-time-equivalents in its Office of Investigations in fiscal year 2019. Department of Health and Human Services, Office of Inspector Gen., Fiscal Year 2021 Justification of Estimates for Appropriations Committees, at 17.

25. IG Act § 4(a)(1). The mechanics of these relationships vary by agency.

26. CIGIE, Quality Standards for Investigations (Nov. 15, 2011), https://www.ignet.gov/sites/default/files/files/invprg1211appi.pdf.

> the Inspector General has reasonable grounds to believe there has been a violation of federal criminal law.[27]

Although this language does not expressly apply to FCA cases, defense counsel can expect that where an OIG investigation reveals an FCA violation, it will also be reported to DOJ. The timing of such a report depends on the practice of the entities involved. OIG employees are also compelled to make such referrals pursuant to their general obligation of public service to disclose waste, fraud, abuse, and corruption to the appropriate authorities.[28]

2. Receipt of FCA Allegations

Just as there is no uniform structure for an OIG office, there are no uniform procedures or requirements for the intake of fraud allegations. There are, however, referral sources common for OIGs in the federal government that often lead to OIG FCA investigations. Some of those are described next.

a. Internal Concerns Identified within the OIG

OIGs investigate, as they believe appropriate, fraud, waste, and abuse identified as a result of internal audits, investigations, evaluations, and inspections. Government auditing standards that apply to all OIG auditors require them to report to law enforcement indications of certain types of fraud, abuse, and noncompliance with provisions of law, regulation, contracts, or grant agreements.[29] OIG auditors will work closely with OIG investigators to decide whether to continue an audit after a fraud referral is made. It is possible the audit will be placed temporarily on hold while the investigators, and possibly DOJ, do their work.

b. Whistleblower Hotlines

The IG Act requires that each IG have a website and that the homepage of that website include a direct link for individuals to report fraud, waste, and abuse anonymously.[30] According to CIGIE's most recent Annual Report, in 2021, OIGs processed 1,433,736 hotline complaints.[31]

---

27. IG Act § 4(d).

28. 5 C.F.R. § 2635.101(b)(11).

29. *See, e.g.*, U.S. Gov't Accountability Office, Gao-21-368g, Government Auditing Standards (2021), ¶ 7.15, https://gaoinnovations.gov/yellowbook/examination-engagements.html#section-7.15.

30. IG Act § 8M(b)(2).

31. CIGIE, Annual Report to the President and Congress Fiscal Year 2021 (2021), at I.

c. Qui Tam Lawsuits

DOJ asks OIGs to investigate allegations raised in qui tam cases. When the number of annually filed qui tam lawsuits falls,[32] it seems logical that the number of OIG investigations would drop as well. An OIG investigation of a qui tam may broaden beyond those allegations if the OIG has received other complaints or allegations about the subject of the qui tam lawsuit.

d. Other Law Enforcement Agencies

OIG investigative staff frequently work across agencies and receive referrals from other federal, state, or local law enforcement offices. In addition to referrals of specific individuals or entities who may have committed fraud, OIGs work with other law enforcement agencies on task forces to share investigative information to identify fraud schemes and best practices to combat them. If an OIG discovers that a government contractor has defrauded the government in a way that could be duplicated on other contracts, they will undoubtedly alert the OIGs of the other agencies where the defrauding contractor is doing business.

e. Contractor Self-Disclosures

Certain federal government contractors are obligated under the Federal Acquisition Regulation (FAR) to disclose to the OIG whenever they have credible evidence that a principal, employee, agent, or subcontractor has committed a violation of federal criminal law involving fraud, conflict of interest, bribery, gratuity violation, or "a violation of the civil False Claims Act."[33] As a result, OIGs have implemented procedures to receive and evaluate these disclosures. Many use their OIG websites for contractors' disclosures. Once received, some OIGs may have individuals outside of the investigations component do the initial intake. Ultimately, DOJ will be involved in any disclosure that is investigated and pursued as an FCA case.

f. DCAA Form 2000

The Defense Contract Audit Agency (DCAA) provides audit and financial services to U.S. Department of Defense (DOD) and non-DOD agencies through cross-servicing agencies, primarily through conducting contract audits. DCAA audits contractors' books to ensure that agencies are charged only for costs that are allowable, allocable, and reasonable. If a DCAA auditor gets information that raises a reasonable suspicion of fraud, corruption, or unlawful activity, they will typically prepare and send a DCAA Form 2000 to an investigator, usually the appropriate OIG.

---

32. The number of qui tam suits filed in 2021 (598) was the lowest since 2010. Recoveries and awards to whistleblowers also declined. *See* DOJ, FRAUD STATISTICS—OVERVIEW: OCTOBER 1, 1986–SEPTEMBER 30, 2021, https://www.justice.gov/opa/press-release/file/1467811/download. This may be an anomaly, however, attributable to the COVID pandemic.

33. FAR 52.203-13(b) is required in certain government contracts by FAR 3.1004(a).

g. Direct Contact from Concerned Individuals

In addition to registering their complaint online through an OIG hotline, individuals may directly contact an OIG investigator. This is especially true where OIG special agents are housed in or near the same office buildings as employees of the agency they oversee. Similarly, contracting officers and others within the agency who believe they have identified fraud are very likely to call a representative of the OIG to make a referral. OIGs educate staff within their agencies to ensure these types of referrals are made from contract oversight and program management professionals.

h. Congress

In their role overseeing federal agencies, members of Congress commonly refer matters to OIGs that they believe need to be investigated. They also relay concerns to IGs as a service to their constituents. An IG on the receiving end of such a referral has a wide range of responses, including beginning a fraud investigation.

Most OIGs receive many more investigative referrals than they could possibly investigate. Some of them have published or spoken about their investigative priorities and will discuss them in fraud awareness briefings to contractors. These priorities tend to be general, (e.g., "procurement fraud"), but provide some insight as to where the IG expects to dedicate scarce investigative resources.

C. How Inspectors General Investigate False Claims Act Violations

IGs have broad authority within their agencies to "conduct, supervise, and coordinate audits and investigations relating to the programs and operations of the agency."[34] They have the discretion to undertake any audit or investigation that is "in the judgment of the IG, necessary or desirable."[35] Congress has legislated that not even the head of the agency is authorized to prevent or prohibit the IG from initiating, carrying out, or completing any audit or investigation, or from issuing any subpoena.[36] There are a few, limited exceptions to this unfettered discretion, but these exceptions do not create any third-party right to object to an investigation.[37]

OIG agents have jurisdiction to obtain agency documents and interview federal employees only within their own agency (as explained later, they can also issue subpoenas for information outside the federal government entirely). The IG Act contemplates that requests for information or assistance will be made across agencies and requires that agencies honor such requests to the extent practicable and

34. IG Act § 4(a)(1).
35. *Id.* § 6 (a)(2).
36. *Id.* §§ 3(a) and 8G(d).
37. *See, e.g., id.* §§ 8 (DOD), 8D (Dep't of Treasury), 8E (DOJ).

allowable.[38] As members of the federal law enforcement community, IG special agents frequently work with their counterparts on specific cases and through local, regional, or federal task forces. For example, an FCA investigation that involves allegations of overbilling the Medicare program may be led by the Department of Health and Human Service (HHS) OIG, but may also involve agents from the DOD and Office of Personnel Management if their agency health care programs—TRICARE and the Federal Employees Health Benefits Program—are also alleged to be victims.

CIGIE has the responsibility to develop plans for coordinated "interagency and inter-entity" investigations to deal with fraud and waste that exceed the capacity or jurisdiction of an individual OIG.[39]

1. OIG Law Enforcement Authority

Many OIGs have law enforcement authority, which includes the authority to carry firearms, make arrests, and execute warrants.[40] The source of this authority for most of the IGs is explicitly referenced in the IG Act, although several have been delegated their authority by the attorney general or through a specific grant of authority in other statutes.[41] All OIGs, regardless of the source of their law enforcement authority, must follow the same guidelines issued by the attorney general.[42] In OIGs, the same agents with law enforcement authority also investigate civil FCA violations. While the U.S. Attorneys' Offices (USAOs) and DOJ have separate civil and criminal divisions, OIG agents handle an investigation regardless of whether it results in criminal, civil, or administrative remedies.

2. Tools Used in FCA Investigations

In conducting an FCA investigation, an OIG will need to gather information within the possession of both the agency and third parties, such as contractors. The IG Act provides the OIGs tools to do both at the early stage of an investigation without the need to involve DOJ. These tools remain available even if DOJ is directing the investigation.

---

38. *Id.* § (6)(b).

39. *Id.* § 11(c)(1)(B).

40. For a list of OIGs with law enforcement authority, *see* https://www.ignet.gov/sites/default/files/files/IG_Authorities_Paper_-_Final_6-11-14.pdf.

41. For a description of the different types of authority: Congressional Research Service, Offices of Inspectors General and Law Enforcement Authority: In Brief (Sept. 8, 2014).

42. Office of Attorney General, Attorney General Guidelines for Offices of Inspector General with Statutory Law Enforcement Authority (Dec. 8, 2003), https://www.ignet.gov/sites/default/files/files/agleguidelines.pdf.

The OIGs' access to agency records was broadened in the IG Empowerment Act of 2016 to ensure they have full and prompt access to all documents of their agency, unless another law expressly limits the right of access of the Inspector General.[43] OIG agents conducting an FCA investigation are required to be given "timely access to all records, reports, audits reviews, documents, papers, recommendations, or other materials" related to their investigation.[44]

To obtain documents outside the custody and control of the agency, OIG agents routinely use the subpoena power provided to them by section 6(a)(4) of the IG Act, which allows them to require production of:

> all information, documents, reports, answers, records, accounts, papers, and other data in any medium (including electronically stored information), as well as any tangible thing and documentary evidence necessary.[45]

The legal threshold for an enforceable IG subpoena is relatively low. Courts that have recently considered motions to quash IG subpoenas still rely on the standard set forth in an administrative subpoena enforcement case from 1950, *United States v. Morton Salt*.[46] In that case, the Supreme Court held that a court reviewing the enforceability of a subpoena may consider, "only whether 'the inquiry' is within the authority of the agency, the demand is not too indefinite, and the information sought is reasonably relevant."[47] One reason there might not be a significant body of case law considering IG subpoenas may be that OIGs are thorough in reviewing agents' requests for subpoenas to ensure they can meet legal scrutiny.[48] Additionally, it may not be necessary for an OIG to issue a subpoena to a contractor if the terms of the contract require access.

In addition to obtaining documents for their investigations, OIGs will often seek to interview individuals outside the federal government. Employees of contractors may have an obligation to make their employees available pursuant to the

---

43. IG Act § 6(a).

44. *Id.* § 6(a)(1).

45. *Id.* § 6(a)(4).

46. 338 U.S. 632, 70 S. Ct. 357, 94 L. Ed. 401 (1950).

47. *Id.* at 652. *See also* United States v. Hill, 319 F. Supp. 3d 44 (D.D.C. 2018) (DOJ OIG subpoena upheld); United States v. Inst. for Coll. Access & Success, 27 F. Supp. 3d 106 (D.D.C. 2014) (Dep't of Education OIG subpoena to third party upheld); Richards v. Dep't of Defense, Civil No. 14-00235, May 9, 2014 (order denying motion to quash Right to Financial Privacy Act subpoena duces tecum).

48. *See, e.g.*, U.S. DOD IG Instruction 7050.9 (Aug. 29, 2016). In testimony before the Senate Homeland Security and Government Affairs Committee on October 21, 2021, the chairwoman of CIGIE and IG at the National Science Foundation explained that in her office a documentary subpoena is reviewed by three investigators, two attorneys, and the IG before it is issued. Jory Heckman, *Senators Seek "Guardrails" on Expanded Subpoena Power for Inspectors General*, FED. NEWS NETWORK (Oct. 21, 2021), https://federalnewsnetwork.com/agency-oversight/2021/10/senators-seek-guardrails-on-expanded-subpoena-power-for-inspectors-general/.

terms of their contract. Beyond that, only the DOD and Veterans Affairs (VA) IGs have the power to issue testimonial subpoenas.[49] CIGIE has supported expanding this authority to all IGs to enable them to interview former agency employees, subcontractors, and others who refuse to provide information voluntarily. Other investigative tools provided in the IG Act that may be used in FCA investigations include the authority to request assistance from any federal, state, or local government agency and to administer oaths.[50]

D. IG Coordination with the Department of Justice

As discussed earlier, in qui tam cases, DOJ will be aware of the lawsuit and ask the OIG to undertake an investigation. In investigations that originate through other sources, an OIG agent will decide if there is enough evidence to refer the case to DOJ for civil enforcement pursuant to the FCA. OIG agents will typically consult with an assistant U.S. attorney (AUSA) or DOJ commercial litigation attorney early in an investigation to make sure that, if the allegations are substantiated, DOJ will want to pursue the case. This early consultation saves agents from wasting their resources trying to make a case that an AUSA will decline. It also helps to focus investigative resources and ensures the evidence the AUSA will need is being collected. If DOJ declines the case, the OIG will assess whether to pursue administrative remedies within the agency or close the matter entirely.

II. The Department of Justice

Established more than 200 years ago in the Judiciary Act of 1789, DOJ is the primary federal government agency charged with enforcing federal law. It is the only agency permitted to prosecute federal criminal cases and to represent the United States as a party in litigation.[51] The Judiciary Act created an "attorney for the United States" in each judicial district "to prosecute in such district all delinquents for crimes and offences, cognizable under the authority of the United States, and all civil actions in which the United States shall be concerned."[52] It also provided for "a meet person, learned in the law, to act as attorney-general for the United States . . . whose duty it shall be to prosecute and conduct all suits in the Supreme Court

49. IG Act § 8(i) (for DOD); Strengthening Oversight for Veterans Act of 2021, Pub. L. No. 117-136, 136 Stat. 1251 (2022) (for VA).

50. IG Act §§ 6(2) and (5).

51. *See* 28 U.S.C. § 516; United States v. Nixon, 418 U.S. 683 (1974); United States v. Hercules, Inc., 961 F.2d 796, 798 (8th Cir. 1992). There are some rare exceptions. *See, e.g.*, Fed. Election Comm'n v. NRA Political Victory Fund, 513 U.S. 88, 92 n.1 (1994).

52. Judiciary Act of 1789, Ch. 20, § 35, 1 Stat. 73, 92.

in which the United States shall be concerned, and to give his advice and opinion upon questions of law when required by the President of the United States, or when requested by the heads of any of the departments."[53] From those humble beginnings has emerged the Department as we know it today, a legal-investigatory complex of tremendous sophistication and almost limitless enforcement power. The Department currently employs nearly 117,000 people across 41 components in 100 countries and 94 judicial districts.[54]

A. The Structure of DOJ

DOJ is organized into many diverse components, from the Foreign Claims Settlement Commission to the Executive Office for Immigration Review. It contains well-known federal policing and investigatory bodies, including the FBI; Drug Enforcement Administration; U.S. Marshals Service; and Bureau of Alcohol, Tobacco, Firearms, and Explosives. Most importantly for this book's purposes, it also contains the USAOs and seven lawyer-run "divisions" tasked with enforcing particular laws.[55]

The USAOs serve as DOJ's field offices and do much of the Department's work. There is one presidentially appointed U.S. attorney for each federal judicial district,[56] such as the Southern District of New York or the District of Kansas. Under each U.S. attorney are a number of AUSAs, who are typically organized into a hierarchy based on location and the types of laws they enforce. Offices thus generally have a "first assistant" (the office's number two) along with a criminal chief, a civil chief, assistant chiefs, and heads of particular areas of enforcement. For instance, the USAO for the Eastern District of Virginia has offices in four cities, organized with a criminal division divided into six units—national security, violent crime, cybercrime, public corruption and civil rights, financial crime, and narcotics trafficking[57]—and a civil division divided into four units—defensive litigation, civil rights enforcement, bankruptcy, and affirmative civil enforcement (ACE).[58]

53. *Id.* 1 Stat. at 93.

54. *See* U.S. DOJ, FY 2021 Agency Financial Report (2021), at I-4, https://www.justice.gov/doj/page/file/1448361/download.

55. For an organizational chart of the attorney general's office, see *id.* at I-5.

56. Except one. Guam and the Northern Mariana Islands are separate districts but share a U.S. attorney.

57. *See* U.S. DOJ, *Eastern District of Virginia—Criminal Division*, https://www.justice.gov/usao-edva/criminal-division.

58. *See* U.S. DOJ, *Eastern District of Virginia—Civil Division*, https://www.justice.gov/usao-edva/civil-division.

USAOs employ surprisingly few attorneys. For instance, the District of New Jersey (which encompasses the state of New Jersey) has about nine million people yet only 170 AUSAs,[59] roughly one prosecutor for every 53,000 people.

In addition to the USAOs, DOJ houses seven divisions principally based in Washington, D.C., collectively and colloquially known as "Main Justice." Those divisions are the Antitrust Division, the Civil Division, the Civil Rights Division, the Criminal Division, the Environment and Natural Resources Division, the National Security Division, and the Tax Division.[60] Each of these divisions is tasked with enforcing the laws that fall under their particular area of responsibility. They often coordinate with local AUSAs, so it is not uncommon in an investigation or litigation for a defendant to deal with DOJ attorneys located both in the jurisdiction and in Washington.

The FCA is a civil statute, and it is enforced by Department attorneys in civil practice, not criminal practice, although the two may coordinate parallel proceedings—investigations and litigation on both criminal and civil tracks. In the USAOs, the FCA is enforced by AUSAs in those offices' civil divisions. If a USAO has established an ACE unit within its civil division, FCA matters will be handled by AUSAs within that unit. At Main Justice, the Fraud Section of the Commercial Litigation Branch of the Civil Division handles FCA suits.[61]

B. DOJ's Powers and Limitations under the False Claims Act

DOJ is charged with investigating and litigating violations of the FCA.[62] Leads for potential FCA investigations come from many sources, including referrals from other government agencies, but most often, the Department begins an FCA investigation after being tipped off by a "relator," a whistleblower who has filed an FCA lawsuit under seal for the Department's review.[63] Such a lawsuit is brought in the name of the United States (since it is the United States who has been defrauded) and is referred to as a qui tam suit.[64] The lawsuit remains under seal while the Department investigates and makes the decision whether to "intervene"—to take

---

59. *See* U.S. DOJ, *District of New Jersey*, https://www.justice.gov/usao-nj.

60. *See* U.S. DOJ, FY 2021 Agency Financial Report (2021) at I-4.

61. *See* U.S. DOJ, *Civil Division—Fraud Section*, https://www.justice.gov/civil/fraud-section. For an organizational chart of the Civil Division, *see* U.S. DOJ, *Civil Division Branches, Sections and Offices*, https://www.justice.gov/civil/org-chart/map.

62. *See* 31 U.S.C. § 3730(a) (the Attorney General "diligently shall investigate a violation" of the False Claims Act).

63. *See id.* § 3730(b).

64. "*Qui tam* is short for the Latin phrase *qui tam pro domino rege quam pro se ipso in hac parte sequitur*, which means 'who pursues this action on our Lord the King's behalf as well as his own.'" Vt. Agency of Nat. Res. v. United States *ex rel.* Stevens, 529 U.S. 765, 769 n.1 (2000).

over the case—or to "decline"—to leave the relator to prosecute the case herself.[65] The FCA gives the Department 60 days to investigate the under-seal case, but the Department will typically ask the court for extensions of time for "good cause shown."

As part of its investigation, the FCA authorizes DOJ to issue civil investigative demands (CIDs)—subpoenas—for documents, written interrogatories, and depositions, as long as the Department "has reason to believe" that the recipient "may [have] material or information relevant to a false claims law investigation."[66] A recipient can petition a federal district court to modify or set aside the CID,[67] but such a petition is unlikely to be successful. CIDs enjoy the same standard of review as other subpoenas, which essentially requires only a showing that the government body is acting within the scope of its authority and that the information sought is relevant to its investigation.[68]

Sometimes, the DOJ attorney handling the government's investigation of a qui tam action will explore the possibility of the relator supporting the investigation by, for example, conducting factual or legal research, proposing language for document requests in an OIG subpoena or CID, or assisting with the review and analysis of subpoenaed documents. This is more likely to happen when the relator possesses special technical or scientific knowledge of value to the DOJ attorney or when the relator's counsel is known and trusted. When DOJ requests a relator's assistance, it ordinarily will ask the relator and their counsel to enter into a "common interest agreement" that, among other things, obligates the relator and their counsel to accord confidential treatment to the documents and other information shared with the relator. It is generally good practice for the relator's counsel both to encourage the government to request relator's assistance and, if such assistance is requested, to invest resources in supporting the government's investigation. If the government lacks the necessary resources or expertise, the relator's assistance may make the difference in the success of an investigation in uncovering the relevant law and facts.

With regard to defendants' role during the investigation, it is usually good practice for defendants to encourage DOJ to decline the case, since relators

---

65. *See* 31 U.S.C. § 3730(b)(2).

66. *See id.* § 3733(a)(1).

67. *See id.* § 3733(j).

68. *See* United States v. Markwood, 48 F.3d 969, 976–79 (6th Cir. 1995). *See also* United States v. Kamal Kabakibou, MD, PC, 522 F. Supp. 3d 1307 (N.D. Ga. 2020) (holding physician failed to establish any ground for denying DOJ's petition to enforce CID); Gen. Med., PC v. United States, No. 3:20-MC-53-NJR, 2020 WL 7209278 (S.D. Ill. Dec. 7, 2020) (denying petition to set aside CIDs, applying *Markwood* standard).

typically fare much worse in declined actions.[69] However, the Department's declination does not mean that it is powerless. The Department may be required to consent to any settlement of the claim,[70] may intervene later for good cause,[71] and may stay the case if the relator's discovery efforts interfere with its own criminal or civil investigation.[72] It is also important to remember that DOJ is not bound by any restrictions on relator-filed FCA suits such as the "first to file" bar, the public disclosure bar, and the government action rule. None of those restrictions apply to the government.[73]

C. DOJ Policies Regarding the FCA

The Department's stated position is that "[c]ivil remedies against fraud should be vigorously enforced."[74] The Department has no published policies regarding which FCA cases warrant intervention and which do not, though courts may view a declination as evidence that the case has little merit.

The overall aim of FCA enforcement is to make the government whole, to deter fraud, and to punish offenders:

> Expeditious enforcement of civil sanctions should be undertaken to make the government whole, if possible, and to provide a strong deterrent to fraudulent conduct in similar circumstances. Such enforcement is important to the promotion of the highest ethical standards among those who have dealings with the government or who are employed by it. Flagrant frauds, justifying the initiation of

---

69. *See* U.S. DOJ, Fraud Statistics: October 1, 1986–September 30, 2021, https://www.justice.gov/opa/press-release/file/1467811/download (from 2011 to 2021, False Claims Act recoveries for relators in DOJ's intervened cases were nearly $4.5 billion, and only $671 million in declined cases).

70. *See* 31 U.S.C. § 3730(b)(1) (A relator's lawsuit "may be dismissed only if the court and the Attorney General give written consent to the dismissal and their reasons for consenting."); *compare* United States *ex rel.* Killingsworth v. Northrop Corp., 25 F.3d 715 (9th Cir. 1994) (government consent not required if it declines case), *with* United States *ex rel.* Michaels v. Agape Senior Cmty., Inc., 848 F.3d 330 (4th Cir. 2017) (consent is required), United States v. Health Possibilities, P.S.C., 207 F.3d 335, 339 (6th Cir. 2000) (same), *and* Searcy v. Philips Elecs. N. Am. Corp., 117 F.3d 154, 159 (5th Cir. 1997) (same).

71. *See* 31 U.S.C. § 3730(c)(3).

72. *See id.* § 3730(c)(4).

73. *See id.* § 3730(b)(5) ("When a person brings an action under [the FCA], no person *other than the Government* may . . . bring a related action . . .") (emphasis added); *id.* § 3730(e)(3) ("In no event may *a* [*relator*] bring an action . . . based upon allegations or transactions which are the subject of a civil suit . . . in which the Government is already a party.") (emphasis added); *id.* § 3730(e)(4) ("The court shall dismiss an action . . . *unless opposed by the Government*, if substantially the same allegation or transactions . . . were publicly disclosed. . . .") (emphasis added).

74. U.S. DOJ, *Justice Manual* § 4-4.110, https://www.justice.gov/jm/jm-4-4000-commercial-litigation#4-4.110.

suits for multiple damages and penalties under relevant statutes generally, should not be compromised for less than multiple damages and some forfeitures.[75]

DOJ takes into consideration many factors when evaluating the appropriate resolution of FCA matters, including the nature, seriousness, and scope of the violation; damages and harm or risk of harm from the violation; the defendant's history or recidivism; litigation risks; and the ability of the wrongdoer to satisfy an eventual judgment.[76] Voluntary disclosure of misconduct, cooperation, and remedial measures can result in DOJ reducing the penalties or damages it seeks.[77] If a defendant fully discloses its knowledge of an FCA violation within 30 days of learning about it (though learning about the violation through a government investigation does not count) and fully cooperates in the government investigation, the government can press only for double damages, not treble damages.[78]

Enforcing the FCA and related statutes (including criminal prohibitions against fraud and other conduct that may arise from the same facts) requires careful coordination among federal law enforcement agencies. Department attorneys are instructed that "[i]mmediately after a *qui tam* complaint is received, attorneys from the USAO and the Fraud Section should confer to ensure that both offices have received the complaint and to decide how the case will be handled."[79] DOJ is also expected to coordinate its criminal and civil fraud investigations with agency regulatory and administrative proceedings.[80]

FCA investigations may also involve state and local authorities, as many states and even some cities have similar false claim laws of their own.[81] For example, DOJ and HHS OIG collaborate with local law enforcement on Medicare Fraud Strike Force Teams throughout the country to harness data analytics and combine resources to prevent and combat health care fraud, waste, and abuse.[82]

---

75. *Id.*
76. *Id.* § 4-4.112.
77. *Id.*
78. *See* 31 U.S.C. § 3729(a)(2).
79. *Justice Manual*, § 4-4.110.
80. *Id.*
81. *See, e.g.*, Cal. Gov't Code §§ 12650–12656; Del. Code. Ann. tit. 6, §§ 1201–1209; D.C. Code §§ 2-381.01 to 2-381.07; 740 Ill. Comp. Stat. 175/1 to 175/8; Mass. Gen. Laws ch. 12, § 5A(A)–(O); N.J. Stat. §§ 2A:32C-1 to 2A:32C-18; N.Y. Stat. Fin. Law §§ 187–194; Va. Code Ann. §§ 8.01-216.1 to 8.01-216.19; *see also* N.Y.C. Admin. Code §§ 7-801 to 7-810; Munic. Code of Chi. §§ 1-22-010 to 1-22-060.
82. HHS OIG, *Medicare Fraud Strike Force*, https://oig.hhs.gov/fraud/strike-force/.

III. Suspension and Debarment Officials

More than 35 years ago, President Reagan issued an executive order establishing a government-wide system for suspending and debarring participants in government programs.[83] Today the suspension and debarment system is part of most every federal government agency.[84] The system is meant to protect the government from dishonest, unethical, or incompetent contractors by suspending such contractors' government business for a short period of time, typically less than a year,[85] or debarring them from government business for a much longer time, up to three years in some cases.[86] A violation of the FCA is one of the many things that can cause a contractor to be suspended or debarred.[87]

Suspension and debarment are not designed to punish contractors, but rather to ensure they are presently responsible to do business with the federal government. Agencies implement the system through their suspension and debarment officials (SDOs).[88] Referrals to SDOs can come from many sources, including law enforcement, government customers, voluntary and mandatory contractor disclosures, or IGs.[89] When multiple agencies are interested in suspending or debarring a person or organization, the Interagency Committee on Debarment and Suspension decides which agency will take the lead and coordinates the agencies' efforts.[90] The Interagency Committee oversees the progress and training of SDOs across the government and issues annual reports on SDOs' activities.[91]

Before closing an investigation where fraud has been identified—whether pursued or declined by DOJ—an OIG will consider referral to the agency's SDO. (Suspension and debarment procedures are addressed in detail in Chapter 12.) Many OIGs have written policies requiring agents to consider a suspension-and-debarment referral in each investigation. As a consequence, defense counsel needs to be alert to possible suspension and debarment proceedings being initiated any time before, during, or after an FCA investigation. The fact that DOJ declined

83. *See* Exec. Order No. 12549, 51 FR 6370 (1986).

84. *See* 48 C.F.R. § 9.403 (2016) (agencies covered are "any executive department, military department or defense agency, or other agency or independent establishment of the executive branch").

85. *See id.* § 9.407-4.

86. *See id.* § 9.406-4.

87. *See id.* §§ 9.406-2(a)(1), 9.407-2(a)(1).

88. *See id.* §§ 9.406-1(a), 9.407-1(a).

89. *See, e.g.*, CIGIE, Don't Let the Toolbox Rust: Observations on Suspension and Debarment, Debunking Myths, and Suggested Practices for Offices of Inspectors General (2011), https://www.ignet.gov/sites/default/files/files/sandwgrpt092011.pdf (encouraging IGs to refer matters to SDOs).

90. *See* 48 C.F.R. § 9.402(d).

91. *See generally* Interagency Suspension and Debarment Committee (ISDC), *About the ISDC*, https://www.acquisition.gov/isdc-home.

the case or that it settled for a reasonable amount does not preclude an OIG from referring a case to the SDO. To protect their clients, FCA practitioners settling a case will often seek written assurance from the agency that the contractor is presently responsible, or that the agency will not presently pursue suspension or debarment. While the practice varies among agencies, most OIGs will defer to the SDO for coordination with defense counsel on these matters.

The IGs' role in the suspension-and-debarment process is inherently limited because it is an agency action, not a law enforcement proceeding. The OIG agent may assemble information for the SDO or provide testimony at a hearing, but the decision whether to suspend or debar an individual or company belongs to the SDO, not the IG. Similarly, DOJ's interaction with SDOs in an FCA case is limited. DOJ attorneys do not have the authority to direct an SDO or promise a defendant in an FCA case that it will not be suspended or debarred.

CHAPTER 4

Qui Tam Relators

ROB VOGEL[1]

I. Who Can Be a Qui Tam Relator?

Under the False Claims Act (FCA), the "relator" is a "person [who] may bring a civil action for a [FCA] violation . . . for the person and for the United States Government."[2] While it is common for the relator to be an "insider" who at one point worked for the defendant company, that need not be the case.[3] One can also find examples of relators who were competitors of the target company,[4] or who had the ability and expertise to surmise the existence of a fraud scheme from data available to people outside the company.[5] One can also find examples in the case law of cases filed by individuals acting as co-relators,[6] or by relators that were business associations.[7]

If a relator brings a case that ultimately results in a recovery for the government through a judgment or settlement, the relator is typically entitled to receive from the government a percentage of the case proceeds (including multiple damages and civil penalties), ranging from 15 to 25 percent of the case proceeds if the government has intervened in the lawsuit to from 25 to 30 percent if the government has not intervened and the relator has gone forward alone.[8] A successful relator

1. Rob Vogel is a partner at Vogel, Slade & Goldstein.
2. 31 U.S.C. § 3730(b)(1).
3. *See* United States *ex rel.* Atkinson v. Pa. Shipbuilding Co., 473 F.3d 506, 523 n.23 (3d Cir. 2007) ("neither the text of the FCA nor its legislative history suggests that non-insiders should never be able to bring *qui tam* actions"); Kennard v. Comstock Res., Inc., 363 F.3d 1039, 1044–45 (10th Cir. 2004).
4. United States *ex rel.* Daugherty v. Bostwick Labs., No. 1:08-CV-00354, 2012 WL 6593804 (S.D. Ohio Dec. 18, 2012).
5. United States *ex rel.* Shea v. Verizon Commc'ns, Inc., 844 F. Supp. 2d 78 (D.D.C. 2012).
6. Rille v. PricewaterhouseCoopers LLP, 803 F.3d 368 (8th Cir. 2015) (*en banc*).
7. Minn. Ass'n of Nurse Anesthetists v. Allina Health Sys. Corp., 276 F.3d 1032 (8th Cir. 2002).
8. 31 U.S.C. § 3730(d).

is also entitled to recover attorneys' fees, costs, and reasonable expenses from the defendant.[9]

The statute sets forth several circumstances in which a relator can be barred from proceeding with a qui tam case.[10] The most commonly invoked bar is known as the "public disclosure" bar. This provision states that if, prior to the relator's filing a qui tam lawsuit, substantially the same allegations or transactions have been publicly disclosed through certain enumerated channels (e.g., "from the news media"), then the lawsuit can be dismissed, unless (1) the government opposes dismissal or (2) the relator was an "original source" of the information in the lawsuit.[11] The FCA defines "original source" as

> an individual who either (i) prior to a public disclosure under subsection (e)(4)(a), has voluntarily disclosed to the Government the information on which allegations or transactions in a claim are based, or (2) who has knowledge that is independent of and materially adds to the publicly disclosed allegations or transactions, and who has voluntarily provided the information to the Government before filing an action under this section.[12]

Another provision that can preclude a relator from pursuing a qui tam case is known as the "pending case" or "first-to-file" bar. Under this provision, when another qui tam lawsuit is pending, a relator cannot "bring a related action based on the facts underlying the pending action."[13] The Supreme Court has held that the "pending case" bar is a temporal one, rather than a permanent one: the second relator may proceed with the case in the event the earlier-filed case is resolved or dismissed.[14]

A relator can also be barred from pursuing a qui tam case if the case is "based upon allegations which are the subject of a civil suit or an administrative money

9. *Id. See generally* United States *ex rel.* Nichols v. Computer Scis. Corp., 499 F. Supp. 3d 32 (S.D.N.Y. 2020).

10. 31 U.S.C. § 3730(e).

11. *Id.* § 3730(e)(4)(A); *see generally* United States *ex rel.* Winkelman v. CVS Caremark Corp., 827 F.3d 201 (1st Cir. 2016).

12. 31 U.S.C. § 3730(e)(4)(B); *see generally* United States *ex rel.* Moore & Co., P.A. v. Majestic Blue Fisheries, LLC, 812 F.3d 294 (3d Cir. 2016).

13. 31 U.S.C. § 3730(b)(5); *see generally* United States *ex rel.* LaCorte v. SmithKline Beecham Clinical Labs., Inc., 149 F.3d 227 (3d Cir. 1998); Grynberg v. Koch Gateway Pipeline Co., 390 F.3d 1276, 1279–80 (10th Cir. 2004).

14. Kellogg Brown & Root Servs., Inc. v. United States *ex rel.* Carter, 575 U.S. 650, 662–64 (2015); *see* United States *ex rel.* Gadbois v. PharMerica Corp., 809 F.3d 1, 3–4 (1st Cir. 2015).

penalty proceeding in which the Government is already a party."[15] This provision is sometimes referred to as the "government action" bar.[16]

Although there is no per se prohibition against attorneys becoming relators in qui tam cases, courts have disqualified attorney-relators who tried to rely on privileged or confidential information to pursue such cases.[17] Likewise, the statute does not contain any per se prohibition against former government employees who seek to pursue qui tam cases,[18] but courts have sometimes looked to the public disclosure bar to preclude former government employees from going forward.[19]

Finally, in cases where the relator has died after initiating a qui tam case, courts have held that the estate of the relator may continue to proceed with the action.[20]

II. Being a Relator: Rewards and Risks

A successful relator can reap significant financial rewards. The general rule is that a prevailing relator can recover between 15 and 25 percent of the case proceeds in an intervened case or 25 to 30 percent in a non-intervened case. In some FCA cases that resulted in large settlements, relators have received awards of tens or even hundreds of millions of dollars.[21]

There are some exceptions to this general rule, however. Courts may, in their discretion, reduce the monetary awards for relators who are found to have "planned and initiated" the fraudulent scheme.[22] Also, courts must dismiss from the case a relator who is "convicted of criminal conduct arising from his or her role in" the fraudulent scheme.[23]

---

15. 31 U.S.C. § 3730(e)(3); *see* United States *ex rel.* S. Prawer & Co. v. Fleet Bank of Me., 24 F.3d 320 (1st Cir. 1994).

16. United States v. Coloplast Corp., 327 F. Supp. 3d 358 (D. Mass. 2018).

17. United States *ex rel.* Holmes v. Northrop Grumman Corp., 642 F. App'x. 373 (5th Cir. 2016); United States v. Quest Diagnostics Inc., 734 F.3d 154 (2d Cir. 2013).

18. United States *ex rel.* Williams v. NEC Corp., 931 F.2d 1493 (11th Cir. 1991).

19. Prather v. AT&T, Inc., 847 F.3d 1097 (9th Cir. 2017); United States *ex rel.* Fine v. Chevron, U.S.A., Inc., 72 F.3d 740 (9th Cir. 1995) (*en banc*).

20. United States *ex rel.* Semtner v. Med. Consultants, Inc., 170 F.R.D. 490 (W.D. Okla. 1997); United States v. NEC Corp., 11 F.3d 136 (11th Cir. 1993), *as amended* (Jan. 12, 1994).

21. *See, e.g.*, United States *ex rel.* Shea v. Verizon Commc'ns, Inc., 844 F. Supp. 2d 78 (D.D.C. 2012). Dep't of Justice, *Biogen Agrees to Pay $900 Million to Settle Allegations Related to Improper Physician Payments* (Sept. 26, 2022), justice.gov/opa/pr/biogen-inc-agrees-pay-900-million-settle-al legations-related-improper-physician payments (noting that the relator would receive 29.6 percent of the $843,805,187 federal recovery).

22. 31 U.S.C. § 3730(d)(3); United States *ex rel.* Stearns v. Lane, No. 2:08-CV-175, 2010 WL 3702538, at *5 (D. Vt. Sept. 15, 2010).

23. 31 U.S.C. § 3730(d)(3); Schroeder v. United States, 793 F.3d 1080 (9th Cir. 2015).

Under certain circumstances, when the government has declined to intervene, the relator has chosen to continue pursuing the case, and the defendant has prevailed, the court may order the unsuccessful relator to pay the prevailing defendant's reasonable attorneys' fees and expenses.[24] The court may only award the defendant its fees and expenses upon finding that the relator's claim was "clearly frivolous, clearly vexatious, or brought primarily for purposes of harassment."[25]

III. The FCA's Anti-Retaliation Provision, § 3730(h)

The FCA contains a provision that is intended to protect relators or would-be relators from retaliation.[26] The anti-retaliation provision of the Act provides the means for a relator or would-be relator to bring a personal action—in other words, on the person's own behalf, rather than on the government's behalf—to enforce the provision.[27] In order to prevail on a claim under the anti-retaliation provision of the Act, a plaintiff must prove (1) that they engaged in conduct that is protected by the provision, (2) that the defendant took adverse action against them, and (3) that the plaintiff's engagement in protected conduct motivated the defendant to take the adverse action.[28]

Courts have established that the conduct protected by the anti-retaliation provision consists of (1) actions in furtherance of an actual or potential qui tam claim[29] or (2) attempts to stop a violation of the Act.[30] The types of adverse action that can create liability for a defendant include termination of the relator or would-be relator's employment,[31] demotion or lessening of the relator or would-be relator's job responsibilities,[32] and reduction in the relator's or would-be relator's pay or benefits.[33]

To prove that the defendant had a retaliatory motive, the plaintiff must demonstrate that the defendant knew about the plaintiff's protected conduct and acted

24. 31 U.S.C. § 3730(d)(4); *In re* Nat. Gas Royalties Qui Tam Litig., 845 F.3d 1010, 1016–24 (10th Cir. 2017).

25. 31 U.S.C. § 3730(d)(4).

26. *Id.* § 3730(h).

27. *Id.* § 3730(h); *see* United States *ex rel.* Carson v. Manor Care, Inc., 851 F.3d 293 (4th Cir. 2017).

28. 1 U.S.C. § 3730(h)(1); *see* United States *ex rel.* Yesudian v. Howard Univ., 153 F.3d 731, 736 (D.C. Cir. 1998); Smith v. Clark/Smoot/Russell, A JV, 796 F.3d 424, 433–34 (4th Cir. 2015).

29. *See* United States *ex rel.* Yesudian v. Howard Univ., 153 F.3d 731, 736 (D.C. Cir. 1998).

30. *See Clark/Smoot/Russell*, 796 F.3d at 433–34; United States *ex rel.* Booker v. Pfizer, 847 F.3d 52, 60 (1st Cir. 2017).

31. *See* Nifong v. SOC, LLC, 190 F. Supp. 3d 549, 560 (E.D. Va. 2016).

32. *See* Boone v. MountainMade Found., 64 F. Supp. 3d 216, 232–39 (D.D.C. 2014).

33. *See* United States *ex rel.* Todd v. Fid. Nat'l Fin., Inc., No. 1:12-CV-666-REB-CBS, 2014 WL 4636394, at *13–*15 (D. Colo. Sept. 16, 2014).

in response to it.[34] As evidence of the defendant's motive, the plaintiff can point to the fact that the defendant took the adverse action in close temporal proximity to when it learned of the plaintiff's protected conduct[35] and that other justifications for the adverse action were pretextual.[36] An employer can be liable for violating the anti-retaliation provision of the Act even though the plaintiff's "protected conduct" was not directed at the employer but, instead, involved a potential qui tam claim against a party other than the employer.[37]

The anti-retaliation provision states that relators or would-be relators who successfully prove that they were retaliated against in the manner just described "shall be entitled to all relief necessary to make [them] whole."[38] The forms of relief available under the anti-retaliation provision include reinstatement,[39] double back pay and interest,[40] special damages,[41] and attorneys' fees and costs.[42]

IV. Relator's Exposure to Counterclaims under Federal or State Law

Many FCA cases are filed by qui tam relators who are employees of the companies that they are suing and, in that sense, are "insiders" to the fraudulent schemes that they are exposing. Frequently, these relators are able to provide the government with internal company documents that demonstrate the origin and extent of the scheme, the fact that the company acted "knowingly," or the extent of the damages. Some defendants in FCA cases have asserted counterclaims against relators, alleging that these relators violated various civil or criminal laws by taking these documents for use in a qui tam case. Defendants have charged, among other things, that the relators have breached confidentiality agreements with their employers, misappropriated trade secrets or privileged information, or violated laws intended to safeguard computer data.

---

34. *See* United States *ex rel.* Schweizer v. Océ N.V., 677 F.3d 1228, 1237–40 (D.C. Cir. 2012).

35. *See* United States *ex rel.* Parato v. Unadilla Health Care Ctr., Inc., 787 F. Supp. 2d 1329, 1344–45 (M.D. Ga. 2011); Elder v. DRS Techs., Inc., No. 1:13CV799 JCC/TRJ, 2013 WL 4538777, at *6 (E.D. Va. Aug. 27, 2013).

36. *See* Townsend v. Bayer Corp., 774 F.3d 446, 457 (8th Cir. 2014); Ickes v. Nexcare Health Sys., L.L.C., 178 F. Supp. 3d 578, 595–97 (E.D. Mich. 2016).

37. *See Townsend*, 774 F.3d at 459–60.

38. 31 U.S.C. § 3730(h)(1).

39. *See Townsend*, 774 F.3d at 464–65.

40. United States *ex rel.* Macias v. Pac. Health Corp., No. CV1200960RSWLJPR, 2016 WL 8722639, *11–*12 (C.D. Cal. Oct. 7, 2016).

41. *See* Neal v. Honeywell Inc., 191 F.3d 827, 831–32 (7th Cir. 1999).

42. *See id.* at 832–33.

Generally, courts have refused, on public policy grounds, to permit defendants to pursue counterclaims against relators for breaching confidentiality agreements that would effectively prevent the relators from gathering or disclosing information to the government for the purpose of bringing a qui tam suit.[43]

On the other hand, courts have permitted defendants to assert counterclaims against qui tam relators under several circumstances, including (1) where the relator breached a duty to the employer by engaging in conduct that went far beyond what would have been reasonably necessary to pursue a qui tam case;[44] (2) where the conduct at issue was distinct from the conduct underlying the FCA case (e.g., a counterclaim based on defamatory statements made by the relator to third parties outside the context of the litigation);[45] or (3) where the defendant could prevail on its counterclaim only if it were first found not to be liable on the underlying FCA claim (e.g., a claim for malicious prosecution).[46] Chapter 15, Protecting the Relator, covers the risks to the relator in much greater depth.

---

43. United States *ex rel.* Head v. Kane Co., 668 F. Supp. 2d 146, 151–53 (D.D.C. 2009); Erhart v. BofI Holding, Inc., No. 15-CV-02287-BAS-NLS, 2017 WL 588390 (S.D. Cal. Feb. 14, 2017).

44. Cafasso v. Gen. Dynamics C4 Sys., Inc., 637 F.3d 1047 (9th Cir. 2011) (finding the relator had indiscriminately copied a large quantity of company documents, among which were "attorney-client privileged communications, trade secrets belonging to [the company] and other contractor, internal research and development information, sensitive government information, and at least one patent application that the Patent Office had placed under a secrecy order"); United States *ex rel.* Ruscher v. Omnicare, Inc., 2015 WL 4389596 (S.D. Tex. July 15, 2015) (permitting defendant to pursue counterclaim alleging that relator had taken company documents that exceeded the scope of her FCA claim); Uchytil v. Avande, Inc., No. C12-1209-JCC, 2018 WL 1121497 (W.D. Wash. Mar. 1, 2018) (same).

45. Head v. Kane, 668 F. Supp. 2d at 153.

46. *Id.* at 153–54; United States *ex rel.* Notorfransesco v. Surgical Monitoring Assoc., Inc., No. CIV.A. 09-1703, 2014 WL 7008561 (E.D. Pa. Dec. 12, 2014) (permitting defendant to pursue counterclaim for breach of contract on grounds that it was independent from a determination of the defendant's liability under the FCA).

CHAPTER 5

Interplay between the False Claims Act and Contractor Ethics and Compliance Programs

AMY C. HOANG AND EDWARD V. ARNOLD[1]

I. Introduction

A contractor's internal ethics and compliance program plays an integral part in a contractor's ability to mitigate False Claims Act (FCA) litigation risks. Changes in regulatory requirements, interpretative case law, and the government's policies both with regard to the FCA and the underlying rules applicable to government contractors will naturally impact a contractor's compliance requirements and, consequently, a contractor's internal ethics and compliance programs. This section will address the reporting obligations and ethics and compliance requirements of the Mandatory Disclosure Rule (MDR),[2] along with best practices for internal investigations to ensure MDR compliance. It will also discuss the interplay between the mandatory disclosure process and Office of Suspension and Debarment proceedings.

II. Mandatory Disclosure Rule

A. Overview of the Mandatory Disclosure Rule

The Federal Acquisition Regulation (FAR) Council published the MDR on November 12, 2008, to reflect the requirements of the Close the Contractor Fraud

1. Amy C. Hoang is a partner at Seyfarth Shaw, where she co-chairs the firm's Government Contracts Practice. Edward ("Teddie") V. Arnold is a partner at the firm.

2. FAR 52.203-13 (Contractor Code of Business Ethics and Conduct); FAR 9.406-2 (Causes for Debarment); and FAR 9.407-2 (Causes for Suspension).

Loophole Act[3] and the Department of Justice's (DOJ) concerns with the Department of Defense's (DOD) Voluntary Disclosure Program.[4] The MDR requires government contractors to disclose to the government certain potential violations of criminal and civil law along with instances of significant overpayment.[5] The MDR included a new FAR clause addressing business ethics and conduct, applicable to certain covered contracts, and requiring disclosure of potential wrongful conduct. The MDR also included a new definition of "present responsibility," which provides that federal contractors and subcontractors, regardless of whether they are subject to the new FAR clause, can be suspended or debarred for failure to timely disclose potential wrongful conduct or significant overpayments.

B. Contractor Code of Business Ethics and Conduct

Pursuant to FAR 3.1003 and 3.1004, all federal contracts and subcontracts that are expected to exceed $6 million and take 120 days or more to perform must include the "Contractor Code of Business Ethics and Conduct" clause found in FAR 52.203-13. Subsection (b) of the clause requires contractors to (1) implement a written code of business ethics and conduct and make a copy of the code available to each employee engaged in performance of the contract; (2) exercise due diligence to prevent and detect criminal conduct; and (3) promote an organizational culture that encourages ethical conduct and a commitment to compliance with the law. Subsection (c) of the clause requires (with certain exceptions for small businesses and awards for commercial items) that, within 90 days after contract award, the contractor shall establish (1) an ongoing business ethics awareness and compliance program and (2) an internal control system, each with specific requirements. For example, the compliance program must include an effective training program, and the internal control system must include an internal reporting mechanism, such as a hotline, that allows for anonymous reporting by employees of suspected instances of improper conduct.

C. Reporting Obligations under the Mandatory Disclosure Rule

Both subsections (b) and (c) of FAR 52.203-13 require timely disclosure in writing to the Office of the Inspector General (OIG) and Contracting Officer (CO), where the contractor has "credible evidence" that a principal, employee, agent, or subcontractor of the contractor has committed, in connection with award, performance,

---

3. Pub. L. No. 110-252, tit. VI, ch. 1 (sec. 6101 *et seq.*), June 30, 2008, 122 Stat. 2386 (41 U.S.C. 101 note).

4. *See* 73 Fed. Reg. 67064.

5. FAR 52.203-13.

or closeout of a federal government contract (or subcontract at any tier): (1) a violation of federal criminal laws involving fraud, conflict of interest, bribery, or gratuity violations found in title 18 of the U.S. Code—most commonly, 18 U.S.C. §§ 287 (false claims), 1001 (false statements), 1031 (major fraud against the United States), and 371 (conspiracy); or (2) a violation of the civil FCA.

Even where FAR 52.203-13 does not apply, pursuant to FAR 3.1003(a)(2), contractors and subcontractors at all tiers performing contracts and subcontracts of any value can be suspended or debarred until three years after final payment on a contract for knowing failure by a principal to timely disclose to the government, in connection with the award, performance, or closeout of a government contract performed by the contractor or a subcontract awarded thereunder, credible evidence of (1) a violation of federal criminal law involving fraud, conflict of interest, bribery, or gratuity violations found in title 18 of the United States Code; (2) a violation of the civil False Claims Act; or (3) significant overpayment(s) on the contract, other than overpayments resulting from contract financing payments as defined in 32.001.[6] Independently, "the Payment clauses at FAR 52.212-4(i)(5), 52.232-25(d), 52.232-26(c), and 52.232-27(l) require that, if the contractor becomes aware that the Government has overpaid on a contract financing or invoice payment, the contractor shall remit the overpayment amount to the Government."[7]

Accordingly, all federal contractors and subcontractors face the possibility of losing the right to contract with the federal government—and many state and local governments—if they fail to promptly disclose credible evidence of FCA violations.

If the contract is intended for use by multiple agencies, that is, Federal Supply Schedules (FSS) contracts, the contractor need only make a disclosure to the OIGs of the ordering agency and the agency responsible for the basic contract.

Notably, FAR 52.203-13(b)(3)(ii) also provides that the government, to the extent permitted by law and regulation, will safeguard and treat disclosed information as confidential, if marked as "confidential" or "proprietary," and will not release such information to the public pursuant to a Freedom of Information Act (FOIA) request without prior notification to the contractor.

D. Determining Whether Conduct Warrants a Mandatory Disclosure

Nearly every contractor's internal investigation focuses on the difficult questions of whether the conduct that is potentially at issue could violate the FCA and, if so, whether the facts uncovered constitute "credible evidence" that the contractor actually engaged in that conduct. In analyzing these issues, the contractor must

6. *See* FAR 9.406-2(b)(1)(vi) and 9.407-2(a)(8).
7. 48 C.F.R. § 3.1003(a)(3).

take into account the shifting regulatory framework and the evolving FCA jurisprudence in up to 13 judicial circuits on the legality of the conduct, as well as the current thinking of the program agency and suspension and debarment officials as to the amount of evidence that creates "credible" evidence of a violation.

1. Could the Conduct Constitute an FCA Violation?

Answering this first question requires contractors to focus on and know well the state of FCA jurisprudence in each of the 13 circuits in which a civil FCA might be brought against the contractor and/or its employees. The nuances of this determination are addressed in other chapters of this book.

Implied certification—the theory that, when a contractor submits a request for payment to the government, it impliedly certifies that it has complied with contractual and regulatory requirements that are a prerequisite to payment—has the practical effect of imposing potential FCA liability for what might otherwise have been characterized as a mere breach of contract claim. Contractors and attorneys conducting informal investigations under the MDR must attempt to determine if the conduct being examined could expose the contractors to FCA liability under implied certification theories. This is very challenging.

The Supreme Court's 2016 decision in *United Health Services, Inc. v. United States ex rel. Escobar*[8] validated the implied certification theory but limited its application in several important ways. Under *Escobar*, plaintiffs must prove that violations of contract terms or regulations were "material" to the government's decision to pay the claim (often an invoice) and that the defendant knew the violated provision was material to the government's decision to pay. The Supreme Court described the materiality analysis as a "holistic" inquiry with no one factor being dispositive. In other words, the materiality analysis is extremely case-specific. The *Escobar* ruling has been subject to varying interpretations in the lower courts since 2016. However, the decision in *Escobar* has provided some additional guidance for those who attempt to determine if a contractor might be exposed under theories of implied certification applied to a specific fact scenario.

Because the MDR requires disclosure of "credible" evidence of civil false claims, this evolving body of case law interpreting the *Escobar* decision will naturally impact a company's analysis under the MDR. Contractors and their counsel should be aware of the variances within lower court decisions on the materiality issue when assessing whether or not a mandatory disclosure may be required.

---

8. 136 S. Ct. 1989 (2016).

Contractors must also consider current federal policies that may impact FCA liability and, consequently, whether conduct should be disclosed under the MDR. For instance, under the Trump administration, DOJ issued the "Brand Memo" (named for then Attorney General Rachel Brand), which limited DOJ's use of nonbinding agency guidance to help establish that a defendant submitted a false claim and acted knowingly. However, under the Biden administration, Attorney General Merrick Garland rescinded the Brand Memo, effectively returning policy to its pre-2017 state, wherein both relators and DOJ relied on nonbinding, agency-level guidance to establish FCA liability. The evolution of these policies highlights the importance of staying up-to-date on current federal policies that may impact whether conduct rises to the level of an FCA violation that could trigger a duty to report under the MDR.

2. What Constitutes "Credible Evidence"?

The second question—what constitutes "credible evidence"?—is the subject of countless speculative commentaries. The MDR does not define the term. Government enforcement authorities have been vigorous in arguing that the concept of "credible evidence" is meant to be less than a preponderance of evidence.[9] They assert that the MDR was implemented to require contractors to disclose possible civil FCA violations, not merely actual violations.[10] As a result, the authors of this chapter and others who were involved in developing the ABA Public Contract Law Section's monograph regarding MDR best practices interpret "credible evidence" to lie somewhere between "reasonable grounds to believe" that a violation occurred and a "preponderance of the evidence" that a violation occurred.[11]

Needless to say, this presents a tricky situation for contractors. With 13 different jurisdictions and scores of varying lower court interpretations of numerous aspects of the FCA, determining when "credible evidence" of a violation exists involves not only extensive legal research but also some degree of subjective analysis.

E. Ethics and Business Conduct Awareness Program

FAR 52.203-13(c) requires contractors to communicate periodically in a practical manner to principals and employees, and, as appropriate, subcontractor and agents, the contractor's business ethics awareness and compliance program and

9. *See* American Bar Ass'n Section of Public Contract Law, Guide to the Mandatory Disclosure Rule: Issues, Guidelines, and Best Practices, Report of the Task Force on Implementation of the Contractor Code of Business Ethics and Conduct and Mandatory Disclosure Rule 71 (2010).

10. *Id.* at 72.

11. *Id.* at 71.

internal control system. The provision requires that this communication should take place through effective training programs and the dissemination of information appropriate to an individual's respective roles and responsibilities.

FAR 52.203-13(c) also requires contractors to maintain an internal control system that shall (1) establish standards and procedures to facilitate timely discovery of improper conduct in connection with government contracts, and (2) ensure corrective measures are promptly instituted and carried out. At a minimum, the contractor's internal control systems must provide for the following:

- Assignment of responsibility at a sufficiently high level and adequate resources to ensure effectiveness of the business ethics awareness and compliance program and internal control system;
- Reasonable efforts not to include an individual as a principal whom due diligence would have exposed as having engaged in conduct that is in conflict with the contractor's code of business ethics and conduct;
- Periodic reviews of company business practices, procedures, policies, and internal controls for compliance with the contractor's code of business ethics and conduct and the special requirements of government contracting, including:
  - Monitoring and auditing to detect criminal conduct;
  - Periodic evaluation of the effectiveness of the business ethics awareness and compliance program and internal control system, especially if criminal conduct has been detected; and
  - Periodic assessment of the risk of criminal conduct, with appropriate steps to design, implement, or modify the business ethics awareness and compliance program and the internal control system as necessary to reduce the risk of criminal conduct identified through this process.
- An internal reporting mechanism, such as a hotline, which allows for anonymity or confidentiality, by which employees may report suspected instances of improper conduct, and instructions that encourage employees to make such reports;
- Disciplinary action for improper conduct or for failing to take reasonable steps to prevent or detect improper conduct;
- Timely disclosure, in writing, to the agency OIG, with a copy to the contracting officer, whenever in connection with the award, performance, or closeout of any government contract performed by the Contractor or a subcontractor thereunder, the contractor has *credible evidence* that a principal, employee, agent, or subcontractor of the Contractor has committed a violation of Federal criminal law involving fraud, conflict of interest,

bribery, or gratuity violations found in Title 18 of the U.S.C. or a violation of the civil False Claims Act; . . .
  - The disclosure obligation continues until at least three years after final payment on the contact; . . .
- Full cooperation with any government agencies responsible for audits, investigations, or corrective actions.[12]

F. Setting Up a Compliance Program

1. Code of Business Ethics and Conduct

The Code of Business Ethics and Conduct (the Code) is the core of any compliance program. The Code summarizes the company's expectations, including key policies and procedures, and it applies to all employees, members of the board of directors, consultants, contractors, and others acting on behalf of the company. The Code must emphasize the company's commitment to compliance and corporate integrity and a contractor's adherence to strict compliance with all procurement laws and regulations. In addition, the Code should mandate strict compliance by company workforce with the policies and procedures in the compliance program, as well as provide notice that those who violate applicable laws, regulations, or company policies and procedures will be disciplined immediately. The Code must be in writing and should be simple, easy to understand, and relatively high-level—an employee should be able to quickly find the information they are looking for in the Code or at least be directed to how to find it. It must also be distributed to all employees and be easily accessible.

2. Policies and Procedures

Accompanying the Code should be detailed written policies and procedures that ensure conformance with specific government requirements and that define acceptable conduct in the workplace. Policies are the "what" and communicate a company's expectations to employees. Procedures are the "how" and help facilitate compliance with policies by explaining how processes should be performed. Written procedures include topics such as time charging, nonretaliation, anti-corruption, records retention, conflicts of interest, and confidential information. Together, policies and procedures work to reduce risk that employees and others acting on behalf of the contractor will do something illegal or unethical.

---

12. FAR 52.203-13(c).

Policies and procedures should address specific legal, financial, reputational, or other types of risk. Performing a regular risk assessment will help ensure most important risks are addressed. Policies and procedures should also cover all aspects of the company's operations and all of a company's operating units and subsidiaries and should therefore be tailored specifically to the activities at each operating unit. Depending on the company's size, individual operating units may be required to draft policies and procedures directly applicable to that unit and submit those policies and procedures to a compliance board for review and approval.

3. Ethics and Compliance Officer

The leader of the ethics and compliance program is typically designated as the chief ethics and compliance officer and is responsible for the program's day-to-day operations. It is generally understood in the industry that this individual should have demonstrated leadership skills, have a solid reputation, and be a role model for character, leadership, integrity, and diplomacy. The individual must be fair and trustworthy, have knowledge of the business, and understand its operations. They must also be approachable and be perceived as someone who will safeguard the confidentiality of those who contact the Ethics Office. They should have a solid foundation in legal and regulatory compliance, investigations and issue resolution, and training and communication.

In essence, the chief ethics and compliance officer is responsible for ensuring that the compliance program is aggressively implemented and remains current. The chief ethics and compliance officer reports to the board of directors, CEO, president, and so on, or has direct access to them. The nature of this position is somewhat dependent on the size of the organization. For instance, large companies often have a standalone Ethics Office, while smaller companies make ethics part of Legal, Human Resources (HR), Audit, and so on. Thus, large companies are more likely to have a chief ethics and compliance officer who is focused full time on ethics and compliance, whereas a small company may have an individual who wears multiple hats.

4. Inquiry and Reporting Mechanism

FAR 52.203-13(c)(2)(D) requires "[a]n internal reporting mechanism, such as a hotline, which allows for anonymity or confidentiality, by which employees may report suspected instances of improper conduct, and instructions that encourage employees to make such reports." This is often known as the company "hotline" or "helpline" and provides a way for employees to anonymously ask questions or report issues to management, HR, legal, or another department.

In setting up a company hotline, most companies use a designated phone number as the primary inquiry and reporting mechanism. Larger companies may provide for multiple avenues to make inquiry or reports, including online tools and a dedicated email address. Smaller companies may forego a phone number and instead implement a locked comments or suggestions box in a break room.

Once set up, companies should determine how the reporting mechanism will be used, including how inquiries and reports will be addressed, the time frame in which they will be addressed, and the individuals designated to respond. In addition, the company hotline should have the ability to memorialize all calls or emails. As discussed later, contractors may designate a member of the law department to function as the chief ethics and compliance officer in an attempt to protect some of the information learned in an investigation from disclosure on the ground that it is subject to the attorney-client privilege. However, involving an attorney will not necessarily cloak all material relating to the investigation in the attorney-client privilege.

The company hotline should be widely publicized as an alternative to the option of reporting to a supervisor. The company can spread the word about the hotline through the company website, ethics posters, ethics training and communications, as well as via an employee handbook or orientation. These publication efforts should encourage anonymous reporting and assure employees that such communications will be treated as confidential. Thus, would-be whistleblowers who fear retaliation by reporting through normal channels will be encouraged to report their concerns, and this reporting will in turn put the company on notice that violations may be occurring and give the company an opportunity to take steps to stop or otherwise remediate any illegal conduct.

5. Compliance Audits

To ensure an ethics and compliance program is effective, companies must periodically audit the program. To that end, a compliance audit ensures that a company's corporate systems, policies, procedures, and practices conform to federal procurement rules and that employees adhere to policies and procedures. The individuals conducting the compliance audit can come from numerous departments (HR, legal, etc.) who comprise an "audit team." The audit team is tasked with reviewing internal systems, policies, procedures, and practices for deficiencies, along with determining the underlying causes of any problems. This review includes ensuring that systems, policies, and procedures reflect the most current laws and regulations and address key risks effectively. It also assesses how the company's training and communications address risk, as well as evaluates how and why people contacted the Ethics Office and how any investigations were conducted. These actions are critical to measuring the program's effectiveness in preventing, detecting, and addressing misconduct and to identifying opportunities to make the program more effective.

The compliance audit may result in recommended changes and/or an accounting of identified misconduct. If misconduct is uncovered during an audit, the case management policies and procedures should require an investigation of every allegation commensurate with the severity of the violation. Moreover, the case management policies and procedures should establish a framework for disciplining employees who engage in misconduct and for providing the subject and referring source (if applicable) with a high-level brief on the outcome of the case.

6. Education and Training

Once the ethics and compliance program is in place, it is critical to ensure that employees understand the company's expectations, how to meet them, and what to do if they see something that does not meet expectations. This follows logically, because if no employee knows what is expected of them in terms of ethics and compliance, or what to do if they suspect misconduct, they will be unable to determine the right course of action. Therefore, a company should implement a comprehensive training program for its personnel. A best practice is to provide employees with both "compliance" training—which focuses on specific legal or regulatory topics—and "awareness" training—which focuses on values and how to handle ethical dilemmas.

Compliance training aims to teach employees how to comply with the legal, regulatory, and policy requirements that impact their job performance. Contractors often require compliance training in areas that present substantial risk to the company. This may include topics such as antitrust, insider trading, international business practices, gifts, business courtesies, and so on, and may focus on specific laws and regulations like the FAR or the Foreign Corrupt Practices Act.[13] Performing a risk assessment is the best way to determine what topics need be covered during the training.

Awareness training is designed to reinforce an organization's core values and help employees identify and navigate ethical dilemmas. Some companies refer to "awareness training" as "code of conduct training," because it often covers the main points in the Code of Business Ethics and Conduct, including the expectation for employees to take action when they observe misconduct and the company's anti-retaliation policy. Awareness training may cover a variety of compliance topics, but

13. 15 U.S.C. §§ 78dd-1 *et seq.*

it is generally broader in scope than topic-focused compliance training. Together, both types of training enable employees to understand the company's expectations, the consequences of noncompliance, and why it is important to speak up and make the right decisions when there is pressure to meet business goals.

To ensure that both the substance of the program and the seriousness of the message are communicated to employees, it is a best practice to require that employees certify that they have reviewed and understand the Code and all relevant policies and procedures and that they have completed the designated training sessions.

III. Internal Investigations

A. Maintaining Privilege during an Internal Investigation

1. Attorney-Client Privilege and Attorney Work Product

Under U.S. law, communications between an attorney and client, along with documents and information created by or at the direction of an attorney, may be protected from compelled disclosure to third parties, including law enforcement authorities. Two primary types of protections are available. Under the "attorney-client privilege," confidential communications between attorney and client may be protected from release to third parties if "made for the purpose of obtaining or providing legal advice to the client."[14] A second and distinct form of protection, known as "the attorney work product doctrine" protects "documents and tangible things that are prepared in anticipation of litigation or for trial by or for another party or its representative."[15]

2. The Supreme Court's Decision in *Upjohn v. United States*

In 1981, the Supreme Court ruled in *Upjohn v. United States* that companies, like individuals, enjoy attorney-client and work product protections that they are entitled to invoke to protect communications between company lawyers and employees.[16] The 13 federal circuit courts are not all consistent in their interpretations of the scope of the attorney-client and work product protections under *Upjohn*.

For instance, the D.C. Circuit has held that, notwithstanding that government contractors are required by the MDR to conduct investigations, documents, and other information created through such investigations are entitled to attorney-client and work product protection so long as a significant purpose behind their

---

14. *In re* Kellogg Brown & Root, Inc., 756 F.3d 754, 757 (D.C. Cir. 2014).
15. Fed. R. Civ. P. 26(b)(3).
16. *See* Upjohn Co. v. United States, 449 U.S. 383 (1981).

creation involves seeking advice of counsel.[17] This rule applies to investigations conducted by in-house counsel as fully as it applies to investigations conducted by outside counsel. However, a number of courts outside the D.C. Circuit have adopted a "but for" test under which the attorney-client privilege would not apply to investigative material unless the sole or primary purpose of the communication was to obtain or provide legal advice.[18]

U.S. companies are well advised to provide documented and complete *Upjohn* instructions at the start of any employee interview dealing with a compliance matter, no matter who conducts the interview (though ideally, interviews would be conducted by outside counsel or by in-house counsel who perform truly legal rather than business functions). These instructions should convey to the interviewee that (1) the attorney-client privilege over communications between the attorney and the employee belongs to the company and not the employee, and (2) that the company controls the privilege and may choose to waive it to disclose information provided by the employee.

B. Determining When the Privileges Apply

Attorney-client privilege and attorney work product, while often conflated, are separate doctrines afforded differing degrees of protection. Moreover, there are two different types of attorney work product, with each category subject to a different level of protection:

- Attorney opinion work product, and
- Attorney fact work product.

Investigators and counsel should resist the urge to conflate attorney-client privilege and the types of attorney work product, as they are separate and distinct.

1. Communications between Investigators and Employees

Some courts have concluded that an investigator may "step into the shoes" of an attorney, thereby affording attorney-client privilege to the investigator's communications with employees. Therefore, such communications may be protected under attorney-client privilege. Marking and designating communications as such can help their protection.

---

17. *Kellogg Brown*, 756 F.3d at 758–59.

18. *See, e.g.*, *In re* Grand Jury, 23 F.4th 1088, 1094 (9th Cir. 2021), *cert. granted sub nom. In re* Jury, No. 21-1397, 2022 WL 4651237 (U.S. Oct. 3, 2022).

2. Communications between Internal Investigators and In-House Counsel

Attorney-client privilege does *not* extend to communications between two company attorneys unless the attorneys are discussing communications between an employee and company counsel that on their own are subject to the attorney-client privilege. The D.C. Circuit elaborated on this principle in *In re Kellogg Brown & Root, Inc.*, holding that the privilege similarly does not extend to communications between an attorney and an investigator "stepping into the shoes" of an attorney.[19] The D.C. Circuit confirmed that when an investigator has stepped into the shoes of an attorney, thus protecting the investigator's notes as work product and its communications with employees as privileged, that investigator cannot also claim privilege over its communications with in-house counsel (except in the circumstances set forth in the first sentence of this paragraph).

In other words, where an investigator steps into the shoes of an attorney, any communication by that investigator to an attorney is an attorney-to-attorney communication. There is no client involved. Accordingly, while the communication can be a work product communication, it cannot be an attorney-client privileged communication, unless it concerns a communication already subject to the privilege, such as legal advice provided to a company employee or facts relayed to counsel for the purpose of obtaining legal advice.

3. Investigator Notes: Opinion Work Product versus Fact Work Product

Federal Rule of Civil Procedure 26(b)(3) distinguishes between "fact work product" and "opinion work product." Opinion work product reveals an attorney's mental impressions, opinions, legal theories, or strategies and is exempt from discovery. But under certain circumstances, purely factual material embedded in attorney notes—referred to as "attorney fact work product"—may not benefit from the same protection if the requesting party can demonstrate substantial need for the materials and cannot obtain the substantial equivalent without undue hardship.

C. Protecting Privileged Material throughout an Internal Investigation

Contractors should draft and implement written MDR protocols or procedures for (1) initial intake and triage of any allegations of potential misconduct; (2) assignment of allegations for review; (3) assessment to determine whether disclosure is warranted; and (4) documentation of the entire process and maintenance of documentation for an appropriate period.

---

19. *Kellogg Brown*, 756 F.3d 754.

As discussed earlier, fact work product, unlike opinion work product, may be discoverable if the requesting party can demonstrate a substantial need for the materials to prepare its case, and cannot, without undue hardship, obtain their substantial equivalent by other means. Contractors conducting internal investigations should take appropriate steps to ensure that documents generated in the course of an internal investigation that reflect an attorney's analysis in anticipation of potential litigation are properly structured and marked to confer opinion work product protection.

Investigators and counsel should remember that communications between them may not be considered attorney-client privileged in the context of an internal investigation if an investigator "steps into the shoes" of an attorney (rather, such communications may be attorney-to-attorney communications subject to work product analysis or may derive protection under the attorney-client privilege from the fact that they reflect privileged communications between client and counsel).

IV. Interaction with the Office of Suspension and Debarment

Debarment and Suspension (Present Responsibility) considerations in FAR 9.406-2 and 9.407-2, as applied by FAR 3.1003(a), impose obligations on contractor principals to timely disclose credible evidence of relevant FCA violations (including credible evidence of a significant overpayment).

The Office of Suspension and Debarment (OSD) for the agency designated as the lead agency relative to the subject of a disclosure (e.g., Air Force, Navy, Army OSD) is typically given a copy of the contractor's disclosure as soon as the DOD inspector general (IG) receives it. An OSD must sign off before a disclosure can be closed. Disclosures submitted to date have rarely resulted in suspensions or debarments of companies, and to our knowledge there have been no suspensions or debarments that have been based on what an IG considers to be a "true" or "legitimate" disclosure. On the other hand, some contractors have been suspended or debarred for the failure of contractor principals to disclose credible evidence of fraud that the government learned about through independent means. Also, although few companies have been suspended or debarred by reason of making or failing to make MDR disclosures, many *individuals* have been suspended or debarred as a result of contractor (and subcontractor) disclosures.

The comments to the MDR specifically state that a contractor may assert the attorney-client privilege with regard to MDR materials. However, it is fairly (if not certainly) clear that the disclosure itself cannot be subject to privilege once it is submitted. Protection of the information submitted in a disclosure therefore becomes an issue of confidentiality (i.e., whether the government can and will safeguard submitted information) rather than legal privilege.[20] Except for when a common interest or joint prosecution privilege applies, submission of a disclosure document waives any legal privileges that might otherwise protect the document and its contents.[21]

DOD and General Services Administration (GSA) IGs have exerted efforts to protect the confidentiality of disclosures and have assured contractors that they will fight efforts to require them to release disclosures to those seeking release using FOIA or similar vehicles. However, the OSDs generally are taking a different view, one that is being widely accepted and acknowledged within the bar. The OSDs have been suspending individuals at a considerable rate based on information contractors submit in disclosures. Item One in an OSD's administrative record prepared in support of a proposed suspension or debarment is often a contractor's mandatory disclosure. Reluctantly, contractors are facing the reality that their actual disclosures may be subject to release.

V. Practice Pointers

- Contractors should maintain appropriate ethics and compliance programs to satisfy the requirements of the MDR and to monitor and prevent FCA violations.
- To mitigate the risks of FCA violations under the "implied certification" theory, contractors should consider the statutory, regulatory, or contractual requirements that may be considered "material" to the government's decision to pay specific invoices or other requests for payment.
- Contractors and their counsel should be versed in the differing judicial views of the "knowledge," "materiality," and "falsity" FCA elements in their respective jurisdictions.
- When analyzing whether conduct rises to the level of an FCA violation, contractors and their counsel should consider the impact of current federal policies such as the Garland Memo.
- When investigating a potential violation of the FCA pursuant to the MDR, contractors should develop protocols and procedures aimed at protecting

20. FAR 52.203-13(b)(3)(ii) ("The Government, to the extent permitted by law and regulation, will safeguard and treat information obtained pursuant to the contractor's disclosure as confidential where the information has been marked 'confidential' or 'proprietary' by the company.").

21. *See, e.g., In re* Martin Marietta Corp., 856 F.2d 619 (4th Cir. 1988) (holding that disclosure to the government waived any attorney-client privilege or work product protection that attached to the disclosed material).

privileged information throughout the course of the investigation. The procedures should:

- Require preparation of documentation at the outset of an investigation establishing that the investigation will be conducted at the express direction of and under the supervision of counsel for the purpose of securing legal advice and (when appropriate) in anticipation of litigation.
- Provide for the type of documentation that will be maintained with respect to any intake matter or investigation, and how and where the documentation will be maintained.
- State (as appropriate) that documentation generated in the course of an investigation has been created for the purpose of obtaining or providing legal advice and/or in anticipation of litigation, and at the express direction of counsel, and is transmitted to counsel if created by nonlawyers.

CHAPTER 6

The Decision to File Suit

RENÉE BROOKER[1]

I. Introduction

When the U.S. Department of Justice (DOJ) completes its investigation of procurement fraud allegations, it makes a decision as to whether to file suit against a contractor and any other persons with potential liability. In the case of a qui tam action, the decision is whether to intervene or decline to intervene in the relator's case. DOJ may intervene for "good cause" after an initial decision to decline. In a non-*qui tam* case referred by a federal agency, DOJ determines whether to file a False Claims Act (FCA) case or whether to refer the matter back to the federal agency.

II. The Process and Players

A. Who Makes the Decision

1. U.S. Department of Justice

The final decision on whether to initiate or intervene in a suit under the FCA lies with DOJ.[2] The component within the Department responsible for the final decision is governed by various delegations of authority from the attorney general.[3]

Generally, and with some exceptions, the deciding official is determined by the potential dollar value of the case, the importance of the legal issues associated with the case, and whether the action is related to other actions pending in other districts. DOJ regulations set forth a dollar threshold under which cases ordinarily

1. Renée Brooker is a partner at Tycko & Zavareei.

2. Only the attorney general has authority to initiate, compromise, or close claims involving fraud against the United States. Exec. Order No. 6166, June 10, 1933.

3. 28 C.F.R. § 0.160(a); *see also* DOJ, *Justice Manual*, https://www.justice.gov/jm/jm-4-3000-compromising-and-closing.

will be handled by the U.S. Attorney's Office (USAO) for the appropriate district. Cases above that threshold are ordinarily handled by DOJ's Commercial Litigation Branch, Fraud Section, in DOJ headquarters in Washington, D.C. ("Main Justice") either primarily by Main Justice or jointly with an appropriate USAO.[4] Main Justice often will take the lead in cases with significant legal issues of national import and cases involving multiple districts.

When a matter is being handled by Main Justice, trial attorneys in the Civil Fraud Section of the Civil Division's Commercial Litigation Branch handle the initial investigation and recommendation as to whether to initiate suit, generally preparing a recommendation memorandum for their direct supervisors (ordinarily assistant or deputy directors of the Commercial Litigation Branch). The recommendation of the trial attorney and supervisor will be made to the Commercial Litigation Branch Director. Depending on the dollar threshold, either the Branch Director or the Assistant Attorney General for the Civil Division has authority to make the final determination.[5] If the cognizant agency objects to a recommendation by the deciding official, the decision will be made by the next higher official.[6]

2. The Cognizant Agency's Role

While DOJ makes the final decision on filing or intervening in FCA cases, the Department almost always seeks a recommendation from the cognizant agency or agencies. In a procurement case, the agency recommendation will ordinarily come from the contracting agency. However, in some cases, the contracting agency may be purchasing on behalf of several other agencies. For example, the Air Force may enter into a contract for the purchase of equipment, and the Army and Navy may also purchase through the same contract. In situations such as this, DOJ usually seeks input from all affected agencies, because any litigation will likely involve witnesses and documents from each agency, requiring a commitment of resources by each agency.

The main contact point between DOJ and each agency differs. In some agencies, the Office of Inspector General (OIG) conveys agency recommendations to DOJ, whereas in other agencies, the Office of General Counsel makes the recommendation. In either case, the Office of General Counsel usually weighs in on the decision, either directly to DOJ or through the OIG.

---

4. *See* 28 C.F.R. Appendix to Subpart Y of Part 0, Redelegations of Authority to Compromise and Close Civil Claims.

5. 28 C.F.R. §§ 0.164, 0.169.

6. *See* 28 C.F.R. Appendix to Subpart Y of Part 0, Redelegations of Authority to Compromise and Close Civil Claims. This part also includes delegations of authority from the Assistant Attorney General of the Civil Division to various Department officials and U.S. attorneys to initiate civil cases.

3. The Relator

In qui tam cases, the relator's position is important because, should the government decline to intervene in the case, the relator has the right under the FCA to go forward with the litigation on their own.[7] DOJ consults with the relator and usually informs the relator of the DOJ trial attorney's recommendation before the declination/intervention memo goes forward, so that the relator's position may be included.

B. Factors for Consideration

Before filing or joining a suit, as a matter of DOJ policy, DOJ attorneys will meet with representatives of the company or individuals being investigated. These meetings are to present DOJ's theories of liability and damages and to hear from the defendant or potential defendant(s). The defendant or potential defendants(s) will have an opportunity to present whatever information they think might be relevant to DOJ's decision, including any pertinent facts and legal arguments. The parties also often use these meetings to explore the possibility of settling the matter short of litigation.

When considering whether to file suit or intervene in a procurement fraud-based qui tam action, DOJ considers a number of issues, including the following:

1. Do the facts as uncovered in the investigation support a breach of contract cause of action?
    a. Are the witnesses credible?
    b. Do agency, defendants' or third-party documents or witnesses undercut the allegations?
2. Do the facts support the additional elements of an FCA cause of action, specifically materiality and scienter?
    a. Are the witnesses credible?
    b. Do agency, defendants' or third-party documents or witnesses undercut the allegations?
3. What are potential defenses to a suit—statute of limitations, government release of claims, and so on?
4. What is the position of the contracting or purchasing agency (and any other affected agencies)?
5. Are there sufficient damages or penalties to justify the expenditure of resources by the government to pursue the case?

---

7. *See* 30 U.S.C. § 373(c)(3) (the United States has the right to intervene for cause even if it initially declines the case).

6. Are there legal or factual issues that might counsel against intervention?
7. Are there important program considerations that weigh in favor of or against initiating an FCA case?
8. Is there an ongoing criminal investigation that might be adversely affected by the civil suit?[8]

III. The Scope of DOJ's Complaint

As a part of the decision on whether to initiate or intervene in an FCA case, the government decides what issues and causes of action to pursue. When intervening in a qui tam action, for several reasons, DOJ usually files its own complaint and does not just adopt the relator's complaint.

First, in a procurement fraud action, the relator may bring a cause of action on behalf of the United States only under the FCA, whereas the government may include other causes of action, such as breach of contract or common law causes of action such as payment by mistake or unjust enrichment, based on the same underlying facts. The government often adds in additional claims of this nature in procurement fraud cases.

Second, the government's investigation may have discovered facts that bolster the allegations in the relator's complaint and the government may want to lay out those facts in the complaint to inoculate its complaint against dismissal. On the other hand, the government's investigation may have found that some of the relator's allegations are not supported by the evidence, are weak, or are not worth the effort to pursue. In this case, DOJ might adopt some of the relator's allegations and decline intervention as to others.

Third, the government might choose to include in its complaint other causes of action that are not based on the same underlying facts as those alleged by the relator. Finally, based on facts uncovered during its investigation, the government may elect to sue a different group of defendants than those sued by the relator.

Once the government makes its decision as to which claims and defendants to pursue, the relator may either voluntarily dismiss those allegations the government does not adopt or may litigate them on their own. Under the FCA, the relator has the right to proceed with claims and defendants declined by the government.[9] However, the government may settle or move to dismiss those claims over the objection of the relator.[10]

---

8. How DOJ manages the relationship between civil FCA cases and concurrent criminal cases is discussed in Chapter 12.

9. *See* 30 U.S.C. § 3730(c)(3).

10. *See id.* § 3730(c)(2).

CHAPTER 7

The Role of Defendants in DOJ's Decision to File an FCA Suit or to Intervene in a Qui Tam Suit

ROBERT HUFFMAN, MICHAEL WAGNER, AND TERRA FULHAM[1]

I. Introduction

It may seem counterintuitive that a defendant in a False Claims Act (FCA) qui tam suit that is still under seal would have the opportunity to play a role in the U.S. Department of Justice's (DOJ) decision whether to intervene in that suit. In fact, however, there are a variety of ways in which a party can discover that it is a qui tam defendant before the unsealing of the complaint and properly seek to influence DOJ's intervention decision. Likewise, where DOJ is conducting an investigation on its own initiative, with no qui tam action having been filed, there are several ways in which a party can discover that it is the subject of such an investigation and properly seek to influence DOJ's decision regarding whether to file an FCA suit against it.

This chapter examines the role played by defendants and potential defendants in the processes leading up to DOJ's decision whether to file an FCA suit or to intervene in a qui tam suit. These processes include (1) fact-finding by the government prior to DOJ's decision; (2) internal investigations or disclosures by the defendant or potential defendant prior to DOJ's decision; (3) factual and legal presentations by the defendant or potential defendant to the government prior to DOJ's decision; (4) the defendant's input into DOJ's consideration of whether to seek dismissal of a qui tam suit; and (5) settlement discussions and negotiations prior to DOJ's decision. This chapter also identifies special problems and issues for

1. Robert Huffman is senior of-counsel at Covington & Burling. Michael Wagner is a partner and Terra Fulham is an associate at the firm.

a defendant or potential defendant in dealing with DOJ, agency personnel, and the relator prior to DOJ's decision regarding whether to file an FCA suit or to intervene in a qui tam suit.

II. How a Party Can Learn That It Is the Subject of a Sealed Qui Tam Suit or a Government FCA Investigation

There are several ways in which a party can learn (or suspect) that it is a named defendant in a sealed qui tam suit or that it is otherwise the subject of a government FCA investigation. First, the party may receive an agency Office of Inspector General (OIG) subpoena, Health Insurance Portability and Accountability Act (HIPAA) subpoena, or a DOJ civil investigative demand (CID) seeking documents, testimony, or interrogatories relating to particular government contracts or programs. Such subpoenas strongly suggest that the government has begun an FCA investigation on its own or in response to the filing of a qui tam complaint. Second, the party may learn that government investigators have questioned or seek to question the party's employees or former employees. Third, the party may receive a request from DOJ or an agency investigator for informal employee interviews. Fourth, the party may receive a grand jury subpoena. Finally, the party may be told by a DOJ lawyer that it is the subject of a qui tam complaint that has been partially unsealed to allow the government to engage in discussions with the party.

Only in the last scenario would the party know for sure that it has been named as a defendant in a qui tam suit. Absent partial unsealing of the suit, the DOJ attorneys, agency personnel, and the relator are prohibited from revealing the suit's existence to any third party, including the named defendants in the suit. Some DOJ attorneys and other government personnel will refuse to confirm that a qui tam suit is *not* pending, even when no suit has been filed. Accordingly, a party should not assume that a qui tam suit is pending merely because a DOJ attorney or other government official refuses to affirm or deny the existence of such a suit.

III. Fact-Finding by the Government and Relator Prior to DOJ's Decision to File Suit or to Intervene

DOJ conducts FCA investigations both in response to referrals by government agency personnel and in response to the filing of a qui tam complaint under seal. The fact-finding resources available to the government are the same in either case. DOJ lawyers can request an agency OIG issue a subpoena, or they can simply make an informal request for documents. DOJ lawyers can also issue a CID for documents, interrogatory responses, or sworn witness testimony. In other cases, DOJ lawyers or agency OIG personnel may request informal interviews of a party's employees or former employees and rely on the party to make those individuals available for the interviews. Witnesses in these informal interviews are not placed under oath and the interviews are not transcribed, although they may be electronically recorded.

At least one district court has held that counsel for a party does not have a right to be present during a CID deposition of the party's employee. However, DOJ attorneys and agency investigators will sometimes permit counsel for the party to attend such depositions, as well as informal witness interviews. Through such attendance, counsel for a party can gain insight into the areas of interest to DOJ and its potential FCA theories. Counsel for the party can also engage with DOJ attorneys and agency investigators regarding particular facts or documents, and thus possibly correct any misunderstandings that may arise during or as a result of the interviews.

IV. Internal Investigations Prior to DOJ's Decision to File Suit or to Intervene

Receipt of a subpoena or other government information request or demand may prompt a party to initiate an internal investigation relating to the government's investigation, if an internal investigation is not already ongoing when the subpoena or information request is received. The party's internal investigation may uncover facts, documents, or other data that the party may want to share—in whole or in part—with DOJ or agency personnel involved in the government's investigation. The party could choose to share such information through a formal written disclosure to the agency OIG, an informal written disclosure to the DOJ attorneys or agency investigators, or oral discussions with the DOJ attorneys or agency investigators. Such disclosures, regardless of form, would not be privileged, although they could be subject to FOIA exemptions and confidentiality agreements. A party sharing facts uncovered in its internal investigation with the government must exercise caution not to disclose attorney-client communications or attorney work product to avoid any argument by the government or a third party (such as a relator) that the party has made a broad, subject-matter waiver of all privileged communications relating to the internal investigation.

V. Presentation of Factual and Legal Arguments to the Government Prior to DOJ's Decision to File Suit or to Intervene

In many circumstances, DOJ will ask a named defendant in a qui tam suit (or the subject of an FCA investigation where no qui tam suit has been filed) to make a factual presentation to the government regarding the conduct and allegations that are the subject of the government's investigation. In some instances, DOJ may provide the party with a copy of the qui tam complaint that has been partially unsealed for that purpose in order to guide the party's presentation. In other instances, the government may simply provide the party with a general description of the areas that it would like covered in the presentation. Although the government is ordinarily represented by DOJ and agency lawyers at such presentations, DOJ may request the relator's counsel and nonlawyer agency personnel to attend as well.

DOJ attorneys requesting pre-decision presentations sometimes may ask the party to limit its presentation to facts and avoid arguments on legal issues. Regardless, DOJ expects defendants and potential defendants to address elements of and "defenses" to FCA liability such as materiality, the statute of limitations, and government knowledge in their presentation. (The defense of public disclosure is not normally addressed in such presentations since DOJ can "eliminate" that defense by intervening in the qui tam suit or by objecting to dismissal on the grounds of public disclosure.) Presentations by defendants and potential defendants should address the facts relevant to each element of FCA liability, including falsity and knowledge, along with the facts relevant to the party's defenses and the calculation of single damages. However, given DOJ's professed reluctance to hear defendants' legal arguments at this stage, defendants and potential defendants should avoid lengthy dissertations on FCA case law in their presentations.

VI. DOJ's Consideration of Whether to Seek Dismissal of a Qui Tam Suit

DOJ has until relatively recently been reluctant to exercise its statutory authority to seek dismissal of a qui tam suit. However, on January 10, 2018, the Director of the Fraud Section of DOJ's Civil Division, Michael Granston, issued a memorandum identifying a number of circumstances where such dismissals would be appropriate and urging DOJ lawyers to consider seeking dismissal where one or more such circumstances are present. Since that time, DOJ has sought (and obtained) involuntary dismissal of more than 50 qui tam actions. Companies involved in FCA investigations triggered by the filing of a qui tam action can assert to DOJ that the circumstances warranting involuntary dismissal of the qui tam are present in the investigation and that seeking such dismissal would be consistent with the Granston Memorandum and good public policy.

VII. Settlement Negotiations Prior to DOJ's Decision to File Suit or to Intervene

DOJ lawyers may specifically request that a defendant in a partially unsealed qui tam suit enter into settlement discussions. These discussions may be conducted solely between DOJ lawyers and counsel for the party, with the DOJ lawyers merely updating relator's counsel on the progress of the talks, or DOJ may invite relator's counsel to attend the settlement discussions. Settlement negotiations provide a unique opportunity to address with DOJ and relator's counsel the weaknesses of the relator's (or government's) case and the strength of the defendant's defenses.

When engaging in settlement negotiations with the government, potential defendants should consider DOJ's Guidelines for Taking Disclosure, Cooperation, and Remediation into Account in False Claims Act Matters.[2] These guidelines, announced in May 2019, set forth the framework used by DOJ to assess cooperation credit for FCA defendants and the effect of cooperation on damages multipliers and civil penalties. Defendants should be aware of and attempt to maximize the mitigating factors outlined in the policy.

To the extent settlement discussions do not succeed in changing entrenched positions, the parties can consider pursuing nonbinding mediation. DOJ lawyers have become more amenable to mediation in recent years, and there are a number of potential neutrals with experience in mediating FCA matters. In many cases, mediation has proven to be an effective way to resolve complex FCA cases prior to DOJ's decision to file suit or to intervene in a qui tam suit.

VIII. Special Problems and Issues for Defendants or Potential Defendants Prior to DOJ's Decision to File Suit or to Intervene

The process of dealing with DOJ lawyers, agency personnel, and the relator and their counsel prior to DOJ's decision to file suit or to intervene in a qui tam suit poses several potential challenges and issues for defendants and potential defendants. These potential challenges and issues include the following.

A. Preserving Records

Potential defendants who become aware of a possible qui tam suit or FCA investigation may have obligations to preserve emails and other evidence that reasonably relate to the likely subject matter of the suit or investigation. Such obligations become clearer once a subpoena, CID, or informal request for documents or information has been issued by DOJ or an agency OIG. Potential defendants should, therefore, have a process in place to issue hold notices and to stop scheduled deletions of electronic records, and should take other actions necessary to ensure documents and information are not lost or destroyed. Potential defendants may want to activate such processes even during internal investigations that are not prompted by a government subpoena or other request for information, since such internal

2. U.S. DOJ, *Justice Manual*, 4-4.112, https://www.justice.gov/jm/jm-4-4000-commercial-litigation#4-4.112.

investigations may result in the uncovering of arguable violations of law and may require disclosures to the government or disciplinary measures needing evidentiary support.

B. Preserving Confidentiality

Defendants and potential defendants should place the appropriate FOIA legend on any written submissions to DOJ or government investigators that contain proprietary data. They should also consider entering into nondisclosure agreements with relator's counsel and with other defendants or potential defendants to protect such data. While a defendant may already have a confidentiality agreement with a relator if the relator is an employee or subcontractor, the defendant must be careful not to attempt to enforce such an agreement in a manner that would restrict the relator from communicating with the government regarding alleged fraud, waste, or abuse.

C. Preserving Privilege

Defendants and potential defendants should take steps to protect attorney-client privilege throughout an FCA investigation. A 2014 D.C. Circuit decision in *In re Kellogg Brown & Root Inc.* made clear that communications made during an internal investigation will not be subject to civil discovery as long as "one of the significant purposes of the internal investigation [is] to obtain or provide legal advice."[3] However, in order to reduce the risk of disclosure of sensitive, privileged communication outside the company and a resulting waiver of the privilege protecting related communications, a defendant or potential defendant should be careful to avoid discussing attorney-client communications or litigation strategies with client personnel who are likely to be interviewed or deposed as part of the government's pre-decision investigation. Defendants and potential defendants should also take care not to include any privileged communications or documents in their presentations to DOJ or relator's counsel or in any disclosures pursuant to the Federal Acquisition Regulations (FAR) Mandatory Disclosure Rule.

D. Preserving Potential Insurance Claims

Insurance coverage might be available to defray some of the costs of an FCA investigation. Typically, this coverage is found in directors' and officers' (D&O) liability policies and is often subject to a sublimit that is less than the policy limit of liability. In order to preserve coverage, it is essential to provide timely notice of a legal

---

3. *In re* Kellogg Brown & Root, Inc., 756 F.3d 754 (D.C. Cir. 2014).

claim. As the preceding discussion makes clear, it is often unclear in the FCA/qui tam context when an FCA "claim" has been made against the insured and when the insured has sufficient information to disclose that fact to its insurer. When renewing D&O policies, it is important to consider how a potential FCA claim fits within the notice requirements of the policy. Should there be such a claim, the insured must document its costs carefully and submit them to the insurer in a timely fashion. As a practical matter, insurers are likely to resist covering FCA claims.

E. Complying with the Seal Order

Once a party has been advised that the qui tam complaint has been partially unsealed for the purposes of allowing the party to make a presentation or engage in settlement discussions, the party must be careful not to disclose the existence or allegations of the qui tam suit to third parties or even to employees other than those who have a need to know in order for the party to make the presentations or participate in settlement negotiations. Third parties for this purpose include government agency personnel other than the DOJ attorneys and agency investigators assigned to handle the qui tam action, shareholders, lenders, insurers, subcontractors, and even affiliates; a party should seek DOJ's consent before disclosing to such parties the existence or content of a partially unsealed qui tam action.

F. Segregating Costs

Under the FAR, the costs of defending a fraud action are, in many cases, unallowable. Thus, if a contractor becomes aware of a possible qui tam suit or FCA investigation against it, the contractor should consider whether to segregate costs related to the matter, including internal investigation costs.

G. Coordinating with Multiple Parties

A qui tam complaint may name several defendants, and DOJ may decide to request partial unsealing of the complaint as to some or all of the named defendants. This can create a situation in which a party knows that a business partner is a named defendant in a qui tam suit but cannot disclose that fact to the business partner. In addition, the scope of a government FCA investigation may include individuals, subcontractors, and other entities in addition to the party itself. In such instances, the party should consider entering into a common interest agreement (a.k.a. joint defense agreement) in order to protect privileges with respect to shared information and documents. However, a party should ensure that such common interest agreements give it the flexibility *not* to share information and documents and to engage in presentations to or discussions with DOJ or the relator without the participation (or even the knowledge) of the other parties to the common interest agreement.

H. Preventing Retaliation against Relator Who Is a Current Employee

A party may learn though an internal investigation, government investigation, or partial unsealing that one or more of its current employees is a relator in a qui tam action against it or that they are contemplating bringing a qui tam suit against it. Although the party would be justified in excluding this individual from any communications or decision-making regarding the investigation or suit, it should not take any action with respect to the individual that could be construed as retaliation for their whistleblower activities or pursuit of a qui tam action. Furthermore, the party should keep confidential whatever facts or suspicions it might have regarding the whistleblower to prevent other employees from retaliating.

I. Complying with Mandatory Self-Disclosure Obligations While a Government Investigation or Sealed Qui Tam Suit Is Pending

Many contractors subject to mandatory disclosure obligations such as those imposed by FAR 52.203-13 do not construe them to require the party to disclose the facts or allegations that are already the subject of a FCA qui tam suit or government investigation. However, to the extent a party's internal investigation uncovers credible evidence of FCA violations beyond those that are the subject of the qui tam suit or government investigation, the party may be obligated to disclose such facts. A party can arguably fulfill such obligation by disclosing the facts to DOJ or other investigators in the course of its presentations or other communications during the investigation. To the extent a contractor opts to make a voluntary or mandatory disclosure, the contractor should take extreme care to reveal facts—and only facts. Although the Fourth Circuit recently affirmed that mandatory disclosures do not require a contractor to waive any attorney-client privilege that would otherwise protect its underlying investigation,[4] contractors should take extreme care to avoid disclosing to the government statements made to its counsel, as such disclosures may be deemed a subject-matter waiver.

J. Working with Agency Personnel

While being mindful not to breach the seal on any qui tam action, contractors should consider whether it would be beneficial to inform relevant contracting

4. *In re* Fluor Intercontinental, Inc., 803 F. App'x 697 (4th Cir. 2020).

officers or other agency personnel of FCA allegations, particularly where performance of the relevant contract is ongoing. First, DOJ guidance indicates that cooperation, including voluntary disclosure of misconduct, is a significant factor considered by the government when evaluating whether to pursue and/or resolve FCA claims. Second, to the extent that an agency continues to pay a contractor's invoices following a disclosure of potential misconduct on a government contract, the contractor can argue that the agency's continued payment despite the alleged false claim undercuts the materiality element of FCA liability.

K. Coordinating with Suspension and Debarment Officials

DOJ attorneys are required by policy to coordinate with the government's administrative attorneys when initiating an FCA investigation, including with regard to suspension and debarment. Thus, while making sure not to breach the seal on any qui tam action, the contractor should consider engaging with the relevant suspension and debarment official (SDO) if the contractor becomes aware of a potential FCA investigation or qui tam suit. Early proactive engagement with the cognizant SDO may also help to demonstrate present responsibility and avoid suspension or debarment.

L. Managing Parallel Criminal Proceedings

DOJ will frequently request the court to stay a sealed qui tam proceeding if it is undertaking a criminal investigation related to the parties and conduct involved in the qui tam proceeding. This is not always the case, however. In those cases where the government is pursuing parallel criminal and civil investigations, defendants and potential defendants should be aware that their actions and statements in one proceeding may influence DOJ's decisions in the other proceeding. For example, FRE 418 does not preclude statements made by a party in settlement of a civil matter from being introduced into evidence against that party in a criminal proceeding, nor does it preclude such statements from being considered by DOJ in deciding whether to prosecute a party or to intervene in a qui tam action against them.

M. Providing Separate Counsel

Particularly where there is a parallel criminal proceeding, a party must consider whether to recommend that its officers or employees whom DOJ wants to interview or depose should be represented by separate counsel and, if so, whether the party should offer to pay for such counsel. Even in the absence of a parallel criminal proceeding, however, a party must consider whether the risk of individual liability under the FCA or other civil statute is significant enough to warrant arranging for separate counsel for that individual. This risk has been heightened by the Yates Memorandum, which emphasized the requirement for DOJ lawyers to consider naming individuals as well as corporations as defendants in FCA cases regardless of such individual's ability to pay any judgment.[5]

5. *See* U.S. DOJ, MEMORANDUM FROM S. YATES, DEPUTY ATTORNEY GENERAL, RE: INDIVIDUAL ACCOUNTABILITY FOR CORPORATE WRONGDOING (Sept. 9, 2015), https://www.justice.gov/d9/pages/attachments/2015/09/10/individual_accountability_for_corporate_wrongdoing_dag_memo2.pdf; U.S. DOJ, *Justice Manual*, 4-3100 (discussing "Pursuit of Claims Against Individuals"), https://www.justice.gov/jm/jm-4-3000-compromising-and-closing#4-3.100.

CHAPTER 8

Threshold Defenses

DAVE NADLER, JENNIFER SHORT, ADAM PROUJANSKY, AND SARA GERBER[1]

In this chapter the authors discuss the following defenses to False Claims Act (FCA) liability that may be raised at the pleading stage: (1) failure to allege fraud with particularity as required by Federal Rule of Civil Procedure (FRCP) 9(b); (2) failure to allege the elements of an FCA violation as required by FRCP 12(b)(6); (3) running afoul of the FCA's so-called "public disclosure" bar; (4) violating the FCA's "first to file" requirement by filing a qui tam action while another qui tam action based on the same underlying information is pending; (5) filing a qui tam action after the filing of a related "government action"; and, (6) filing after the running of the FCA's statute of limitations.

I. Motion to Dismiss under Rule 9(b)

A. Application of Rule 9(b) to FCA Claims

Federal Rule of Civil Procedure 9(b) applies to FCA claims and requires that the plaintiff "state with particularity the circumstances constituting fraud." The Rule 9(b) standard is often likened to the first paragraph of a newspaper story: the complaint must describe the "who, what, when, where, and how of the alleged fraud."[2] However, federal courts are split—although not always sharply—over the degree of particularity required at the pleading stage.[3] The Supreme Court appears unlikely

1. Dave Nadler is senior counsel at Blank Rome. Jennifer Short and Adam Proujansky are partners at the firm, and Sara Geber is an associate.

2. United States v. Molina Healthcare of Ill., 17 F.4th 732, 739 (7th Cir. 2021), *cert. denied sub nom.* Molina Healthcare of Ill. v. Prose, No. 21-1145, 2022 WL 9551004 (U.S. Oct. 17, 2022); United States *ex rel.* Taylor v. Boyko, 39 F.4th 177, 189 (4th Cir. 2022).

3. *See, e.g.*, United States *ex rel.* Chorches for Bankr. Est. of Fabula v. Am. Med. Response, Inc., 865 F.3d 71, 89–93 (2d Cir. 2017) (discussing circuit court decisions applying Rule 9(b) in FCA cases).

to settle the matter anytime soon. On October 17, 2022, the Supreme Court denied three petitions for certiorari seeking review of the issue.[4] The Court previously declined to address the issue in three other cases—one in 2014, and two in 2018.[5]

B. Circuit Divide on Whether a Complaint Must Identify a Specific False Claim

On one side of the split, the courts follow the rule that, in order to meet Rule 9(b) requirements, a relator must plead either (1) a representative example of a false claim that was submitted to the government for payment; or (2) a scheme to submit false claims paired with allegations based on the relator's firsthand knowledge of billing practices sufficient to support a strong inference that false claims were submitted to the government for payment.[6] Generalized allegations of fraud, in the absence of specific facts about the submission of false claims, are insufficient to withstand a motion to dismiss.

The Eighth Circuit's views, which have evolved over time, are illustrative of this side of the split. For example, in 2014's *United States ex rel. Dunn v. North Memorial Health Care*, the Eighth Circuit held that the relator's "generalized conclusion that [Defendant] engaged in noncompliant conduct, and in doing so, caused thousands of instances of fraudulent billing" and allegations that "every claim submitted from 1996 until the present is false" failed to satisfy Rule 9(b).[7] Even though the relator identified individuals who were directly involved in the alleged fraudulent billing, the complaint was fatally deficient because it did not provide "even one example of an actual false claim submitted to [Medicare] for reimbursement."[8] In a later case, the Eighth Circuit softened its strict Rule 9(b) holding slightly, reasoning that, if a relator could not identify particular false claims, it might still satisfy Rule 9(b) by pleading "the particular details of a scheme to submit false claims paired with reliable indicia that lead to a strong inference that claims were actually

4. Cert petitions were filed in the cases of: Est. of Helmly v. Bethany Hospice & Palliative Care of Coastal Georgia, LLC, 853 F. App'x 496 (11th Cir. 2021), *cert. denied sub nom.* Johnson v. Bethany Hospice & Palliative Care LLC, 143 S. Ct. 351 (2022); United States v. Molina Healthcare of Ill., Inc., 17 F.4th 732, 739 (7th Cir. 2021), *cert. denied sub nom.* Molina Healthcare of Ill., Inc. v. Prose, 143 S. Ct. 352 (2022); and United States *ex rel.* Owsley v. Fazzi Assocs., Inc., 16 F.4th 192 (6th Cir. 2021), *cert. denied sub nom.* United States v. Fazzi Assocs., Inc., 143 S. Ct. 362 (2022).

5. *See* United States *ex rel.* Nathan v. Takeda Pharmaceuticals North America, 572 U.S. 1033 (2014); United States *ex rel.* Chase v. Chapters Health Sys., Inc., 139 S. Ct. 69 (2018); Med. Device Bus. Servs., Inc. v. United States *ex rel.* Nargol, 138 S. Ct. 1551 (2018).

6. *E.g.*, *Owsley*, 16 F.4th 192; *Helmly*, 853 F. App'x 496; United States *ex rel.* Benaissa v. Trinity Health, 963 F.3d 733, 739 (8th Cir. 2020).

7. *Dunn*, 739 F.3d at 420.

8. *Id.*

submitted."[9] But this potential exception is not available where a relator does not have firsthand knowledge of the billing practices sufficient to allege "details about [the defendant's] billing practices," such as "dates and descriptions of particular services coupled with 'a description of the billing system that the records were likely entered into.'"[10]

The Fourth, Sixth, and Eleventh Circuits also tend to adhere to the notion that "under Rule 9(b), '[t]he identification of at least one false claim with specificity is an indispensable element of a complaint,'"[11] unless the relator can credibly allege that they had sufficient personal knowledge or participation in the scheme that—while they can't provide specific datils of a single claim, such as invoice number, date, specific services covered, or dollar amount—their allegation that false claims were submitted to the government is nonetheless reliable. The courts' concern seems to be ensuring that the alleged misconduct is logically and factually connected to requests for payment—the "false claims" upon which FCA liability rests. As the Sixth Circuit has explained, it is not sufficient to "describe a private scheme in detail, but then to allege simply that claims requesting illegal payments must have been submitted."[12] The Fourth Circuit similarly has reasoned that "when a defendant's actions, as alleged and as reasonably inferred from the allegations, *could* have led, but *need not necessarily* have led, to the submission of false claims, a relator must allege with particularity that specific false claims actually were presented to the government for payment."[13] And the Eleventh Circuit has ruled that even a "mathematical probability" that a false claim was submitted is not enough under this approach; to satisfy Rule 9(b), a relator lacking direct, personal knowledge of the scheme must plead such details as the "dates on or the frequency with which the defendants submitted false claims, the amounts of those claims, or the patients whose treatment served as the basis for the claims."[14]

---

9. *Benaissa*, 963 F.3d at 739.

10. *Id.* at 740.

11. *See, e.g.*, U.S. v. Walgreen Co., 846 F.3d 879, 881 (6th Cir. 2017).

12. *Id.* (citations omitted).

13. United States *ex rel.* Nathan v. Takeda Pharms. N. Am., Inc., 707 F.3d 451, 457–58 (4th Cir. 2013) (emphasis in original). In *Nathan*, the relator relied on statistics to infer that doctors must have engaged in off-label drug prescribing (per the defendant's allegedly improper marketing efforts) that led to the submission of false claims, but could not identify any particular off-label prescriptions that resulted in claims. The Fourth Circuit held that this approach was insufficient to satisfy Rule 9(b).

14. Est. of Helmly v. Bethany Hospice & Palliative Care of Coastal Ga., LLC, 853 F. App'x 496, 501–02 (11th Cir. 2021), *cert. denied sub nom.* Johnson v. Bethany Hospice & Palliative Care LLC, 143 S. Ct. 351 (2022); *see also* Carrel v. AIDS Healthcare Found., Inc., 898 F.3d 1267, 1275 (11th Cir. 2018) (a relator must plead with particularity the submission of an actual false claim and "must do so with some indicia of reliability"); *see also* United States *ex rel.* Owsley v. Fazzi Assocs., Inc., 16 F.4th 192, 197 (6th Cir. 2021) (relator's identification, based on her personal knowledge, of diagnosis codes

In these (the Fourth, Sixth, and Eleventh) circuits, in the absence of being able to identify specific representative claims, a relator must have at least "personal knowledge or [a] level of participation that can give rise to some indicia of reliability" to plausibly allege that false claims were submitted to the government. Most often, the relator must be able to assert that he or she personally witnessed or participated in the submission of false claims.[15]

Other circuits—including the First, Third, Fifth, Ninth, and Tenth—take a more relaxed approach, holding that Rule 9(b) is satisfied where a plaintiff alleges the details of a fraudulent scheme and can "provide an adequate basis for a reasonable inference that false claims were submitted as part of that scheme."[16] Under this view, it is "the scheme in which particular circumstances constituting fraud may be found that make it highly likely the fraud was consummated through the presentment" of false claims.[17] As the Third Circuit has explained, falsity "comes not from a particular misrepresentation, but from a set of circumstances that, if true, makes a whole set of claims at least prima facie false"; Rule 9(b) is satisfied if the relator can "allege those circumstances with particularity."[18]

Perhaps wavering between these two standards, the Seventh Circuit has articulated that "the specific details that are needed to support a plausible claim of fraud"

---

that were fraudulently up-coded did not amount to "an allegation of 'particular identified claims' submitted pursuant to the fraudulent scheme" because relator did not identify the dates on which she reviewed the patient information, the dates of any related claims for payment or the amounts of those claims), *cert. denied sub nom.* United States v. Fazzi Assocs., Inc., 143 S. Ct. 362 (2022).

15. *Helmly*, 853 F. App'x at 501. For a summary of Eleventh Circuit cases in which a relator with personal knowledge of the submission of false claims was held to have met Rule 9(b) requirements despite a failure to allege the specifics of a particular false claim, *see* Conatser v. ACET, slip op. at 11-20, No. 5:19-cv-00170 (N.D. Ala. July 20, 2022). Within the Fourth and Sixth Circuits, examples of cases in which the pleadings satisfied Rule 9(b) in the absence of identified claims are United States *ex rel.* Jones v. Concerted Care Grp., No. RDB-16-3056, 2022 WL 861396, at *9 (D. Md. Mar. 23, 2022); Hinton v. Integra Lifesciences Holding Corp., No. 18-cv-00244-SRB, 2022 WL 1036777, at *8 (W.D. Mo. Apr. 6, 2022).

16. United States *ex rel.* Lemmon v. Envirocare of Utah, Inc., 614 F.3d 1163, 1172–73 (10th Cir. 2010); *see also, e.g.*, United States *ex rel.* Kelly v. Novartis Pharms. Corp., 827 F.3d 5, 13–15 (1st Cir. 2016); United States *ex rel.* Customs Fraud Investigations, LLC. v. Victaulic Co., 839 F.3d 242, 258 (3d Cir. 2016); United States *ex rel.* Grubbs v. Kanneganti, 565 F.3d 180, 190 (5th Cir. 2009); United States *ex rel.* Presser v. Acacia Mental Health Clinic, LLC, 836 F.3d 770, 777–78 (7th Cir. 2016); Ebeid *ex rel.* United States v. Lungwitz, 616 F.3d 993, 998–99 (9th Cir. 2010).

17. *Grubbs*, 565 F.3d at 190 (reversing district court's dismissal under Rule 9(b) where the complaint described a meeting in which doctors discussed their scheme to defraud the government and further alleged relator's "first-hand experience of the scheme unfolding," including "specific dates that each doctor falsely claimed to have provided services to patients and often the type of medical service or its Current Procedural Terminology code that would have been used in the bill").

18. United States *ex rel.* Bookwalter v. UPMC, 946 F.3d 162, 176 (3d Cir. 2019).

under Rule 9(b) "will depend on the facts of the case" and courts should not "take an overly rigid view of the formulation."[19] In certain circumstances, it is enough that the relator's "detailed allegations support a strong inference" that defendant was making false claims.[20] Accordingly, in *United States ex rel. Prose v. Molina Healthcare of Illinois, Inc.*, allegations that the defendant enrolled new patients in its skilled nursing facility and then sought reimbursement for skilled nursing services—even though defendant had in fact stopped providing skilled nursing facility services—plausibly supported the inference that defendant submitted false claims in accordance with Rule 9(b).[21]

C. Rule 9(b) and FCA Materiality

A footnote in the Supreme Court's 2016 decision in *Universal Health Servs., Inc. v. United States ex rel. Escobar* suggests that Rule 9(b) applies to the FCA's materiality element:

> We reject Universal Health's assertion that materiality is too fact intensive for courts to dismiss False Claims Act cases on a motion to dismiss or at summary judgment. The standard for materiality that we have outlined is a familiar and rigorous one. And False Claims Act plaintiffs must also plead their claims with plausibility and particularity under Federal Rules of Civil Procedure 8 and 9(b) by, for instance, pleading facts to support allegations of materiality.[22]

Courts that tend to apply Rule 9(b) more stringently in the FCA context, as described earlier, also look closely at the relator's factual allegations in support of materiality. For example, in *United States ex rel. Taylor v. Boyko*, the Fourth Circuit cited *Escobar* in upholding dismissal of a complaint asserting that defendant's compliance with licensure requirements was a condition of payment but "failed to allege any further details that would be needed to satisfy Rule 9(b)'s stringent particularity requirement" on the issue of materiality.[23] Other courts have taken a more holistic view of factual allegations in a complaint to find "a compelling

---

19. United States v. Molina Healthcare of Ill., Inc., 17 F.4th 732, 739 (7th Cir. 2021), *cert. denied sub nom.* Molina Healthcare of Ill., Inc. v. Prose, 143 S. Ct. 352 (2022).

20. *Id.* at 740.

21. *Id.*

22. Universal Health Servs., Inc. v. United States *ex rel.* Escobar, 579 U.S. 176, 195 n.6 (2016).

23. 39 F. 4th 177, 190 (4th Cir. 2022) ("Materiality, like other non-scienter elements of a False Claims Act claim, must be pleaded with particularity under Rule 9(b)"); *see also* United States *ex rel.* Foreman v. AECOM, 19 F.4th 85, 109 (2d Cir. 2021) ("Materiality must also 'be pleaded with particularity under Rule 9(b)'"), *cert denied* 142 S. Ct. 2679 (2022).

inference that the purported misrepresentations in question were material to the Government's payment decision."[24]

II. Motion to Dismiss under Rule 12(b)(6)

Federal Rule of Civil Procedure 12(b)(6) allows a district court to dismiss a complaint for failure to state a claim upon which relief can be granted. While motions to dismiss under Rule 9(b) address whether an asserted fraud is described with an appropriate level of detail, a Rule 12(b)(6) motion examines whether the complaint pleads "enough facts to state a claim to relief that is plausible on its face," so that the factual allegations "raise a right to relief above the speculative level."[25] For purposes of an FCA lawsuit, motions to dismiss under Rule 12(b)(6) focus on whether the complaint includes facts that, if true, would plausibly establish each element of the FCA violation.

A. Application of Rule 12(b)(6) to FCA Claims

1. Falsity

Falsity is an essential element of an FCA cause of action under 31 U.S.C. § 3729(a)(1)(A) (false or fraudulent claims), (a)(1)(B) (false statements material to false or fraudulent claims), (a)(1)(G) (false statements material to an obligation to pay), and (a)(1)(C) (conspiracy, when the conspiracy concerns violations of (a)(1)(A), (a)(1)(B), or (a)(1)(G)). The failure to adequately allege that the defendant's conduct involved false or fraudulent claims or statements is a basis for moving to dismiss these causes of action pursuant to Rule 12(b)(6).

Oftentimes, the falsity is "express"—that is, on its face, the claim or statement is untrue. For example, a claim for goods or services that were not provided is factually false. Likewise, a party that submits a claim certifying its compliance with a legal requirement when it is not, in fact, compliant also makes an express false statement.

---

24. *See, e.g.*, United States v. Crumb, No. CV 15-0655-WS-N, 2016 WL 4480690, at *24 (S.D. Ala. Aug. 24, 2016) (allegations that defendant did not comply with requirements for properly diagnosing patients sufficient to support materiality element because "treatment of these false diagnoses are not covered and payable claims under applicable rules, regulations, policies and contract terms" (cleaned up)); United States *ex rel.* Worthy v. E. Maine Healthcare Sys., No. 2:14-CV-00184-JAW, 2017 WL 211609, at *27 (D. Me. Jan. 18, 2017) (allegations that defendants created dummy accounts in violation of billing rules make materiality "at least . . . plausible" such that the complaint could withstand a motion to dismiss).

25. Bell Atl. Corp. v. Twombly, 550 U.S. 544, 545, 547 (2007).

In some circumstances, FCA liability can also arise when a party's submission of a claim is premised on an implied certification or statement that is untrue.[26] A prime example in government contracting is where FCA liability is premised on alleged bid rigging that wrongfully "tainted" the procurement process, rendering subsequent claims for payment "false."[27]

After some years of debate as to the viability of "implied false certification" cases, the Supreme Court in *Escobar* held that "implied certification" can be a basis for establishing the falsity element "at least where two conditions are satisfied" (1) "the claim does not merely request payment, but also makes specific representations about the goods or services provided"; and (2) "failure to disclose noncompliance with material statutory, regulatory, or contractual requirements makes those representations misleading half-truths."[28] The *Escobar* endorsement of implied false certification cases thus created another fertile ground for motions to dismiss under Rule 12(b)(6): a complaint may be dismissed if it relies on an implied certification theory but fails to adequately allege "specific representations" or "misleading half-truths."[29]

Where the allegation of falsity is only a possible explanation for the defendant's conduct and there is a plausible alternative explanation, a court will dismiss the complaint for failure to state a claim.[30] In *Integra Med Analytics LLC v. Providence Health & Services*, the defendant system and its affiliated hospitals engaged a consultant to train doctors to describe medical conditions in a way that supported coding for higher paying diagnoses.[31] The relator, relying on a statistical analysis of coding practices at comparable institutions, alleged that defendants falsely coded claims with secondary diagnosis codes to increase the amount of reimbursement received from Medicare.[32] The court held that the relator failed to state a plausible

26. *See* United States *ex rel.* Mackillop v. Grand Canyon Educ., Inc., No. 18-11192-WGY, — F. Supp. 3d —, 2022 WL 4084444, at *18–19 (D. Mass. Sept. 6, 2022) (overview of "factual," "legal," "express," and "implied" falsity); United States *ex rel.* Hutchins v. DynCorp Int'l, Inc., 342 F. Supp. 3d 32 (D.D.C. 2018) (same).

27. *See* United States *ex rel.* Harrison v. Westinghouse Savannah River Co., 176 F.3d 776, 787–88 (4th Cir. 1999) (collecting cases premised on bid-rigging allegations); United States *ex rel.* McGee v. IBM Corp., 81 F. Supp. 3d 643, 663 (N.D. Ill. 2015); United States v. Inc. Vill. of Island Park, 888 F. Supp. 419, 439 (E.D.N.Y. 1995).

28. Universal Health Servs., Inc. v. United States *ex rel.* Escobar, 579 U.S. 176, 190 (2016).

29. *See, e.g.*, United States *ex rel.* Hawkins v. ManTech Int'l Corp., No. CV 15-2105 (ABJ), 2020 WL 435490, at *14 (D.D.C. 2020) (dismissing claim alleging defendant falsely certified employee qualifications where relators did not point to any specific representations about employee qualifications contained in defendant's claims for payment).

30. Integra Med. Analytics LLC v. Providence Health & Servs., 854 F. App'x 840 (9th Cir. 2021).

31. *Id.* at 842.

32. *Id.* at 842–43.

claim for relief because its allegations did not eliminate "an obvious alternative explanation" that defendants, as a result of a lawful and competitive business strategy, were "more effective at properly coding for better Medicare reimbursement than others in the healthcare industry."[33] The court noted that its conclusion did not "categorically preclude" statistical data from being used to meet pleading requirements for falsity, but, in this instance, the data did not rule out that defendants were "simply ahead of others in the industry" in taking steps to maximize Medicare payments.[34]

2. Scienter

Knowledge of the presentment of a false claim or statement or knowledge of the making or using of a false statement material to a false claim (scienter) is another essential element of a cause of action under the FCA. Where a relator has not adequately alleged scienter, an FCA claim can be dismissed under Rule 12(b)(6).[35] The D.C. Circuit and several district courts have held that allegations of collective knowledge—piecing together the knowledge of various employees—are insufficient to plead corporate scienter in FCA cases and such allegations therefore will not defeat a motion to dismiss under Rule 12(b)(6).[36] The authors are not aware of any courts that have held to the contrary. On the other hand, when a corporate employee has full knowledge of the scheme, this knowledge may be imputed to the corporation for purposes of respondeat superior or vicarious liability so long as the employee was acting within the scope of their authority and for the purpose of benefiting the corporation.[37]

---

33. *Id.* at 841, 844–45.

34. *Id.* at 845 n.5.

35. *See* United States v. Sci. Applications Int'l Corp., 626 F.3d 1257, 1271 (D.C. Cir. 2010).

36. *Sci. Applications Int'l Corp.*, 626 F.3d at 1271; United States *ex rel.* Durkin v. Cnty. of San Diego, No. 15CV2674-MMA (WVG), 2018 WL 3361148, at *5 (S.D. Cal. July 10, 2018); United States v. Fadul, No. CIV.A. DKC 11-0385, 2013 WL 781614, at *9 (D. Md. Feb. 28, 2013); United States v. Educ. Mgmt. Corp., 871 F. Supp. 2d 433, 452 (W.D. Pa. 2012).

37. *See, e.g.*, United States v. O'Connell, 890 F.2d 563, 569 (1st Cir. 1989) (holding that corporation will be liable under FCA if agent acts with apparent authority even if corporation received no benefit from agent's fraud); Grand Union Co. v. United States, 696 F.2d 888, 891 (11th Cir. 1983) (finding that knowledge of employees can be imputed to employer for purposes of liability under the FCA); United States v. Hangar One, Inc., 563 F.2d 1155, 1158 (5th Cir. 1977); United States v. Ridglea State Bank, 357 F.2d 495 (5th Cir. 1966); United States v. Walgreen Co., 591 F. Supp. 3d 297, 311 (E.D. Tenn. 2022) ("When a corporation, like Walgreen here, benefits from the fraud of a managerial agent who is acting within the scope of her employment, a constellation of courts, including the district court in *Shackelford*, has held that the corporation can be vicariously liable under the False Claims Act."); United States *ex rel.* Shackelford v. Am. Mgmt., Inc., 484 F. Supp. 2d 669, 676 (E.D. Mich. 2007) ("The Court therefore joins the majority of cases which hold that a principal is vicariously liable whenever its agents act within the scope of their employment or with apparent authority regardless of the employer's knowledge or culpability."); United States *ex rel.* O'Keefe v. McDonnell

While proof of specific intent to defraud is not required, scienter is not adequately alleged by pleading facts amounting to mere mistake, negligence, or differences in interpretation.[38] Instead, a relator must allege that defendant had actual knowledge that its statements were false, acted in deliberate ignorance of the truth or falsity of its statements, or acted in reckless disregard of the truth or falsity of the statements.[39]

Until the Supreme Court recently provided definitive guidance in *United States ex rel. Schutte v. SuperValu Inc.*,[40] courts were divided on the issue of whether the scienter requirement involved only the defendant's subjective state of mind, or also included an objective reasonableness component. Prior to *Schutte*, several appellate courts held that the FCA does not reach a defendant's reasonable but erroneous interpretation of an ambiguous statute, regulation, or legal obligation where it was not cautioned against such interpretation by authoritative agency or other official guidance.[41] These cases relied on an earlier Supreme Court case, *Safeco Insurance Co. of America v. Burr*,[42] interpreting the scienter requirement of a different statute, the Fair Credit Reporting Act (FCRA), which imposes liability for "willfully" failing to comply with the Act. In *Safeco*, the Court held that a defendant does "not act in reckless disregard" where its interpretation of a statute "albeit erroneous, was not objectively unreasonable," particularly where no agency guidance was available to warn the defendant of its error.[43] This holding has become known as the "objective reasonableness" test.

Leading up to *Schutte*, several circuit courts had held that the *Safeco* "objective reasonableness" test "applies with equal force to the FCA's scienter requirement."[44]

Douglas Corp., 961 F. Supp. 1288, 1292 (E.D. Mo. 1997) (stating that liability under the FCA may be imposed on employers under respondeat superior); United States v. Inc. Vill. of Island Park, 888 F. Supp. 419, 438 (E.D.N.Y. 1995) (determining that respondeat superior applies to FCA violations committed by employee who acts within scope of authority and, in part, for benefit of employer; determining also that corporation is liable if employee acts with apparent authority, even if does not benefit corporation at all).

38. 31 U.S.C. § 3729(b)(1)(B); United States *ex rel.* Berkowitz v. Automation Aids, Inc., 896 F.3d 834, 842 (7th Cir. 2018).

39. 31 U.S.C. § 3729(b)(1)(A); Adomitis v. San Bernardino Mountains Cmty. Hosp. Dist., 816 Fed. App'x 64, 67 n.2 (9th Cir. 2020).

40. United States *ex rel.* Schutte v. SuperValu Inc., Nos. 21-1326 and 22-111, 2023 WL 3742577 (U.S. June 1, 2023).

41. Olhausen v. Arriva Med., LLC, No. 21-10366, 2022 WL 1203023, at *2 (11th Cir. Apr. 22, 2022); United States *ex rel.* Gugenheim v. Meridian Senior Living, LLC, 36 F.4th 174, 181 (4th Cir. 2022); United States v. Allergan, Inc., 746 Fed. Appx. 101, 106–10 (3d Cir. 2018); Olson v. Fairview Health Servs. of Minn., 831 F.3d 1063, 1071–72 (8th Cir. 2016).

42. 551 U.S. 47 (2007).

43. *Id.* at 69.

44. United States v. SuperValu Inc., 9 F.4th 455, 459 (7th Cir. 2021), *rev'd sub nom.* United States *ex rel.* Schutte v. SuperValu Inc., Nos. 21-1326 and 22-111, 2023 WL 3742577 (U.S. June 1, 2023);

For example, in *Olhausen v. Arriva Medical, LLC*, the Eleventh Circuit considered certain Medicare rules that were "susceptible to multiple reasonable interpretations,"[45] and concluded that because the defendant's interpretation of its obligations under the Medicare rules was objectively reasonable, the relator had failed to plead the requisite scienter.[46]

During its 2023 term, the Supreme Court confronted the question of whether the *Safeco* "objective reasonableness" test applied to FCA scienter in its decision in *Schutte*. *Schutte* involved allegations by qui tam plaintiffs that operators of retail drug pharmacies filed false reports regarding "usual and customary" drug prices when they sought reimbursement under Medicare and Medicaid.[47] The district court granted summary judgment in favor of defendants, on the ground that the defendants lacked the requisite scienter. The Seventh Circuit affirmed, reasoning that the defendants could not have acted with the required scienter if their actions were consistent with an objectively reasonable interpretation of the phrase "usual and customary," notwithstanding their subjective beliefs.

The Supreme Court unanimously reversed. It held that the scienter element turns on the defendant's knowledge and subjective beliefs, not on an objective test of what a reasonable person would have known or believed.[48] The Court further held that, in the context of the FCA scienter requirement, "reckless disregard" entails a defendant's subjective awareness of a substantial and unjustifiable risk that the claims are false, rather than a test of objective reasonableness.[49] In the cases before the Court, therefore, the scienter requirement would be met if the defendants (1) actually knew that their reported prices were not their "usual and customary" prices at the time they reported the prices, (2) were aware of a substantial risk that their reported prices were not their "usual and customary" prices and intentionally avoided learning whether their reported prices were accurate, or (3) were aware of a substantial and unjustifiable risk that their reported prices were not their "usual and customary" prices but submitted the claims anyway—regardless of how an objectively reasonable person might interpret the phrase "usual and customary."[50]

United States v. Allergan, Inc., 746 F. App'x 101, 106 (3d Cir. 2018); United States *ex rel.* McGrath v. Microsemi Corp., 690 F. App'x 551, 552 (9th Cir. 2017); United States *ex rel.* Donegan v. Anesthesia Assocs. of Kansas City, PC, 833 F.3d 874, 879–80 (8th Cir. 2016); United States *ex rel.* Purcell v. MWI Corp., 807 F.3d 281, 288–91 (D.C. Cir. 2015).

45. *Olhausen*, 2022 WL 1203023, at *2.

46. *Id.*

47. United States *ex rel.* Schutte v. SuperValu Inc., 2023 WL 3742577, at *3–4.

48. *Id.* at *8–9.

49. *Id.* at *7.

50. *Id.* at *10.

Because it is normally more challenging to prove or disprove the subjective knowledge and beliefs of the defendant at an early phase of the litigation, and because state of mind can be pled generally in a complaint, the *Schutte* Court, by moving away from the "objective reasonableness" test that many lower courts had applied, and focusing instead on a subjective inquiry into the defendant's state of mind, likely made it more difficult for a defendant to obtain dismissal of an FCA complaint on the basis of lack of scienter at the pleading stage.

3. Materiality

The Supreme Court's 2016 decision in *Escobar* made clear that the FCA element of materiality is an important guardrail that separates an FCA violation from a mere breach of contract action. The FCA defines materiality as "having a natural tendency to influence, or be capable of influencing, the payment or receipt of money or property."[51] *Escobar* identified three nonexclusive factors that are probative of materiality: (1) whether the government has expressly identified compliance with a statutory, regulatory, or contractual provision as a condition of payment; (2) whether the government consistently refuses to pay similar claims based on noncompliance with the particular statutory, regulatory, or contractual requirement at issue, or continues to pay claims despite knowledge of the noncompliance; and (3) whether the noncompliance is minor or insubstantial or goes to the essence of the bargain.[52] Although materiality can be a fact-intensive inquiry that normally would not be appropriately resolved at the pleading stage, the *Escobar* Court made clear that courts are empowered to dismiss FCA claims under Rule 12(b)(6) if a complaint fails to plead facts that, if true, would establish materiality with the requisite plausibility.[53]

In the years following *Escobar*, the lower courts have examined the sufficiency of pleading on the element of FCA materiality and dismissed cases that fall short. For example, in *United States ex rel. Foreman v. AECOM*, the complaint asserted contractual violations of man-hour utilization and property tracking

---

51. 31 U.S.C. § 3729(b)(4).

52. Universal Health Servs., Inc. v. United States *ex rel.* Escobar, 579 U.S. 176, 193–95 & n.5 (2016).

53. The Supreme Court stated in a footnote that:

> We reject Universal Health's assertion that materiality is too fact intensive for courts to dismiss False Claims Act cases on a motion to dismiss or at summary judgment. The standard for materiality that we have outlined is a familiar and rigorous one. And False Claims Act plaintiffs must also plead their claims with plausibility and particularity under Federal Rules of Civil Procedure 8 and 9(b) by, for instance, pleading facts to support allegations of materiality.

Escobar, 579 U.S. at 195 n.6.

requirements.[54] The same complaint also referenced corrective actions taken by the government that illustrated the government's willingness to pay the defendant despite knowledge of the alleged violation. The Second Circuit upheld the district court's order dismissing that claim, reasoning that the factual allegations of the complaint made materiality implausible.[55]

Similarly, in *United States ex rel. Porter v. Magnolia Health Plan, Inc.*, the Fifth Circuit affirmed dismissal of FCA claims alleging the defendant defrauded Medicaid by staffing case manager positions with individuals who did not meet statutory or contractual licensing requirements because the relator did not adequately plead that the defendant's misrepresentations about staffing were material to the government's decision to pay.[56] The court considered the provisions of the defendant's Medicare contract, which was attached as an exhibit to the complaint, and found that its language did not support the relator's theory that compliance with licensing requirements was an express condition of payment.[57] The relator's additional allegations that Medicaid took no action after learning about the defendant's staffing practices—and, indeed, instead renewed the contract several times—also rendered the element of materiality implausible.[58]

As the Second Circuit noted in *Foreman*, "there may be circumstances where the government's payment of a claim or failure to terminate a contract despite knowledge of certain alleged contractual violations will not be particularly probative of a lack of materiality," but a plaintiff must "plausibly plead facts to support such possible alternative explanations in the complaint."[59] In *United States ex rel.*

---

54. 19 F.4th 85 (2d Cir. 2021), *cert. denied*, 142 S. Ct. 2679 (2022); *see also* United States *ex rel.* Petratos v. Genentech Inc., 855 F.3d 481, 489–90 (3d Cir. 2017) (granting dismissal of FCA complaint on materiality grounds where relator conceded that government would have paid, and continued to pay claims, after being informed of noncompliance); *In re* Plavix Mktg., Sales Prac. and Prods. Liab. Litig. (No. II), 332 F. Supp. 3d 927, 944–48 (D.N.J. 2017) (dismissing FCA claim where blood-thinner drug Plavix was placed on state's preferred drug list and, therefore, Medicaid automatically issued reimbursement payments regardless of whether physician's claims contained false certifications of compliance).

55. United States *ex rel.* Foreman v. AECOM, 19 F.4th 85, 113–15 (2d Cir. 2021), *cert. denied* 142 S. Ct. 2679 (2022). Notably, the court reversed dismissal of other FCA counts based on alleged labor billing violations, finding that the district court erroneously relied on a DCAA report in assessing materiality. While the DCAA report tended to show government knowledge of the alleged violations, the report was not referenced or relied upon in the complaint, and the district court should not have considered it on a motion to dismiss. *Id.* at 107–08.

56. 810 F. App'x 237 (5th Cir. 2020), *cert. denied*, 141 S. Ct. 1238 (2021).

57. *Id.* at 241 (citing United States *ex rel.* Riley v. St. Luke's Episcopal Hosp., 355 F.3d 370, 377 (5th Cir. 2004)).

58. *Id.* at 241–42.

59. *Foreman*, 19 F.4th 85 at 115–16; *see also* United States *ex rel.* Mei Ling v. City of Los Angeles, 389 F. Supp. 3d 744, 761–62 (C.D. Cal. 2019) (an FCA plaintiff "can rebut the 'very strong evidence'

USN4U, LLC v. Wolf Creek Federal Services, Inc., the Sixth Circuit noted some of those possible alternative explanations that might cause the government to continue contracting with a party after becoming aware of the alleged fraud, including that the government may not want to end a relationship with a contractor over unproven allegations, the government may not have other feasible procurement options, or there may be a lack of other suppliers.[60] Accordingly, multiple courts have allowed FCA causes of action to proceed in the face of continued payment, despite *Escobar's* admonition that continued payment is "very strong evidence" of immateriality.[61]

4. Causation

In *United States ex rel. Cimino v. International Business Machines Corp.*,[62] the court held that causation is a required element for an FCA cause of action based on a fraudulent inducement theory.[63] In *Cimino*, the relator alleged that the defendant fraudulently induced the IRS to renew a license agreement for software by manipulating data to make it appear that the agency had overutilized the software licenses and owed compliance penalties under its existing contract—fees which defendant promised to waive if the IRS entered into a new agreement. In responding to the defendant's motion to dismiss, the relator argued that it was required to plead only that the alleged fraud was capable of inducing the government to enter into the

of immateriality provided by the continued payments with its own 'very strong counterevidence' of materiality").

60. 34 F.4th 507, 516–17 (6th Cir. 2022) (concluding relator sufficiently pled materiality element despite NASA continuing to contract with defendant after learning of fraud allegations where NASA repeatedly relied on defendant's estimates in awarding it contracts); *see also* United States *ex rel.* Cimino v. Int'l Bus. Machines Corp., 3 F.4th 412, 423 (D.C. Cir. 2021) (holding that the IRS could have continued to pay for any number of reasons that do not render defendant's fraud immaterial, such as the IRS may have "felt obligated to pay until it received a legal determination that it was relieved of the agreement's terms").

61. Universal Health Servs., Inc. v. United States *ex rel.* Escobar, 579 U.S. 176, 195 (2016); *see also* United States *ex rel.* Vt. Nat'l Telephone Co. v. Northstar Wireless, LLC, 34 F.4th 29, 31 (D.C. Cir. 2022) (holding that plaintiff adequately pled materiality despite government paying claim in full; "focusing on 'the potential effect of the false statement when it is made rather than on the false statement's actual effect after it is discovered'" (quoting United States *ex rel.* Longhi v. United States, 575 F.3d 458, 470 (5th Cir. 2009)); *Mei Ling*, 389 F. Supp. 3d at 761–62 (C.D. Cal. 2019) (stating that "the Government may still maintain an FCA claim if it can muster allegations, taken as true, that explain why continued payments are not probative of immateriality," and holding that the complaint plausibly alleges that HUD was still "trying to obtain voluntary compliance before reducing or terminating funding—a decision which could have harmful collateral consequences").

62. 3 F.4th 412 (D.C. Cir. 2021).

63. *Id.* at 418–19; *see also* United States *ex rel.* USN4U, LLC v. Wolf Creek Fed. Servs., Inc., 34 F.4th 507, 518 (6th Cir. 2022).

new agreement. The court disagreed. Citing common law, the court held that the "ordinary meaning of inducement incorporates a causation requirement" given that "if a fraudster's misrepresentations do not cause a party to enter a contract, no fraudulent inducement has occurred."[64] The court further held that a relator must plead facts to allege not only proximate causation but actual cause under the but-for standard, meaning that the realtor would "have to provide sufficient facts for the court to draw a reasonable inference" that the defendant's false data "caused the IRS to enter the license agreement."[65]

III. The Public Disclosure Bar

When the United States has declined to intervene in a qui tam action or claim, the public disclosure bar is available as a potential defense for the defendant. The FCA's public disclosure bar provides:

> The court shall dismiss an action or claim under this section, unless opposed by the Government, if substantially the same allegations or transactions as alleged in the action or claim were publicly disclosed—
>
> (i) in a Federal criminal, civil, or administrative hearing in which the Government or its agent is a party;
> (ii) in a congressional, Government Accountability Office, or other Federal report, hearing, audit, or investigation; or
> (iii) from the news media
>
> unless the action is brought by the Attorney General or the person bringing the action is an original source of the information.[66]

This statutory provision requires the court to dismiss an FCA action or claim that is based on facts that are substantially the same as information that already has been disclosed in the media or in a government proceeding or investigation, unless the plaintiff is an "original source" of that same information, as that term is defined in the FCA. The public disclosure bar is intended to discourage parasitic litigation by qui tam plaintiffs who have no significant information of their own to contribute to what is already known by the government or the public.[67]

---

64. *Cimino*, 3 F.4th 412, 418–19 (D.C. Cir. 2021).
65. *Id.* at 420–21.
66. 31 U.S.C. § 3730(e)(4)(A) (2010).
67. *See* Graham Cnty. Soil & Water Conservation Dist. v. United States *ex rel.* Wilson, 559 U.S. 280, 294–95 (2010); *see also* United States *ex rel.* Schweizer v. Canon, Inc., 9 F.4th 269 (5th Cir. 2021) (dismissing relator's second qui tam case on grounds that her earlier settled case was a public disclosure that barred her second complaint against the first defendant's successor-in-interest for allegedly continuing the fraud).

The public disclosure bar is subject to a few exceptions. It does not apply where the relator can demonstrate that they are an "original source" of the information in their complaint. By statute, the term "original source" means:

> An individual who either (i) prior to a public disclosure under subsection (e)(4)(a), has voluntarily disclosed to the Government the information on which allegations or transactions in a claim are based, or (2) who has knowledge that is independent of and materially adds to the publicly disclosed allegations or transactions, and who has voluntarily provided the information to the Government before filing an action under this section.[68]

The bar also does not require dismissal if the government is taking over the claim or case or if the government declines to intervene but objects to dismissal.[69]

The Supreme Court has held that in interpreting the public disclosure bar, courts should consider the provision's "entire text, read as an 'integrated whole,'" take into account the "generally broad scope" of the provision, and look to the ordinary meaning of the words used by Congress.[70]

A. Application of the "Public Disclosure" Bar

1. "Allegations or Transactions"

The public disclosure bar applies when "substantially the same allegations or transactions as alleged in the action or claim were publicly disclosed."[71] In *United States ex rel. Springfield Terminal Railway Co. v. Quinn*, the court focused on the precise meaning of the term "allegations or transactions."[72] It noted that the phrase was not defined under the statute and, moreover, the legislative history was silent as to the meaning or significance of the phrase.[73] However, referring to the dictionary meaning of the terms, the court defined "allegation" as "connot[ing] a conclusory statement implying the existence of provable supporting facts" and "transaction" as "suggest[ing] an exchange between two parties or things that reciprocally affect or influence one another."[74] The court further explained:

> The language employed in § 3730(e)(4)(A) suggests that Congress sought to prohibit *qui tam* actions *only* when either the allegation of fraud or the critical elements of the fraudulent transaction themselves were in the public domain.[75]

---

68. 31 U.S.C. § 3730(e)(4)(B).
69. *Id.* § 3730(e)(4).
70. Schindler Elevator Corp. v. United States *ex rel.* Kirk, 563 U.S. 401, 408 *et seq.* (2011).
71. 31 U.S.C. § 3730(e)(4)(A).
72. 14 F.3d 645, 653–56 (D.C. Cir. 1994).
73. *Id.* at 653.
74. *Id.* at 653–54.
75. *Id.* at 654.

Under this approach, "a *qui tam* action cannot be sustained where all of the material elements of the fraudulent transaction are already in the public domain."[76] Courts will find public disclosures even where no one source contained a complete disclosure of the allegations or transactions, but rather multiple sources viewed in combination exposed the elements of the fraud. As stated by the Sixth Circuit, "[a] public disclosure can also be piecemeal so long as the multiple sources of information reveal the allegation of fraud and its essential elements."[77] The Fifth Circuit similarly explained that the public disclosure bar kicks in when "one could have produced the substance of the complaint merely by synthesizing the public disclosures."[78]

Conversely, "where only one element of the fraudulent transaction is in the public domain," the relator "may mount a case by coming forward with either the additional elements necessary to state a case of fraud . . . *or* allegations of fraud itself."[79] And this is true even when the government has in its possession nonpublic information that, when combined with the publicly disclosed information, supports an inference of fraud.[80] Standing alone, the publicly disclosed information must either reflect all of the elements that establish fraud or expressly allege fraud.[81]

2. "Substantially the Same"

In *United States ex rel. Mateski v. Raytheon Co.*, the Ninth Circuit examined what it means for a public disclosure to be "substantially similar to" the allegations or transactions contained in a complaint.[82] According to the court, the "far ends of the similarity spectrum" are (1) "cases finding substantial similarity because the allegations in the *qui tam* complaint were virtually identical to prior public disclosures," and (2) "cases finding no similarity because the allegations in the *qui tam* complaint were completely different from prior disclosures."[83] The *Mateski* case involved circumstances in between these two extremes because if "considered at a high level of generality," the allegations in the qui tam complaint and the public reports both discussed similar problems. At a "more granular level" however,

76. *Id.* at 655.

77. United States *ex rel.* Rahimi v. Rite Aid Corp., 3 F.4th 813, 824 (6th Cir. 2021).

78. United States *ex rel.* Jamison v. McKesson Corp., 649 F.3d 322, 331 (5th Cir. 2011); United States *ex rel.* Beck v. St. Joseph Health Sys., No. 5:17-CV-052-C, 2021 WL 7084164, at *5 (N.D. Tex. Nov. 30, 2021).

79. United States *ex rel.* Springfield Terminal Ry. Co. v. Quinn, 14 F.3d 645, 655 (D.C. Cir. 1994).

80. United States *ex rel.* Crocano v. Trividia Health, Inc., 2022 WL 2800380, at *4–*5 (S.D. Fla. July 18, 2022) (citing United States *ex rel.* Bibby v. Mortgage Investors Corp., 987 F.3d 1340, 1353–54 (11th Cir. 2021)).

81. *Id.*

82. 816 F.3d 565, 573–75 (9th Cir. 2016).

83. *Id.* at 573.

the allegations in the complaint discussed "specific issues found nowhere in the publicly disclosed information."[84] The court in *Mateski* thus addressed whether a court should "approach the substantial similarity question at a high or low level of generality, and accordingly, whether a complaint that is similar only at a high level of generality triggers the public disclosure bar."[85] Quoting a Seventh Circuit decision, the court held that "viewing FCA claims 'at the highest level of generality . . . in order to wipe out *qui tam* suits that rest on genuinely new and material information is not sound.'"[86]

Thus, a suit was permitted to proceed when it provided specific allegations that the defendant chiropractor firm had knowingly filed fraudulent bills, even though there was public information that false or mistaken claims within the chiropractic industry are common.[87] Likewise, a suit was not barred by the public disclosure bar when it alleged that a particular university fraudulently claimed that teaching physicians had properly supervised operations performed by residents in order to obtain Medicare reimbursement, even where public audits had indicated that many teaching hospitals were wrongly receiving double compensation from Medicare for unsupervised procedures performed by residents.[88] Indeed, several courts of appeals have concluded that reports documenting a significant rate of false claims by an industry as a whole—without attributing fraud to particular firms—do not prevent a qui tam suit against any particular member of that industry.[89]

Finally, the Seventh Circuit has permitted a suit to proceed where it alleged a more sophisticated method of violating the Higher Education Act than a prior suit brought by similarly positioned relators,[90] and the Fourth Circuit has rejected a public disclosure challenge to a suit that alleged upcoding by medical providers when an earlier report on a state investigation of the same providers disclosed deficiencies in medical care by the same medical providers but "[n]othing in the [report] or investigation touched on billing or alleged fraud."[91]

---

84. *Id.* at 574.

85. *Id.* at 575.

86. *Id.* at 577 (quoting Leveski v. ITT Educ. Servs., Inc., 719 F.3d 818, 831 (7th Cir. 2013)); *accord* United States *ex rel.* Holloway v. Heartland Hospice, Inc., 960 F.3d 836, 851 (6th Cir. 2020) ("The public-disclosure bar was intended to be 'wide-reaching,' but to stop short of 'wip[ing] out *qui tam* suits that rest on genuinely new and material information'" (citations omitted)).

87. *See* United States *ex rel.* Baltazar v. Warden, 635 F.3d 866 (7th Cir. 2011).

88. *See* United States *ex rel.* Goldberg v. Rush Univ. Med. Ctr., 680 F.3d 933 (7th Cir. 2012).

89. *Baltazar*, 635 F.3d at 868 (citing *In re* Natural Gas Royalties Qui Tam Litigation, 562 F.3d 1032, 1042–43 (10th Cir. 2009) (dictum); United States v. Alcan Elec. & Eng'g, Inc., 197 F.3d 1014, 1019 (9th Cir. 1999) (dictum); United States *ex rel.* Findley v. FPC–Boron Employees' Club, 105 F.3d 675, 687 (D.C. Cir. 1997) (dictum); United States *ex rel.* Fine v. Sandia Corp., 70 F.3d 568, 572 (10th Cir. 1995) (dictum); Cooper v. Blue Cross & Blue Shield of Fla., Inc., 19 F.3d 562, 566 & n.7 (11th Cir. 1994) (holding, and about asserted Medicare fraud in particular).

90. Leveski v. ITF Educ. Servs, Inc., 719 F.3d 818 (7th Cir. 2013).

91. United States *ex rel.* Taylor v. Boyko, 39 F.4th 177, 189 (4th Cir. 2022).

3. Forms of Public Disclosure

A public disclosure may be made "(i) in a Federal criminal, civil, or administrative hearing in which the Government or its agent is a party; (ii) in a congressional, Government Accountability Office, or other Federal report, hearing, audit, or investigation; or (iii) from the news media."[92] These forms of public disclosure are generally interpreted broadly. For instance, "hearing" is understood to apply in "a broad context of legal proceedings."[93] In 2022, the Ninth Circuit held that the term "other Federal . . . hearing" encompasses the ex parte process in which the U.S. Patent and Trademark Office considers a patent application, noting that documents relating to the agency's consideration are published on government websites.[94]

Likewise, the Supreme Court has characterized a "report" as consistent with the "broad ordinary meaning" of the term, that is, as "something that gives information" or a "notification," or "an official or formal statement of facts or proceedings."[95] The key is that the report must be disseminated outside the government. Thus, a federal agency's response to a Freedom of Information Act (FOIA) request disclosing an alleged fraud qualifies as a "report" that triggers the public disclosure bar.[96] However, government investigations and audit reports that are disseminated only to those entities that are the subject of the investigation or audit do not constitute a public disclosure.[97]

The term "news media," also not statutorily defined, nonetheless has a similar "broad[] sweep."[98] Courts have found the term "news media" to include press releases[99] and publicly available, promotional websites geared toward the dissemination of information.[100] Newspaper advertisements also qualify.[101]

4. Original Source Exception

An individual may be an "original source" in one of two ways: first, "prior to a public disclosure under subsection (e)(4)(A)," the relator has "voluntarily disclosed to the Government the information on which allegations or transactions in a claim

---

92. 31 U.S.C. § 3730(e)(4).

93. United States *ex rel.* Springfield Terminal Ry. Co. v. Quinn, 14 F.3d 645, 652 (D.C. Cir. 1994).

94. United States *ex rel.* Silbersher v. Allergan, Inc., 46 F.4th 991 (9th Cir. 2022); *contra* United States v. Janssen Biotech, Inc., 576 F. Supp. 3d 212 (D.N.J. 2021).

95. Schindler Elevator Corp. v. United States *ex rel.* Kirk, 563 U.S. 401, 407 (2011).

96. *Id.* at 410.

97. United States *ex rel.* Foreman v. AECOM, 19 F.4th 85, 123–26 (2d Cir. 2021), *cert. denied* 142 S. Ct. 2679 (2022).

98. Graham Cnty. Soil & Water Conservation Dist. v. United States *ex rel.* Wilson, 559 U.S. 280, 290 (2010).

99. *See, e.g.*, United States *ex rel.* Rahimi v. Rite Aid Corp., 3 F.4th 813, 825 (6th Cir. 2021).

100. *See, e.g.*, United States *ex rel.* Osheroff v. Humana Inc., 776 F.3d 805, 813 (11th Cir. 2015).

101. *See, e.g.*, United States *ex rel.* Colquitt v. Abbott Labs., 864 F. Supp. 2d 499, 519 (N.D. Tex. 2012), *aff'd sub nom.* United States *ex rel.* Colquitt v. Abbott Lab'ys, 858 F.3d 365 (5th Cir. 2017).

are based" or, second, if the relator "has knowledge that is *independent of and materially adds to* the publicly disclosed allegations or transactions, and . . . has voluntarily provided the information to the Government before filing an action under this section."[102]

"Independent knowledge" is "knowledge that does not depend on public disclosures."[103] To establish "independent knowledge," a relator must "allege specific facts—as opposed to mere conclusions—showing exactly how and when he or she obtained" the independent knowledge of the fraudulent acts alleged in the complaint.[104]

Materiality for the purposes of the public disclosure bar requires that a relator's information is of "such a nature that knowledge of the item would affect a person's decision-making" or thinking with respect to the alleged fraud.[105] An individual does not "materially add" to the publicly disclosed information where the public disclosures, by themselves, were "'sufficient to give rise to an inference' of illegality," even "without the Relator's additional facts."[106] Likewise, where the "'key facts' to an FCA claim have already been 'thoroughly revealed,' the relator's knowledge 'even if gained early and independently,' does not 'materially contribute anything of import to the public knowledge about the alleged fraud.'"[107] Similarly, an individual does not qualify as an original source by offering specific examples of the alleged fraud when the underlying conduct has already been publicly disclosed.[108]

By contrast, a relator "materially adds" to the publicly disclosed allegations where prior disclosures had focused on "the fraud committed on patients and doctors" while the relator's suit "provided information on the alleged fraud *on the government* for the first time."[109]

B. The 2010 Public Disclosure Bar Compared to the 1986 Public Disclosure Bar

Because the version of the public disclosure bar in effect at the time the alleged false claim was made is deemed to apply, if a case involves conduct from 2010 or before, it is important to be aware of the prior version of the public disclosure bar.[110] The earlier, 1986-era provision reads as follows:

---

102. 31 U.S.C. § 3730(e)(4)(B) (emphasis added).

103. United States *ex rel.* Atkinson v. Pa. Shipbuilding Co., 473 F.3d 506, 520 (3d Cir. 2007).

104. *In re* Plavix, 123 F. Supp. 3d at 597 (D.N.J. 2015) (quotation marks omitted).

105. United States *ex rel.* Rahimi v. Rite Aid Corp., 3 F.4th 813, 831 (6th Cir. 2021).

106. *In re Plavix*, 123 F. Supp. 3d at 599 (citation omitted).

107. *Id.* (citation omitted).

108. *Rahimi*, 3 F.4th at 831.

109. *In re Plavix*, 123 F. Supp. 3d at 599.

110. Hughes Aircraft Co. v. United States *ex rel.* Schumer, 520 U.S. 939, 946, 951 (1997); United States *ex rel.* Holloway v. Heartland Hospice, Inc., 960 F.3d 836, 843–44 (6th Cir. 2020) (applying the

> No court shall have jurisdiction over an action under this section based upon the public disclosure of allegations or transactions in a criminal, civil, or administrative hearing, in a congressional, administrative, or Government Accounting Office report, hearing, audit, or investigation, or from the news media, unless the action is brought by the Attorney General or the person bringing the action is an original source of the information.[111]

Notably, the 1986 version of the public disclosure bar served as a jurisdictional bar to suit; by contrast, the 2010 amended public disclosure bar merely states that "[t]he court shall dismiss an action or claim under this section. . . ."[112] Accordingly, courts generally have held that the 2010 version of the public disclosure bar is a ground for dismissal but no longer a jurisdictional bar pursuant to FRCP 12(b)(1).[113]

Moreover, under the prior version of the statute, disclosures in federal *and* state trials and hearings qualify as public disclosures[114] and disclosures in federal *and* state reports, audits, or investigations likewise constitute public disclosures.[115] After the amendments, however, only disclosures in *federal* trials and hearings and in *federal* reports and investigations qualify as public disclosures.[116]

Finally, the 1986 version of the public disclosure bar included the somewhat ambiguous requirement that an "original source" have both "independent" *and* "direct" knowledge of the publicly disclosed information, rather than only "independent" knowledge.[117] Courts have held that "direct" knowledge does not require a relator to have "firsthand" knowledge, and that a relator's knowledge is "independent" if it is gained by the relator's own efforts and not acquired through the efforts of others.[118] Although nothing in the FCA requires a relator to be a corporate insider, some courts have held that a relator must have participated in or observed the ongoing fraud.[119] In contrast to the amended public disclosure bar, under the

---

1986 and 2010 versions of the public disclosure bar where the fraud was alleged to have occurred both before and after amendment).

111. 31 U.S.C. § 3730(e)(4) (1986).

112. *Id.*

113. *See, e.g.*, United States *ex rel.* Osheroff v. Humana Inc., 776 F.3d 805, 810–11 (11th Cir. 2015); United States *ex rel.* May v. Purdue Pharma L.P., 737 F.3d 908, 916 (4th Cir. 2013).

114. *See, e.g.*, McElmurray v. Consol. Gov't of Augusta-Richmond Cnty., 501 F.3d 1244, 1252 (11th Cir. 2007).

115. *See* Graham Cnty. Soil & Water Conservation Dist. v. United States *ex rel.* Wilson, 559 U.S. 280, 301 (2010).

116. *See* 31 U.S.C. §§ 3730(e)(4)(A)(i) & (ii) (2010).

117. *See, e.g.*, United States *ex rel.* Bogina v. Medline Indus., Inc., 809 F.3d 365, 368 (7th Cir. 2016) ("what 'direct' adds to 'independent' as a modifier of 'knowledge' is inscrutable").

118. United States *ex rel.* Rahimi v. Rite Aid Corp., 3 F.4th 813, 829–30 (6th Cir. 2021).

119. United States *ex rel.* Schumann v. Astrazeneca Pharms. L.P., 769 F.3d 837, 847 (3d Cir. 2014) ("knowledge of a scheme is not direct when it is gained by reviewing files and discussing the documents therein with individuals who actually participated in the memorialized events").

earlier version, the government was not empowered to oppose the dismissal of a qui tam action where the case was based on publicly disclosed information and for which the relator was not an original source.

IV. The "First to File" Bar

The "first to file" bar is a statutory provision barring a relator from pursuing a qui tam action when a factually "related" qui tam action is currently pending against the same defendant. Specifically, 31 U.S.C. § 3730(b)(5) provides: "[w]hen a person brings an action under the subsection, no person other than the Government may intervene or bring a related action based on the facts underlying the pending action." The legislative history of this provision indicates that Congress's intent was to prevent "class actions or multiple separate suits" under the FCA for the same or related claims.[120] Courts have traditionally interpreted the "first to file" bar broadly, drawing on the legislative history of the provision to discourage parasitic lawsuits while encouraging whistleblowers "to file quickly by protecting the spoils of the first to bring a claim."[121]

A. "Related Action"

A "related action" for purposes of the "first to file" bar is an action that contains the same essential elements as a previously filed case.[122] This has been described as the "material elements" or "material facts" standard. In *United States ex rel. LaCorte v. SmithKline Beecham Clinical Labs*, the Third Circuit held that the "first to file" rule barred an FCA action that arose from the same essential facts as a previously filed FCA action against the same defendant.[123] Like *LaCorte*, in *United States ex rel. Lujan v. Hughes Aircraft Co.*, the Ninth Circuit rejected an "identical facts" test as contrary to the plain language and legislative intent of the FCA, holding that § 3730(b)(5) bars "later-filed actions alleging the same material elements of fraud described in an earlier suit."[124] By contrast, if a court finds that a suit does not share the same material facts as a previously filed suit, a defendant cannot successfully claim that the "first to file" rule bars an action.[125]

---

120. S. Rep. No. 99-345, at 25, reprinted in 1986 U.S.C.C.A.N. 5266, 5290.

121. Cho on behalf of States v. Surgery Partners, Inc., 30 F.4th 1035, 1040 (11th Cir. 2022) (citing *In re* Nat. Gas Royalties Qui Tam Litig. (CO2 Appeals), 566 F.3d 956, 961 (10th Cir. 2009)) (quotation marks omitted).

122. United States *ex rel.* LaCorte v. SmithKline Beecham Clinical Labs, 149 F.3d 227, 232–33 (3d Cir. 1998).

123. *Id.*

124. United States *ex rel.* Lujan v. Hughes Aircraft Co., 243 F.3d 1181, 1189 (9th Cir. 2001).

125. *See id.*; *see also* United States *ex rel.* Heath v. AT&T, 791 F.3d 112, 121–23 (D.C. Cir. 2015) (relator's action against defendant and 19 subsidiaries was not barred by relator's earlier filed action

Establishing that two actions are related for purposes of the first to file bar is a fact-intensive, case-by-case exercise. In *United States ex rel. Hampton v. Columbia/ HCA Healthcare Corp.*, the court cited both to *LaCorte* and *Lujan* in determining that a lawsuit was barred by the "first to file" rule even though the previously filed suit had a different time frame, and all the defendants were not identical.[126] The court reasoned that the "first to file" bar applied because the suits alleged the same fraudulent activity.

Similarly, the First Circuit held that a new qui tam action was barred by a prior qui tam action brought against the same defendant in *United States ex rel. Wilson v. Bristol-Myers Squibb, Inc.*, even though the previous action described a different off-label promotion scheme.[127] The First Circuit reasoned that, although the cases differed in that the previous action involved off-label drug uses for different diseases, the bar applied because both actions involved the same drugs, and alleged a nationwide scheme with the same mechanisms of promotion.[128] The First Circuit further reasoned that the two actions were related because the first-filed action put the government on notice that the defendant was engaged in a nationwide scheme to defraud through the use of particular drugs detailed in the previous complaint.[129]

In *Cho on behalf of States v. Surgery Partners, Inc.*, the court compared the two complaints "side-by-side" and determined that they alleged the "same essential facts" that defendants engaged in a scheme to pressure providers to order expensive and unnecessary diagnostic tests for patients.[130] The court held that while the relator added a new defendant and a conspiracy claim, the complaint did not "meaningfully expand the scope" of the fraudulent scheme or "suggest that it was more pervasive" than the previously filed action indicated.[131]

In contrast, in *United States ex rel. Heath v. AT&T, Inc.*, the D.C. Circuit determined that two actions were not related for purposes of the "first to file" bar where the first action alleged that an AT&T subsidiary in Wisconsin misrepresented pricing to schools and libraries in Wisconsin, while the second action alleged a similar, but nationwide, scheme by AT&T to defraud the federal government through service contracts that misrepresented prices.[132]

---

against one subsidiary involving the same federal program, where the two complaints targeted "factually distinct types of fraud" and "the fraud manifested itself in sufficiently distinct ways in the two cases that the material elements of the fraud differ").

126. 318 F.3d 214 (D.C. Cir. 2003).

127. 750 F.3d 111 (1st Cir. 2014).

128. *Id* at 116.

129. *Id* at 118.

130. Cho on behalf of States v. Surgery Partners, Inc., 30 F.4th 1035, 1043–44 (11th Cir. 2022).

131. *Id.*

132. 791 F.3d 112 (D.C. Cir. 2015).

Similarly, in *United States ex rel. Beauchamp v. Academi Training Center*, the court found that the bar did not apply because the first case involved allegedly false claims relating to security provided to the government in Afghanistan, whereas the later-filed case involved the contractor's alleged failure to conduct proper weapons qualifications testing and related submission of false certifications to the State Department.[133] The Fourth Circuit found that these facts were sufficiently different because the first-filed action relating to security personnel did not relate to weapons training or testing, as did the later-filed action.[134]

B. "Pending Action"

The last phrase of the statutory provision, "underlying the pending action," had previously given rise to some controversy, with lower courts dividing over whether the "first to file" rule permanently barred actions that were related to previously filed actions even if the previous action had been settled or otherwise dismissed, or whether the rule only temporarily barred actions related to previously filed actions while the previous action remained pending. The Supreme Court resolved this conflict in *Kellogg Brown & Root Services, Inc. v. United States, ex rel. Carter*.[135] In that case, the Court unanimously interpreted the phrase "pending action" to mean a currently pending action rather than a previously settled or otherwise dismissed action. Thus, the "first to file" bar does not apply when a related action was previously brought but later dismissed.[136] However, this limitation of the "first to file" rule as a practical matter will not expose defendants to the civil equivalent of "double jeopardy." If the United States released the claims at issue at the conclusion of the earlier action, or if such claims were dismissed with prejudice in the prior lawsuit, a relator will not be able to bring them again. It is only when the claims were not resolved in the earlier action because the plaintiff voluntarily dismissed the claims that a relator may bring a subsequent action.

Courts determine whether an action is barred based on the "first to file" rule by determining whether a related action was pending at the time of filing of the initial complaint. Thus, a complaint that is filed while a related action is pending will be barred even when the complaint is amended after the related action was settled and dismissed.[137] The courts have reasoned that amending a complaint does not bring

133. 816 F.3d 37 (4th Cir. 2016).
134. *Id.*
135. 575 U.S. 650 (2015).
136. *Id.* at 663–64.
137. Cho on behalf of States v. Surgery Partners, Inc., 30 F.4th 1035, 1040–41 (11th Cir. 2022).

a new action and "cannot change the fact" that the "relator *brought* an action while another related action was pending."[138]

V. The "Government Action" Bar

Relators also are precluded from pursuing an FCA action if the government is "already a party" in a civil or "civil monetary penalty" proceeding based on the same conduct or claims as the proposed qui tam.[139] This limitation is referred to as the "government action" bar, and the FCA's statutory provision is intended "to prevent 'parasitic suits'" by relators who add nothing to exposing an alleged fraud.[140] The bar applies when the "critical elements" relevant to the FCA violation are the subject of the existing government action, whether or not that action specifically alleges fraud.[141] In this regard, however, courts proceed cautiously, taking into account the types of remedies available in the government action, the similarities of the specific actions and actors identified in each matter, and the timing of the alleged transactions.[142]

In *United States ex rel. Bennett v. Biotronik, Inc.*, the Ninth Circuit held that the government action bar applies even after the government action has ended,

---

138. *Id.* (citing United States *ex rel.* Wood v. Allergan, Inc., 889 F.3d 163, 172 (2d Cir. 2018)) (quotation marks omitted).

139. 31 U.S.C. § 3730(e)(3) ("In no event may a person bring an action under subsection (b) which is based upon allegations or transactions which are the subject of a civil suit or an administrative civil monetary penalty proceeding in which the Government is already a party.").

140. United States *ex rel.* Fadlalla v. Dyncorp Int'l LLC, No. 8:15-cv-01806-PX, 2022 WL 3716536, at *4 (D. Md. Aug. 29, 2022) (quoting Costner v. URS Consultanta, Inc., 153 F.3d 667, 675–76 (8th Cir. 1998)).

141. United States *ex rel.* Absher v. Momence Meadows Nursing Ctr., Inc., 764 F.3d 699, 707–08 (7th Cir. 2014) ("If an allegation of fraud has already been made, the analysis is straightforward. But even if no allegation of fraud has been made, the [government action and public disclosure] bars . . . may still apply so long as facts disclosing the fraud itself are in the government's possession or the public domain," vacating judgment for relator on other grounds).

142. *See generally* United States *ex rel.* Jahr v. Tetra Tech, Inc., No. 14-cv-01509-JD, 2022 WL 2317286, at *4 (N.D. Cal. June 28, 2022) (noting the dearth of case law related to section 3730(e)(3) and warnings to proceed "with caution"); United States *ex rel.* Herman v. Coloplast Corp., 327 F. Supp. 3d 358, 362–63 (D. Mass. 2018) (proceeding "cautiously" to conclude that qui tam not based on transactions at issue in previous FCA action); *see also Fadlalla*, 2022 WL 3716536, at *6 (rejecting defendant's proposed government action defense based on Contract Disputes Act (CDA) litigation because the CDA does not extend to claims for fraud nor provide for penalties; "if the CDA claim cannot involve fraud, then it cannot, as the government action bar requires, be 'based upon' the same 'allegations or transactions' as the FCA claim"); United States *ex rel.* Hinds v. SavaSeniorCare LLC, No. 3:18-cv-01202, 2022 WL 1663579, at *5–*6 (M.D. Tenn. Apr. 28, 2021) (dismissing certain of relator's counts as barred by the public disclosure and/or government action bars, but preserving claim with allegations of noncompliance that post-date the time period of the government's action).

and "even when the Government is no longer an active participant in an ongoing *qui tam* suit," reasoning that the government—like any other litigant—remains "a party" in these circumstances.[143] But, while defendants have relied on *Biotronik* in asserting a government action bar argument, the defense rarely succeeds on its own and often overlaps with a public disclosure or first-to-file defense.[144]

VI. Statute of Limitations Defenses

The FCA bars actions brought the later of (1) six years after an alleged FCA violation is committed or (2) three years after the date when "facts material to the action are known or reasonably should have been known by the U.S. official responsible to act in the circumstances" and (3) in no event more than ten years after the violation is committed.[145] The limitation period is calculated from the date when the alleged FCA violation was committed.[146]

The six-year limitation period is considered the default provision and applies to actions brought by qui tam relators and cases filed by the government alone.[147] In 2019, the Supreme Court clarified in *Cochise Consultancy, Inc. v. United States ex rel. Hunt* that qui tam relators may also take advantage of the tolling and maximum limitations provisions in cases where the government has declined to intervene. Moreover, the Court determined that the three-year tolling period is triggered based on the government's knowledge of the fraud.[148] The Court noted that the key inquiry under the statute is "the date that 'the official of the United States charged with responsibility to act'" learned of the relevant facts of the violation.[149]

143. 876 F.3d 1011, 1016–17 (9th Cir. 2017); *see also* United States *ex rel.* Gadbois v. Pharmerica Corp., 292 F. Supp. 3d 570, 580 (D. R.I. 2017) (government action bar precluded qui tam case where government had intervened in a previous FCA action based on same allegations); *but see* United States *ex rel.* Springfield Term. Ry. Co. v. Quinn, 14 F. 3d 645, 648 n.3 (D.C. Cir. 1994) (noting that the government action bar of 3730(e)(3) did not apply to analysis of prior federal district court litigation where the government was dismissed as a party).

144. *See, e.g.*, *Gadbois*, 292 F. Supp. 3d at 581 (declining to reach public disclosure bar arguments where government action bar applied); *Absher*, 764 F.3d at 708–09 (rejecting both government action and public disclosure bar arguments).

145. 31 U.S.C. § 3731(b)(1)–(2).

146. *See, e.g.*, Hinton v. Integra LifeSciences Holdings Corp., No. 18-cv-00244-SRB, 2022 WL 1036777, at *5 (W.D. Miss. Apr. 6, 2022) (calculating the limitation period based on the date the complaint alleged that the underlying fraudulent conduct occurred); United States *ex rel.* Allen v. Good Samaritan Hospital of Cincinnati, No. 1:20-cv-61, 2021 WL 4262342, at *3 (S.D. Ohio Sept. 28, 2021) (calculating the limitation period based on the date relators claim the "last fraudulent act" occurred).

147. Cochise Consultancy, Inc. v. United States *ex rel.* Hunt, 139 S. Ct. 1507, 1513 (2019).

148. *Id.* (refusing to interpret section 3731(b)(2) as requiring government participation in a qui tam relator's claim).

149. *Cochise*, 139 S. Ct. at 1513.

After the government learns of an FCA violation, the statute of limitations is tolled for three years, but from a practical perspective, it may never be fewer than six years or more than ten.[150] Thus, whether such a claim is barred at six years, ten years, or somewhere in between requires a fact-specific inquiry to determine when the government learned the facts of an alleged FCA violation.

On a motion to dismiss, courts must determine when the government knew or should have known of the facts underlying an FCA violation.[151] If a court can discern the date on which the government knew or should have known of the alleged violation, the limitations period can be calculated accordingly. Theoretically, under *Cochise*, if a relator first discovers the violation on the day it occurs, and the government does not learn of the violation until the relator files a complaint and then declines to intervene in the action, the relator may effectively have up to ten years from the date of the violation to bring a claim.[152] But if the government learns of the violation at any intervening time within the ten-year maximum, calculating the limitation period within which a qui tam relator can bring a claim can get much more complicated.[153] Often, facts about whether and when the government learned of the alleged fraud must be developed through discovery, and are not available to support a statute of limitations argument as a threshold defense.[154]

---

150. 31 U.S.C. § 3171(b); *see, e.g.*, United States *ex rel.* Allen v. Good Samaritan Hosp. of Cincinnati, No. 1:20-cv-61, 2021 WL 4262342, at *3 (S.D. Ohio Sept. 28, 2021) (determining that the statute of limitation period calculated under section 3731(b)(2) ended in 2016, three years after the government investigated the alleged violation in 2013).

151. *See, e.g.*, *Cochise*, 139 S. Ct. at 1513 (calculating the limitation period from when federal agents interviewed the qui tam relator); Hinton v. Integra LifeSciences Holdings Corp., No. 18-cv-00244-SRB, 2022 WL 1036777, at *5 (W.D. Miss. Apr. 6, 2022) (calculating the limitation period from when the qui tam relator filed the claim); *Good Samaritan*, 2021 WL 4262342, at *3 (calculating the limitation period from when the Attorney General investigated the qui tam relator's claims).

152. In such a circumstance, section (b)(2) is still applicable because the government will always learn of the violation on the day the case is filed. Hinton v. Integra LifeSciences Holdings Corp., No. 18-cv-00244-SRB, 2022 WL 1036777, at *5 (W.D. Miss. Apr. 6, 2022) ("[T]he Government had no knowledge of the alleged FCA violations before this case was filed on March 29, 2018. Under *Cochise*, the applicable statute of limitations under § 3731(b)(2) is therefore ten years prior to March 29, 2018.").

153. *See, e.g.*, United States *ex rel.* Allen v. Good Samaritan Hosp. of Cincinnati, No. 1:20-cv-61, 2021 WL 4262342, at *3 (S.D. Ohio Sept. 28, 2021) (determining that the effective statute of limitations date was August 2016—"six years after the last fraudulent act . . . or three years after the United States Attorney investigated the fraudulent health care scheme and indicted [the defendant] (August 7, 2013)").

154. Nonetheless, where the circumstances suggest that a limitations argument may be available, defendants should consider including it as an affirmative defense in their responsive pleadings so as to preserve the defense should the case survive preliminary motions to dismiss.

CHAPTER 9

Liability

MARCIA G. MADSEN, CAMERON EDLEFSEN, AND LUKE LEVASSEUR[1]

I. Introduction

Under 31 U.S.C. § 3729(a)(1)(A), a government contractor, subcontractor, or supplier can become liable for a false claim when it "knowingly presents, or causes to be presented, a false or fraudulent claim for payment or approval" to a government officer, employee, or agent, or to a contractor, grantee, or other recipient who has received or will receive government payment for the claim and who is using the government funds on behalf of the government or to further a government program or purpose. Subsections (B) to (G) of § 3729(a)(1) create liability for a series of related and additional acts that violate the False Claims Act (FCA), such as knowingly making a false record that is material to the submission of a false or fraudulent claim (31 U.S.C. § 3729(a)(1)(B)) and knowingly and improperly avoiding an obligation to pay money to the United States (31 U.S.C. § 3729(a)(1)(G)).

This chapter focuses on four overarching issues relating to FCA liability:

- What constitutes a "claim" submitted to the government for payment or approval?
- What is the applicable legal standard to determine if a statement or record submitted with a claim is "false or fraudulent"?
- When is the element of materiality required, and how may it be established?
- What is the False Claims Act's scienter requirement, that is, how have courts applied the Act's requirement that a contractor must have acted "knowingly" before liability may be imposed?

---

1. Marcia Madsen is a partner at Mayer Brown, where she chairs the firm's Government Contracts practice and co-chairs its National Security practice. Cameron Edlefsen is of counsel and Luke Levasseur is a partner at the firm.

II. "Claims" as the Touchstone for Liability under § 3729(a)(1)(A) and (B)

A. Requirement of a "Claim"

When considering an FCA allegation made under 31 U.S.C. § 3729(a)(1)(A) or (B)—relating to false claims or to false statements material to false claims, respectively—a threshold question is whether the plaintiff has identified a "claim" for something of value. Subsections 31 U.S.C. § 3729(a)(1)(A) and (B) of the FCA require that plaintiffs identify a false "claim" as an element of liability by imposing liability on any person who:

> (A) knowingly presents, or causes to be presented, a fraudulent or false *claim* for payment or approval; [or]
>
> (B) knowingly makes, uses, or causes to be made or used, a false record or statement material to a false or fraudulent *claim.*[2]

Many judicial opinions repeat the basic rule that "[e]vidence of an actual false claim is the *sine qua non* of a False Claims Act violation."[3] In other words, even when a relator or the U.S. Department of Justice (DOJ) can prove that a defendant engaged in "fraudulent conduct affecting the government," FCA liability does not attach under subsections (a)(1)(A) and (B) unless that conduct resulted in the filing of a false claim paid directly or indirectly with taxpayer funds.

B. Meaning of the Term "Claim"

Since 2009, when Congress passed FCA amendments as part of the Fraud Enforcement and Recovery Act (FERA), 31 U.S.C. § 3729(b)(2) has defined a "claim" under the False Claims Act as:

> (A) any request or demand, whether under a contract or otherwise, for money or property and whether or not the United States has title to the money or property, that—
>
> (i) is presented to an officer, employee, or agent of the United States; or
>
> (ii) is made to a contractor, grantee, or other recipient, if the money or property is to be spent or used on the Government's behalf or to advance a Government program or interest, and if the United States Government—

2. 31 U.S.C. § 3729(a)(1) (emphasis added).

3. Guilfoile v. Shields, 913 F.3d 178, 188 (1st Cir. 2019) (citing United States *ex rel.* Karvelas v. Melrose-Wakefield Hosp., 360 F.3d 220, 225 (1st Cir. 2004)); United States *ex rel.* Booker v. Pfizer, Inc., 847 F.3d 53, 57 (1st Cir. 2017) (citing *Karvelas*, 360 F.3d at 225); *see* United States *ex rel.* Clausen v. Lab. Corp. of Am., Inc., 290 F.3d 1301, 1311 (11th Cir. 2002).

> (I) provides or has provided any portion of the money or property requested or demanded; or
> (II) will reimburse such contractor, grantee, or other recipient for any portion of the money or property which is requested or demanded.

As a result of this statutory definition, the FCA imposes liability for false claims submitted not only by prime government contractors but also by subcontractors and suppliers who are paid with government funds that flow through a prime contractor.

There are many types of claims for payment or property that may result in FCA liability. The typical example is a billing submitted to an agency by a contractor (or request for payment by grantee) that results in government funds being provided to the contractor or grantee. Many such payment requests are made to (and processed by) government personnel every day for goods that have been purchased or services that have been delivered; each of them could result in an FCA allegation by a relator or DOJ.

Consult Chapter 1 for a summary of the categories of government contractor misconduct that the government and relators successfully have pursued under the FCA.

III. Related Acts That Give Rise to FCA Liability

Subsections (C) to (G) of § 3729(a)(1) set forth a series of acts beyond the knowing presentment of false claims, or the making of a false statement material to a false claim, that can give rise to FCA liability. Under those provisions, a person violates the statute if they:

> (C) conspires to commit a violation of subparagraph (A), (B), (D), (E), (F), or (G);
>
> (D) has possession, custody, or control of property or money used, or to be used, by the Government and knowingly delivers, or causes to be delivered, less than all of that money or property;
>
> (E) is authorized to make or deliver a document certifying receipt of property used, or to be used, by the Government and, intending to defraud the Government, makes or delivers the receipt without completely knowing that the information on the receipt is true; [or]
>
> (F) knowingly buys, or receives as a pledge of an obligation or debt, public property from an officer or employee of the Government, or a member of the Armed Forces, who lawfully may not sell or pledge property.
>
> (G) knowingly makes, uses, or causes to be made or used, a false record or statement material to an obligation to pay or transmit money or property to the

> Government, or knowingly conceals or knowingly and improperly avoids or decreases an obligation to pay or transmit money or property to the Government.[4]

IV. Falsity—What Makes a Contractor's Claim "False or Fraudulent"

Courts have recognized that the FCA's "statutory text shows, . . . as the name of the Act suggests, the Act is aimed at *false* claims."[5] The person submitting the claim is "allegedly warranting the making of the claim," in other words, that it is a valid call on the public fisc. "It is only those claims for money or property to which a defendant is not entitled that are 'false' for purposes of the False Claims Act."[6]

The FCA does not specifically define "false" or "fraudulent." But the courts have determined that "[t]here are two categories of false claims under the FCA: a factually false claim and a legally false claim."[7]

A. Factually False Claims

Factually false claims are straightforward and the "paradigmatic FCA action"[8]—the types of claims that are false or fraudulent on their face. For instance, systemic overbilling for goods knowingly not delivered (or services not rendered) involves facial falsity about which it is difficult to argue. In addition, many government contracts include complex pricing provisions and "most favored nation" clauses that require substantial attention and disclosures by contractors.[9] Relators and the

---

4. Under FERA, 31 U.S.C. § 3729(b)(3) was amended to define "obligation" as "an *established* duty, whether or not fixed, arising from an express or implied contractual, grantor-grantee, or licensor-licensee relationship, from a fee-based or similar relationship, from statute or regulation, or from the retention of any overpayment" (emphasis added). Earlier precedent questioned whether "obligations" that are concealed or decreased in reverse false claims could be *contingent*; the FERA revisions made clear that the obligations must be "established," though the precise amount may not be fixed. United States *ex rel.* Simoneaux v. E.I. duPont de Nemours & Co., 843 F.3d 1033, 1038–39 (5th Cir. 2016).

5. United States v. Southland Mgmt. Corp., 326 F.3d 669, 674 (5th Cir. 2003) (emphasis added).

6. *Id.* at 674–75 (citing Costner v. URS Consultants, Inc., 153 F.3d 667, 677 (8th Cir. 1998) ("only those actions by the claimant . . . [calculated to] caus[e] the United States to pay out money it is not obligated to pay . . . are properly considered 'claims' within the meaning of the FCA")); and United States *ex rel.* Wilkins v. N. Am. Constr. Corp., 173 F. Supp. 2d 601, 626 (S.D. Tex. 2001) (citing several cases supporting "the proposition that a 'false claim' is a claim for more than one is due").

7. United States *ex rel.* Wilkins v. United Health Group, Inc., 659 F.3d 295, 305 (3d Cir. 2011).

8. *Id.*

9. *See, e.g.*, General Services Administration (GSA) schedule contracts contain a price reductions clause, 48 C.F.R. 552.238-81, which requires a contractor to provide the GSA its commercial pricing or discount arrangement and include discounts to the government provided to a contractor's commercial customers.

government often contend that any bill submitted with pricing that is based on inaccurate pricing submissions that are inconsistent with these disclosure requirements constitutes a factually false claim.

B. Legally False Claims

Legally false claims "do not involve information that is false on its own terms, but instead rest[] on a false representation of compliance with an applicable federal statute, federal regulation, or contractual term."[10] The courts have recognized two subcategories of legal falsity: express false certification claims and implied false certification claims.

An express false certification occurs when "a claimant explicitly represents that he or she has complied with a contractual condition, but in fact has not complied."[11] For example, a contractor that falsely certifies that it complied with a government contract's cybersecurity requirements for safeguarding controlled unclassified information would be guilty of an express false certification if, in fact, it violated such requirements.

In contrast, an implied false certification occurs when "the defendant submits a claim for payment, impliedly certifying compliance with conditions of payment while omitting its violations of statutory, regulatory, or contractual requirements, and these omissions render the representations misleading."[12] In *Universal Health Services, Inc. v United States ex rel. Escobar*, the Supreme Court confirmed that, under the FCA, "the implied certification theory can be a basis for liability, at least where two conditions are satisfied": (1) "the claim does not merely request payment, but also makes *specific representations* about the goods or services provided"; and (2) "the defendant's failure to disclose *noncompliance with material* statutory, regulatory, or contractual *requirements* makes those representations *misleading half-truths*."[13]

C. Can Opinions or Judgments Be False?

The element of falsity has received considerable attention recently because of the split in the circuits over whether a medical expert's judgment can be considered false—and the broader implications for any industry that relies on expert judgments to support claims for payment. In 2020, the Third and Ninth Circuits split

---

10. United States *ex rel.* Foreman v. AECOM, 19 F.4th 85, 104 n.7 (2d Cir. 2021) (internal quotation marks omitted), *cert. denied*, 142 S. Ct. 2679 (2022).

11. United States v. Kellogg Brown & Root Servs., Inc., 800 F. Supp. 2d 143, 154 (D.D.C. 2011).

12. *AECOM*, 19 F.4th at 104 n.7.

13. 579 U.S. 176, 190 (2016) (emphasis added).

with the Eleventh Circuit regarding the standard for falsity. The Eleventh Circuit held the government or relator "must show an objective falsity," which is more than "the mere difference of reasonable opinion" of medical judgments.[14] The court explained that "absent a showing of an objective and knowing falsehood, the FCA is an inappropriate instrument to serve as the Government's primary line of defense against questionable claims for reimbursement."[15]

The Third Circuit, in contrast, rejected the "objective falsity" standard. The Third Circuit held that plaintiffs need not show objective falsity concerning medical judgments, but that "a physician's judgment may be scrutinized and considered 'false,'" and that "a difference of medical opinion is enough evidence to create a triable dispute of fact regarding FCA falsity."[16]

The Ninth Circuit also rejected the objective falsity standard in medical judgments. The court held that the "[a] physician's certification that inpatient hospitalization was 'medically necessary' can be false or fraudulent for the same reasons any opinion can be false or fraudulent."[17] For example, such a certification could be false or fraudulent if the underlying "opinion is not honestly held, or if it implies the existence of facts—namely, that inpatient hospitalization is needed to diagnose or treat a medical condition, in accordance with accepted standards of medical practice—that do not exist."[18]

Although the objective falsity line of cases has been confined (so far) to medical opinions, similar issues may arise in other professions requiring expert judgments necessary to support claims in other areas or programs utilizing federal funds. The falsity element often requires a fact-specific inquiry based on the relevant contract and regulatory provisions, as well as based on the contractor's performance (often during a period of years). These inquiries can be difficult to resolve at the pleadings or summary judgment stages.

V. Materiality

Since 2009, the FCA has expressly required materiality as an element of 31 U.S.C. § 3729(a)(1)(B) (false records and statements "material" to a false claim), and has defined the term "material" as "having a natural tendency to influence, or be

14. United States v. AseraCare, Inc., 938 F.3d 1278, 1298, 1301 (11th Cir. 2019).

15. *Id.* at 1301.

16. United States v. Care Alternatives, 952 F.3d 89, 100–01 (3d Cir. 2020), *cert. denied*, 141 S. Ct. 1371 (2021).

17. Winter *ex rel.* United States v. Gardens Reg'l Hosp. & Med. Ctr., Inc., 953 F.3d 1108, 1119 (9th Cir. 2020), *cert. denied sub nom.* RollinsNelson LTC Corp. v. United States *ex rel.* Winters, 141 S. Ct. 1380 (2021).

18. *Id.* at 1119.

capable of influencing, the payment or receipt of money or property."[19] In addition, following a line of lower court decisions, the Supreme Court has confirmed that "materiality" is as an element of 31 U.S.C. § 3729(a)(1)(A) (false claims) whenever plaintiff relies on the theory of implied false certification to establish liability under that subsection.[20]

Whether the contractor's allegedly false statement or claim is "material" to the government's payment decision can be a relatively straightforward inquiry when the falsity concerns the nature of the goods or services delivered to the government or the contractor's computation of its charges for such goods and services. However, FCA cases based on allegations that contractors made false certifications as to their compliance with another contractual, statutory, or regulatory provision raise important questions of whether the alleged falsity was material to the agency's decision to pay a claim based on the contract. The legal precedent regarding materiality of false claims developed in response to claims of allegedly false certifications of compliance with respect to contract and regulatory provisions—with materiality initially only a judicially required constraint on false certification theories.

A. Development of the Materiality Requirement

1. Various Standards Were Applied in Different Courts: Prerequisite to Payment, Natural Tendency to Influence

In a false certification case, a claim for payment related to goods or services that were delivered is alleged to be "false" because the contractor purportedly violated a statute, regulation, or contract provision that related to performance of the contract. As noted earlier, 31 U.S.C. § 3729(a)(1)(A) does not expressly require materiality as an element. Before 2009, 31 U.S.C. § 3729(a)(1)(B) did not expressly require materiality as an element either. However, when plaintiffs began to pursue false certification claims following the FCA's 1986 amendments, the courts developed a series of tests to determine whether the alleged falsity was material to the government's decision on payment.

First, to determine whether certifications were material, many courts asked whether the government's contract "conditioned payment of the claim upon certification of compliance with the provision of the statute, regulation, or contract at issue."[21] Tying the materiality requirement for the certification to a specific condition of payment was arguably consistent with the FCA's focus on the claim for payment, not the underlying improper action alleged by the plaintiff. Numerous

19. 31 U.S.C. § 3729(b)(4).

20. *See* Universal Health Servs., Inc. v. United States *ex rel.* Escobar, 579 U.S. 176 (2016).

21. Harrison v. Westinghouse Savannah River Co., 176 F.3d 776, 793 (4th Cir. 1999).

circuit courts ultimately concluded that "a claim under the [FCA] is legally false only where a party certifies compliance with a statute or regulation as a condition to government payment."[22]

Second, some courts adopted a more flexible "natural tendency to influence" standard for materiality, that is, "whether the false statement has a natural tendency to influence agency action or is capable of influencing agency action."[23] A court's determination that a contractor's submission of information to an agency might have influenced the agency's decision to enter or fund a contract could be sufficient to prove materiality under the "natural tendency to influence" test.[24] Courts applied the "prerequisite of payment" and the "natural tendency" materiality tests in a large number of FCA cases, sometimes (when no precedent dictated a specific test) pointing out that the relator's allegation failed under either test.[25]

2. *Allison Engine*'s Requirement of a "Direct Link" between the False Statement and the Government Loss

In 2008, the Supreme Court decided *Allison Engine Co. v. United States ex rel. Sanders* and addressed materiality under the FCA.[26] The Court ruled that materiality was a requirement, notwithstanding the absence of the term in the statute, and that the relator (or the government) must prove a "direct link" between the false statement and the loss to the fisc. Without such a link, the Court reasoned, the connection between "the false statement and the Government's decision to pay or approve a false claim is too attenuated to establish liability."[27] The direct link requirement increased the materiality standard, as the Court explained that the FCA could not be interpreted as "an all-purpose anti-fraud statute."[28]

3. FERA's Revision to Materiality Requirement, 31 U.S.C. § 3729(b)(4)

In response to *Allison Engine* and to address other issues with the FCA, Congress amended the FCA in 2009 through provisions in FERA. As noted earlier,

22. Mikes v. Straus, 274 F.3d 687, 697 (2d Cir. 2001), abrogated by *Escobar*, 579 U.S. 176.

23. United States *ex rel.* Berge v. Bd. of Trs. of Univ. of Ala., 104 F.3d 1453, 1460 (4th Cir. 1997) (internal quotation marks omitted).

24. *See, e.g.*, United States v. United Techs. Corp., 626 F.3d 313, 320–21 (6th Cir. 2010), *as amended* (Jan. 24, 2011) (internal quotation marks omitted); United States v. Rogan, 517 F.3d 449 (7th Cir. 2008); United States *ex rel.* Harrison v. Westinghouse Savannah River Co., 352 F.3d 908, 914 (4th Cir. 2003).

25. United States *ex rel.* Laird v. Lockheed Martin Eng'g & Sci. Servs. Co., 491 F.3d 254, 261 (5th Cir. 2007).

26. 553 U.S. 662, 671–72 (2008).

27. *Id.*

28. *Id.*

the revisions to the statute made clear that any false record or statement that was allegedly part of an FCA violation had to be "material to [the] false or fraudulent claim."[29] The modifications to the FCA also specified that "the term 'material' means having a natural tendency to influence, or be capable of influencing, the payment or receipt of money or property."[30]

The "natural tendency" test for materiality had been applied by some courts prior to *Allison Engine* and FERA. Although some courts applied the FERA materiality requirement in a relatively strict manner,[31] the statutory materiality standard generally eased relators' and the government's burden in FCA cases.[32]

B. Application of *Escobar*'s "Demanding" and "Rigorous" Materiality Test, in Which There Is No Bright Line—and the Conduct of Both the Government and Defendant Can Be Probative

To address "concerns about fair notice and open-ended liability" given its holding in *Escobar* that implied certification can be a basis for liability under 31 U.S.C. § 3729(a)(1)(A), the Supreme Court offered "strict enforcement" of the FCA's materiality and scienter requirements as a solution.[33] The Court emphasized in *Escobar* that the materiality standard is "demanding" and "rigorous" and must be pleaded with particularity. The Court noted that the FCA is not "an all-purpose antifraud statute" or "a vehicle for punishing garden-variety breaches of contract or regulatory violations" or noncompliance that is "minor or insubstantial."[34] For these reasons, the Court rejected as "extraordinarily expansive" the government's position "that any statutory, regulatory, or contractual violation is material so long as the defendant knows that the Government would be entitled to refuse payment were it aware of the violation."[35]

---

29. 31 U.S.C. § 3729(a)(1)(B); *see id.* § 3729(a)(1)(G).

30. *Id.* § 3729(b)(4).

31. *See* United States v. Sci. Applications Int'l Corp., 626 F.3d 1257, 1269–70 (D.C. Cir. 2010).

32. *See, e.g.*, United States *ex rel.* Vt. Nat'l Tel. Co. v. Northstar Wireless, LLC, 34 F.4th 29, 37 (D.C. Cir. 2022) (discussing that "the FCA's materiality inquiry 'focuses on the potential effect of the false statement when it is made'" (citing United States *ex rel.* Loughren v. Unum Grp., 613 F.3d 300, 309 (1st Cir. 2010))).

33. Universal Health Servs., Inc. v. United States *ex rel.* Escobar, 579 U.S. 176, 192 (2016) (internal quotation marks omitted).

34. *Id.* at 194 (internal quotation marks omitted).

35. *Id.* at 195, 196; *see, e.g.*, United States *ex rel.* Westrick v. Second Chance Body Armor, Inc., No. CV 04-0280 (PLF), 2017 WL 8809510, at *5–*6 (D.D.C. Mar. 31, 2017) (discussing application of *Escobar*'s "rigorous" materiality standard, the "expan[sion of] the basis for an implied false certification claim under the FCA," and the need for courts to "consider whether defendants' noncompliance with statutory or regulatory [in addition to contract] requirements also provides a basis for liability" (internal quotation marks omitted)).

Nonetheless, the Court did not provide a bright-line test for determining whether a particular misrepresentation is material. The Court noted that the fact that the government designates compliance with a particular statutory, regulatory, or contractual requirement as a condition of payment, or has the right to refuse payment, is "relevant, but *not* automatically dispositive," and emphasized that the subjective intentions of both the government and the defendant are important considerations. The Court endorsed the definitions of materiality found in the common law of contracts and tort and cited with approval a case holding that a requirement is material if it goes to "the very essence of the bargain."[36]

1. If the Government Is Aware of Alleged Noncompliance, Does Continued Payment Establish Nonmateriality?

Although the Court indicated in *Escobar* that the subjective intentions of both the government and the defendant are relevant in determining whether a misrepresentation is material, each of the examples it provided focused on the conduct or pattern of conduct of the government. For instance, the Court held:

> [P]roof of materiality can include, but is not necessarily limited to, evidence that the defendant knows that the Government consistently refuses to pay claims in the mine run of cases based on noncompliance with the particular statutory, regulatory, or contractual requirement. Conversely, if the Government pays a particular claim in full despite its actual knowledge that certain requirements were violated, that is very strong evidence that those requirements are not material.[37]

The government, in a number of statements of interest and amici briefs since the *Escobar* decision, has emphasized that "payment of claims after learning of potential fraud does not necessarily undermine a materiality finding because important public health and safety considerations may warrant [continued payment]."[38] It has also pointed out that continued payment prior to settlement or judgment may be because the government "simply wish[es] to afford an accused party the opportunity to be heard in court."[39]

More than 20 years ago, the Fourth Circuit similarly recognized that continued government payment of allegedly false claims does not necessarily render a contractor's noncompliance immaterial. Thus, in *United States ex rel. Harrison v. Westinghouse Savannah River Co.*,[40] faced with violations of a contractual,

36. *Escobar*, 579 U.S. at 193 n.5.

37. *Id.* at 194–95.

38. United States Statement of Interest at 15, United States *ex rel.* Brown v. Celgene Corp., No. CV 10-3165 (C.D. Cal. Aug 29, 2016), ECF No. 328.

39. *Id.*

40. 352 F.3d 908 (4th Cir. 2003).

conflict-of-interest prohibition that was known to the government while payments continued, the Fourth Circuit opined that:

> [W]e can foresee instances in which a government entity might choose to continue funding the contract despite earlier wrongdoing by the contractor. For example, the contract might be so advantageous to the government that the particular governmental entity would rather not contest the false statement, even if it became aware of the false statement before the subcontractor began its work. Also, the government might decide not to address a conflict of interest that it first discovers several months after the subcontractor begins work. At that point, to avoid further costs the government might want the subcontractor to continue the project rather than terminate the contract and start over.[41]

The Sixth Circuit recently agreed with this reasoning, holding that "[t]he Government's decision to continue contracting with a party after discovering alleged fraud is not 'dispositive' of the materiality inquiry."[42] The court then provided various scenarios "unrelated to the materiality of the allegations that could cause the Government to continue contracting with a party after the Government becomes aware of alleged fraud."[43] The court differentiated between the government's knowledge of actual fraud versus awareness of alleged fraud. The court reasoned that "the Government may not want to prematurely end a relationship with a contractor over unproven allegations."[44] Other scenarios unrelated to materiality include that "the Government may not have other feasible procurement options and thus may be forced to rely on the contractor for essential goods or services even after becoming aware of a plausible fraud claim," "there could be a lack of other suppliers, '[t]he government may make operational changes or investments in reliance on the agreement,' or there could be high 'costs associated with implementing another bidding process at the last minute.'"[45]

Similarly, the Ninth Circuit has held that the government's decision to continue paying claims may not be dispositive of the materiality issue and must be considered in the context of alternative explanations for the decision. For example, in *United States ex rel. Campie v. Gilead Sciences, Inc.*, the court explained that "there are many reasons the FDA may choose not to withdraw a drug approval, unrelated

41. *Id.* at 917.

42. United States *ex rel.* USN4U, LLC v. Wolf Creek Fed. Servs., Inc., 34 F.4th 507, 517 (6th Cir. 2022).

43. *Id.*

44. *Id.*

45. *Id.* (citing United States *ex rel.* Am. Sys. Consulting, Inc. v. ManTech Advanced Sys. Int'l, 600 F. App'x 969, 977 (6th Cir. 2015)).

to the concern that the government paid out billions of dollars for nonconforming and adulterated drugs."[46]

Some courts are taking the opposite view of continued government payment when the relator's complaint references evidence (or independent evidence establishes) that the government has been aware that the contractor was submitting false claims or has acquiesced to the challenged contractor conduct. For example, in *United States ex rel. Foreman v. AECOM*, the Second Circuit affirmed (in part) the district court's dismissal decision and found that "[t]he allegations in the complaint, *coupled with reports incorporated by reference into the complaint*, demonstrate that the Government had actual knowledge of AECOM's non-compliance" with contract requirements.[47] Despite knowing of the defendant's conduct, "the government repeatedly paid AECOM's claims, extended the [] Contract, and increased funding under the [] Contract."[48] Thus, the government's knowledge and actions made clear that the contract requirements were "not plausibly material to the government's payment decision," but were merely "marginally probative."[49]

Government knowledge and acquiescence were also grounds for dismissal in *United States ex rel. McBride v. Halliburton Co.*[50] The D.C. Circuit noted that a Defense Contract Audit Agency (DCAA) auditor investigated the invoices submitted by the defendant and declined to challenge or disallow any of the amounts billed, and that the contractor received an additional award fee for "exceptional performance." The court found that "[t]his is 'very strong evidence' that the requirements allegedly violated . . . are not material."[51] The First and Fifth Circuits, along with multiple district courts, have applied the materiality requirement similarly.[52]

---

46. 862 F.3d 890, 906 (9th Cir. 2017); *see also* United States *ex rel.* Mei Ling v. City of Los Angeles, 389 F. Supp. 3d 744, 761 (2019) ("the Government may still maintain an FCA claim if it can muster allegations, taken as true, that explain why continued payments are not probative of immateriality in the circumstances presented by a specific case").

47. United States *ex rel.* Foreman v. AECOM, 19 F.4th 85, 118 (2d Cir. 2021) (emphasis added), *cert. denied*, 142 S. Ct. 2679 (2022).

48. *Id.*

49. *Id.*; *see* United States *ex rel.* Kelly v. Serco, Inc., 846 F.3d 325, 334 (9th Cir. 2017) (given "the government's acceptance of Serco's reports despite [the agency's knowledge of Serco's] non-compliance with [the applicable standard], and the government's payment of Serco's public vouchers for its work under Delivery Orders," the court "conclude[d] that no reasonable jury could return a verdict for Kelly on his implied false certification claim").

50. 848 F.3d 1027, 1034 (D.C. Cir. 2017).

51. *Id.* (quoting Universal Health Servs., Inc. v. United States *ex rel.* Escobar, 579 U.S. 176, 195 (2016)).

52. *See, e.g.*, D'Agostino v. ev3, Inc., 845 F.3d 1, 7 (1st Cir. 2016) ("The fact that CMS has not denied reimbursement for [defendant] in the wake of [relator's] allegations casts serious doubt on the materiality of the fraudulent representations that [relator] alleges."); Abbott v. BP Expl. & Prod., Inc., 851 F.3d 384, 388 (5th Cir. 2017) ("As recognized in *Escobar*, when the [Department of the Interior]

Although the government may be aware of an alleged noncompliance, FCA defendants should take heed of *Escobar*'s holding that "half-truths—representations that state the truth only so far as it goes, while omitting critical qualifying information—can be actionable misrepresentations."[53] In *United States v. Aerojet Rocketdyne Holdings, Inc.*, the court denied the defendants' motion to dismiss and held the "relator has plausibly pled that defendants' alleged failure to fully disclose its noncompliance was material to the Government's decision to enter into and pay on the relevant contracts."[54]

Application of the court's materiality ruling raises complex issues for both the government and contractors whenever disclosures pursuant to the Federal Acquisition Regulation (FAR) Mandatory Disclosure Rule (FAR 52.203-13) have been made.[55] This rule requires contractors (upon risk of suspension and debarment) to make a "timely" written disclosure to the agency's Inspector General, with a copy provided to the Contracting Officer (CO), whenever the contractor has "credible evidence" of a violation of the civil False Claims Act (including any overpayment). Thus, when such a disclosure is made, two key government actors are on notice of the disclosed noncompliance. Typically, the contractor will continue to investigate the issue and make periodic reports to the contracting officer and the Inspector General. If the government's authorized representative (the CO) knows of the issue and continues to authorize payment, the question arises whether that response is sufficient for the contractor to claim that the contracting officer accepted the performance as sufficient under the contract.

On the one hand, disclosure is required only for "credible evidence" of noncompliance and does not, by itself, establish noncompliance. The investigation of potential noncompliance revealed by the disclosure takes time; in the meantime, the government may have strong interests in continuing to pay, including continued government need, exigent circumstances, lack of government resources, and so forth. These potential justifications raise questions about the government's

---

decided to allow the Atlantis to continue drilling after a substantial investigation into Plaintiffs' allegations, that decision represents 'strong evidence' that the requirements in those regulations are not material"); *see also* United States *ex rel.* Kolchinsky v. Moody's Corp., 238 F. Supp. 3d 550, 558–59 (S.D.N.Y. 2017) (materiality is absent at the pleading stage when the relator's chronology suggests that the government knew of the alleged fraud, yet paid the contractor anyway), *on reconsideration in part*, No. 12CV1399, 2017 WL 3841866 (S.D.N.Y. Sept. 1, 2017); Knudsen v. Sprint Commc'ns Co., No. C13-04476 CRB, 2016 WL 4548924, at *13–*14 (N.D. Cal. Sept. 1, 2016) ("[a]fter Escobar . . . government knowledge of noncompliance also bears on whether such violations were actually material to the government's decision to pay a claim").

53. United States v. Aerojet Rocketdyne Holdings, Inc., 381 F. Supp. 3d 1240, 1246 (E.D. Cal. 2019) (quoting *Escobar*, 579 U.S. at 188).

54. *Id.* at 1249.

55. The interplay between the FCA and Mandatory Disclosure Rule is also discussed in Chapter 5.

obligations once it receives a disclosure; for example, what is required for the government to perform a prompt, sufficient investigation of the issue—and does the agency need to begin to withhold payment? And if the government does neither, must it have a contemporaneous documented explanation for its action(s)? To what extent should that explanation be shared with the contractor?

On the other hand, *Escobar*'s materiality analysis puts additional pressure on contractors to maintain strong compliance programs and to make early disclosures. The materiality of the contractor's course of action is just as susceptible to examination as is the contractor's failure to make a timely disclosure.

2. To Establish Materiality, Must the Relator Show That the Government Would Have Denied Payment Had It Known?

In its conclusion, the *Escobar* Court indicated that a failure to disclose a noncompliance will be deemed material when the plaintiff alleges with particularity that compliance was so "central" to the deal between the government and the defendant that the government would have denied payment had it known about the noncompliance:

> Respondents have alleged that Universal Health misrepresented its compliance with mental health facility requirements that are *so central* to the provision of mental health counseling that the Medicaid program *would not have paid* these claims had it known of these violations. Respondents may well have adequately pleaded a violation of § 3729(a)(1)(A). But we leave it to the courts below to resolve this in the first instance.[56]

Several district courts have interpreted this language from the Supreme Court's holding as describing what is necessary for materiality as opposed to merely demonstrating one way in which materiality can be established. For instance, in *United States v. Fulton County, Georgia*, the District Court for the Northern District of Georgia explained that the relators had not shown that defendants misrepresented matters "so central" to the contract that the government "would not have paid [Defendants'] claims had it known of these violations."[57]

---

56. *Escobar*, 579 U.S. at 196 (emphasis added).

57. 2016 WL 4158392, at *8 (N.D. Ga. Aug. 5, 2016) (internal quotation marks omitted); *see* United States v. N. Adult Daily Health Care Ctr., 205 F. Supp. 3d 276, 295 (E.D.N.Y. 2016) ("The Supreme Court vacated the judgment of the First Circuit Court of Appeals and remanded for a determination of whether the mental health facility requirements were 'so central to the provision of mental health counseling that the Medicaid program would not have paid the[] claims had it known of the[] violations.'").

VI. Knowledge—The FCA's Scienter Element Required for a Liability Finding

A. The Scienter Requirement Set Forth in the FCA

The FCA imposes liability only on those who "knowingly" cheat the government—scienter is an essential element of the claim. As the Seventh Circuit has explained, when the defendant personnel who prepared and submitted the materials alleged to result in a false claim had no knowledge of the inconsistency between their submission and the underlying program requirements, there can be no FCA violation. After all, the court explained, "without knowledge of falsity there cannot be a knowingly false claim."[58]

31 U.S.C. § 3729(b) states that "[f]or purposes of this section," the terms "knowing" and "knowingly"—

> (A) mean that a person, with respect to information—
>
> (i) has actual knowledge of the information;
>
> (ii) acts in deliberate ignorance of the truth or falsity of the information; or
>
> (iii) acts in reckless disregard of the truth or falsity of the information; and
>
> (B) require no proof of specific intent to defraud

This language was added to the FCA as part of the 1986 amendments to the statute. Although Congress has altered the definition of "claim" and the courts have interpreted "materiality" differently over time—impacting the scienter inquiry—the statutory definition of a "knowing" violation has not changed since 1986. Moreover, the Supreme Court has held that the courts must "strict[ly] enforce" the FCA's "rigorous" scienter requirement.[59]

B. *Supervalu* Decision—Defendant's Knowledge and Subjective Belief at Time of Claim Submission

In *United States ex rel. Schutte v. Supervalu, Inc.*, the Supreme Court clarified the correct legal standard for scienter and resolved a circuit split on whether a defendant can possess the required FCA scienter if "a defendant's acts were consistent with an objectively reasonable interpretation of the relevant law that had not been

58. United States *ex rel.* Hill v. City of Chicago, 772 F.3d 455, 456 (7th Cir. 2014) (discussing 31 U.S.C. § 3729(a)(1), (b)(1)).

59. Universal Health Servs., Inc. v. United States *ex rel.* Escobar, 579 U.S. 176, 192 (2016).

ruled out by definitive legal authority or guidance . . . regardless of whether the defendant actually believed such an interpretation at the time of its claims."[60]

The Court unanimously rejected an objective standard for assessing scienter under the FCA and held that the "FCA's scienter element refers to respondents' knowledge and subjective beliefs—not to what an objectively reasonable person may have known or believed."[61] Moreover, with respect to the timing of scienter, the Court held that a defendant's knowledge "focuses on what the defendant thought when submitting the false claim—not what the defendant may have thought after submitting it."[62]

And, in addressing the FCA's text regarding scienter, the Court explained that the "three-part test [for scienter] largely tracks the traditional common-law scienter for claims of fraud" and "focus[es] primarily on what respondents thought and believed."[63] First, "'actual knowledge' refers to whether a person is 'aware' of information."[64] Second, the term "'deliberate ignorance' encompasses defendants who are aware of a substantial risk that their statements are false, but intentionally avoid taking steps to confirm the statement's truth or falsity."[65] Lastly, the term "'reckless disregard' similarly captures defendants who are conscious of a substantial and unjustifiable risk that their claims are false, but submit the claims anyway."[66]

In practice, *Schutte* removed a defendant's ability to develop post hoc objectively reasonable interpretations of ambiguous laws or regulations to avoid a finding that the defendant possessed the requisite scienter. As the Court noted, an "ambiguity does not preclude respondents from having learned their correct meaning—or, at least, becoming aware of a substantial likelihood of the terms' correct meaning."[67] As a result, where ambiguous laws, regulations, or contractual provisions are at issue, contractors should limit their potential FCA liability by clarifying such ambiguities with the government prior to submitting claims. Additionally, because FCA plaintiffs have the burden to establish that an FCA defendant

60. United States *ex rel.* Schutte v. SuperValu Inc., 143 S. Ct. 1391, slip op. at 7 (U.S. June 1, 2023). In so doing, the Court reversed the Seventh Circuit's objective scienter standard, which the D.C., Eighth, and Ninth Circuits also followed. *See* United States *ex rel.* Donegan v. Anesthesia Assocs. of Kan. City, PC, 833 F.3d 874, 879–80 (8th Cir. 2016); United States *ex rel.* McGrath v. Microsemi Corp., 690 F. App'x 551, 552 (9th Cir. 2017); United States *ex rel.* Purcell v. MWI Corp., 807 F.3d 281, 284 (D.C. Cir. 2015).

61. United States *ex rel.* Schutte v. SuperValu Inc., 143 S. Ct. 1391, slip op. at 8 (U.S. June 1, 2023).

62. *Id.* at 11.

63. *Id.* at 10.

64. *Id.*

65. *Id.*

66. *Id.*

67. *Id.* at 12.

possessed the requisite scienter, FCA defendants can expect extensive discovery efforts into their knowledge and subjective beliefs prior to submission of the claim.

C. Government Knowledge as It Relates to Scienter

Contractors may be able to demonstrate that a government contracting officer's (or other official's) understanding of the contractor's interpretation of the contract, regulation, or statute at issue in a claim negates the "falsity" element of an FCA allegation. Similarly, such government knowledge—as well as the parties' course of dealing—can be evidence that the contractor lacked the requisite knowledge of the falsity of its claims.

In *Hooper v. Lockheed Martin Corp.*, for example, the whistleblower alleged, among other things, that the defendant "employed defective testing procedures" when performing parts of a contract.[68] The Ninth Circuit explained that:

> Although the government's knowledge of the underlying facts is not automatically a complete defense when that knowledge appears only as an allegation on the face of a complaint under the FCA, . . . the extent and the nature of government knowledge may show that the defendant did not "knowingly" submit a false claim and so did not have the intent required by the post-1986 FCA.[69]

The appeals court affirmed the dismissal of the FCA claim because "there was no evidence of fraud in the testing because the Air Force was aware of and approved Lockheed's testing methods, even if the tests were not done in the order specified in the contracts."[70] Because the defendant submitted "overwhelming evidence that it" shared information that was the basis of another claim "and also disclosed to the Air Force its testing procedures," the plaintiff's "claims fail because he has failed to demonstrate the existence of a genuine issue of material fact as to whether Lockheed 'knowingly' submitted a false claim."[71]

---

68. 688 F.3d 1037, 1050–51 (9th Cir. 2012).

69. *Id.* at 1051 (quoting United States *ex rel.* Butler v. Hughes Helicopters, Inc., 71 F.3d 321, 327 (9th Cir. 1995) and citing other Ninth Circuit precedent).

70. *Id.* at 1050–51.

71. *Id.* at 1051.

CHAPTER 10

Evidence

ALEXANDER O. CANIZARES, JULIA FOX, AND SUZANNE BOEHM[1]

I. Obtaining Agency Evidence in Declined Qui Tam Actions

When a relator or the government alleges that an agency has been defrauded, documents from the agency and testimony from agency officials can be of central importance in the litigation. Relators and defendants in False Claims Act (FCA) cases may seek information from agency files or through a contracting officer's testimony to corroborate fraud allegations or mount a defense, particularly to prove or disprove materiality. Beyond discovery mechanisms permitted by the Federal Rules of Civil Procedure (FRCP), relators and defendants may seek to obtain such evidence through the following methods.

A. *Touhy* Requests

When the United States intervenes in a qui tam action, it becomes a party to the suit, and the FRCP will govern a party's requests for discovery from the government. When the United States does not intervene, although it remains the real party in interest, it is not a party to the case,[2] and obtaining information through discovery requests under the FRCP is not an option. Rather, relators and defendants must comply with regulations issued under the Federal Housekeeping Act[3] that are commonly referred to as the "*Touhy*" regulations, based on the Supreme Court's 1951 decision in *United States ex rel. Touhy v. Ragen*.[4] These agency-specific

1. Alexander O. Canizares is a partner at Perkins Coie. Julia Fox is of counsel and Suzanne Boehm is an associate at the firm. The authors acknowledge Gail Zirkelbach, Jason Crawford, and Megan Weisgerber, who drafted the original version of this chapter.

2. *See* United States *ex rel.* Eisenstein v. City of New York, 556 U.S. 928, 932 (2009).

3. 5 U.S.C. § 301.

4. 340 U.S. 462 (1951). *Touhy* concerned a district court order holding a Federal Bureau of Investigation special agent in criminal contempt for refusing to turn over records requested by a prisoner pursuant to a subpoena *duces tecum* in a *habeas corpus* proceeding. The Supreme Court held that an

regulations are designed to protect government personnel from being unduly burdened with discovery demands.

Many agencies' *Touhy* regulations delegate authority to a senior official to determine whether the agency will comply with a *Touhy* request.[5] Most *Touhy* regulations require a formal written request identifying the requested materials or agency witnesses, the reason the information is being sought, and an explanation as to why the government's compliance with such requests would promote the agency's objectives or be in the government's interest.[6] The *Touhy* regulations generally require a showing that production of the requested evidence is necessary in the interest of justice and cannot be obtained from other sources or in a manner less burdensome to the government.

Litigants must comply with *Touhy* regulations before seeking to compel disclosure from the government, and, as a general matter, parties should attempt to negotiate with agency counsel before seeking judicial review of a *Touhy* response. There are two different standards for reviewing an agency's denial of *Touhy* requests. Some circuits hold that the agency's action should be reviewed according to the standards for discovery in the FRCP, while others will review the agency's action under the "arbitrary and capricious" standard of the Administrative Procedure Act (APA).[7] For example, the Ninth Circuit has applied the discovery provisions in the FRCP, while recognizing that Rules 26 and 45 give courts discretion to quash or modify subpoenas that cause an undue burden on the government.[8] In contrast, the Fourth Circuit has held that an agency's refusal to comply with a subpoena must be reviewed pursuant to the APA.[9]

Under either the FRCP or the APA standard, the *Touhy* regulations present a procedural obstacle that may hinder or delay efforts to obtain evidence. The government may deny a *Touhy* request altogether, impose conditions on the production of the requested information, or produce material in lieu of providing requested witness testimony.[10] Even when the government agrees to produce information

---

order promulgated by the Attorney General regulating the disclosure of official Department of Justice (DOJ) files, documents, records, and information was valid and that the agent properly refused to produce the documents and materials called for in the subpoena.

5. *See, e.g.*, DOJ regulations at 28 C.F.R. § 16.22(a).

6. *See, e.g.*, HHS regulations at 45 C.F.R. § 2.3; DOE regulations at 10 C.F.R. § 202.22; DHS regulations at 6 C.F.R. § 5.48; and DOD regulations in 32 C.F.R. pt. 97.

7. 5 U.S.C. § 706.

8. Exxon Shipping Co. v. U.S. Dep't of Interior, 34 F.3d 774, 779–80 (9th Cir. 1994); *see also* Watts v. S.E.C., 482 F.3d 501, 507 (D.C. Cir. 2007).

9. COMSAT Corp. v. Nat'l Sci. Found., 190 F.3d 269 (4th Cir. 1999).

10. *See, e.g.*, United States *ex rel.* Harman v. Trinity Indus. Inc., 872 F.3d 645 (5th Cir. 2017) (case involving agency memorandum produced in response to *Touhy* request for witness testimony).

sought in a *Touhy* request, it can take considerable time for the requested information to be produced. Accordingly, litigants should account for potential *Touhy*-related delays when developing a discovery and litigation plan involving discovery requests to the government.

B. Freedom of Information Act

Another available tool is the Freedom of Information Act (FOIA), which allows private citizens to obtain disclosure of government records, subject to certain exemptions.[11] Unlike a *Touhy* request, a FOIA request is limited to records and does not provide for witness testimony. FOIA requires federal agencies to "make available to the public" any information that is requested in accordance with certain procedural requirements and exemptions.[12] The statute lists nine categories of information that are exempt from the disclosure requirement.[13] Among other things, the exemptions protect from disclosure trade secrets and privileged and confidential commercial or financial information,[14] inter-agency or intra-agency memoranda or letters that would be privileged in civil litigation,[15] documents compiled for law enforcement purposes,[16] and material implicating national security[17] and personal privacy interests.[18] Despite these exemptions, FOIA's preference for disclosure remains. As amended in 2016, FOIA provides that a federal agency or department may withhold responsive records only if (1) the agency reasonably foresees that disclosure would harm an interest protected by one of the nine exemptions that FOIA enumerates; or (2) disclosure is prohibited by law.[19]

Similar to *Touhy* requests, an agency's implementation of FOIA is governed by agency-specific regulations, policies, and procedures, as well as guidance issued by the Department of Justice (DOJ), whose Office of Information Policy is responsible for developing government-wide policy guidance on FOIA and providing training and legal counsel to agencies.[20] On March 15, 2022, Attorney General (AG) Merrick Garland issued a memorandum to the heads of Executive Branch departments

---

11. 5 U.S.C. § 552.
12. *Id.* § 552(a).
13. *Id.* § 552(b)(1)–(9).
14. *Id.* § 552(b)(4).
15. *Id.* § 552(b)(5).
16. *Id.* § 552(b)(7).
17. *Id.* § 552(b)(1)(A)–(B).
18. *Id.* § 552(b)(6).
19. *Id.* § 552(a)(8)(A)(i).
20. DOJ, Office of Information Policy, https://www.justice.gov/oip/about-office (last updated Dec. 22, 2022).

and agencies with comprehensive FOIA guidance.[21] AG Garland's FOIA guidelines direct agencies to apply a "presumption of openness" and state that DOJ will defend only those nondisclosure decisions that conform with this presumption.[22] According to AG Garland's guidelines, "information that might technically fall within an exemption should not be withheld from a FOIA requester unless the agency can identify a foreseeable harm or legal bar to disclosure" and, "[i]n case of doubt, openness should prevail."[23] The guidelines also "strongly" encourage agencies "to make discretionary disclosures of information where appropriate."[24] The guidelines further instruct agencies to continue efforts to remove procedural barriers and reduce FOIA backlogs.[25]

In general, FOIA requests must be sufficiently specific to allow the agency to conduct a meaningful search for responsive records, and the requester must typically pay for any search and reproduction costs. The agency's determination of whether a document is responsive to a FOIA request and whether it constitutes a "record" under FOIA are context-specific determinations. However, absent one of the statutory exemptions applying, neither relevance nor undue burden on the government are permissible grounds for the government to avoid producing records in response to a properly stated FOIA request. Requesters may challenge an agency's refusal to disclose requested information by submitting a request for mediation through the Office of Government Information Services[26] or by filing a complaint in the appropriate U.S. district court.[27] Obtaining information through FOIA can take time, which is at least in part a reflection of the large volume of FOIA requests that agencies handle. The government processed more than 800,000 FOIA requests in Fiscal Year 2021 alone, an increase of more than 8 percent from Fiscal Year 2020.[28]

Both during an FCA investigation and after litigation is commenced, FCA defendants may use FOIA requests as a discovery tool to seek documents such as

21. *See* Memorandum from Att'y Gen. Merrick Garland to Heads of Executive Departments and Agencies (Mar. 15, 2022), https://www.justice.gov/ag/page/file/1483516/download.

22. *Id.* at 1–2.

23. *Id.* at 1.

24. *Id.*

25. *Id* at 2.

26. 5 U.S.C. § 552(h)(3)

27. *Id.* § 552(a)(4)(B).

28. U.S. DOJ, Office of Information Policy, *Summary of Annual FOIA Reports for Fiscal Year 2021*, at 4, https://www.justice.gov/oip/page/file/1521211/download (last visited Aug. 14, 2022). The government maintains a central website with FOIA-related information at https://www.foia.gov/data.html.

contract documents and audit reports, which could be important in presenting a defense to alleged violations of the FCA. Relators may likewise use FOIA requests to support their allegations or counter a defense but should exercise caution to avoid triggering the FCA's statutory public disclosure bar.

More specifically, the FCA's public disclosure bar prohibits a relator from bringing an FCA suit based on alleged fraud that has already been publicly disclosed through certain channels, unless the relator is the "original source" of the information, or unless the United States objects to dismissal.[29] For purposes of this bar, a disclosure is "public" if it is made in a federal criminal, civil, or administrative hearing; in a congressional, administrative, or other federal report, hearing, audit, or investigation; or appears in the news media.[30] In *Schindler Elevator Corp. v. United States ex rel. Kirk*, the Supreme Court held that a federal agency's written response to an FOIA request constituted a "report" within the meaning of the FCA's public disclosure bar, and thus precluded a relator's qui tam suit that relied in part on documents that the relator obtained under FOIA.[31] Following *Schindler*, courts have recognized that information disclosed by an agency under FOIA can trigger the public disclosure bar, even when the FOIA request was made by a third party and not the relator.[32] Thus, unless a relator can demonstrate that it was the "original source" of the information upon which the relator's FCA allegations were based, allegations based on an agency's response to an FOIA request might bar a qui tam action absent government objection to dismissal.[33]

---

29. 31 U.S.C. § 3730(e)(4)(A).

30. *Id.* § 3730(e)(4)(A)(i)–(iii).

31. 563 U.S. 401, 411, 131 S. Ct. 1885, 1893, 179 L. Ed. 2d 825 (2011).

32. *See, e.g.*, United States *ex rel.* Moore & Co., P.A. v. Majestic Blue Fisheries, LLC, 812 F.3d 294 (3d Cir. 2016); United States *ex rel.* Kraxberger v. Kansas City Power & Light Co., 756 F.3d 1075 (8th Cir. 2014); United States *ex rel.* Sirls v. Kindred Healthcare, Inc., 536 F. Supp. 3d 1, 8 (E.D. Pa. 2021); United States *ex rel.* Jones v. Sutter Health, 499 F. Supp. 3d 704 (N.D. Cal. 2020); United States *ex rel.* Doe v. Stanford Healthcare Billing Dep't, No. CV178726DSFAFMX, 2020 WL 1074585, at *1 (C.D. Cal. Feb. 4, 2020); United States *ex rel.* Maharaj v. Est. of Zimmerman, 427 F. Supp. 3d 625 (D. Md. 2019); United States *ex rel.* Coyne v. Amgen, Inc., 229 F. Supp. 3d 159, 170 (E.D.N.Y.), *report and recommendation adopted sub nom.* United States *ex rel.* Coyne v. Amgen, Inc., 243 F. Supp. 3d 295 (E.D.N.Y. 2017), *aff'd sub nom.* Coyne v. Amgen, Inc., 717 F. App'x 26 (2d Cir. 2017); United States *ex rel.* Brown v. BankUnited Trust 2005-1, 235 F. Supp. 3d 1343, 1356 (S.D. Fla. 2017) (all analyzing whether public disclosure bar was triggered in context of agency FOIA responses on fact-specific bases).

33. *See* McComas v. Wells Mkt., No. 16-CV-217 (WOB), 2021 WL 1034193, at *4 (E.D. Ky. Mar. 17, 2021) (holding that relator was the "original source" for purposes of the public disclosure bar where the relator provided the government with information upon which the FCA allegations were based prior to receiving documents from the government in response under FOIA).

II. Preservation of Attorney-Client Privilege and Attorney Work Product Protections

A. Relators' Mandatory Disclosure Statements under § 3730(b)

The FCA requires qui tam relators to serve on the government a "written disclosure of substantially all material evidence and information the person possesses" relevant to the allegations in the complaint.[34] Mandatory disclosure statements can provide a contemporaneous record of a relator's factual knowledge at the time of filing the qui tam suit, before any government investigation. Among other things, such statements can bear upon a relator's credibility, as well as whether the relator qualifies as an "original source" for purpose of the public disclosure bar. Accordingly, defendants may attempt to obtain relators' mandatory disclosure statements and any supporting documents to defend against FCA allegations and liability. Defendants may argue that such documents are necessary to assess whether a relator disclosed the relevant information to the government at the appropriate time, and whether the relator qualifies as an "original source." In response, relators may claim that the disclosure statements are protected by the attorney-client privilege and/or the attorney work product doctrine and thus shielded from discovery.

Courts have rejected the argument that a disclosure statement is protected as an attorney-client privileged communication.[35] Courts are divided, however, over the extent to which the attorney work product doctrine protects information reflected in a disclosure statement. Codified in FRCP 26(b)(3), the attorney work product doctrine is a doctrine of qualified immunity that generally protects against the discovery of documents and tangible things prepared by an attorney or client in anticipation of litigation.[36] The doctrine contemplates two types of work product with distinct levels of protection: (1) opinion work product and (2) fact work product. Opinion work product reflects counsel's mental impressions, conclusions, or legal theories[37] and, absent waiver, is entitled "nearly absolute protection"[38] from discovery. In contrast, fact work product consists of factual material prepared in

---

34. 31 U.S.C. § 3730(b)(2).

35. *See, e.g.*, United States v. Homeward Residential, Inc., No. 4:12-CV-461, 2015 WL 4610284, at *4 n.3 (E.D. Tex. July 31, 2015).

36. Hickman v. Taylor, 329 U.S. 495, 510–11 (1947).

37. *See, e.g.*, United States *ex rel.* Bagley v. TRW, Inc., 212 F.R.D. 554, 563 (C.D. Cal. 2003) ("Where the selection, organization, and characterization of facts reveals the theories, opinions, or mental impressions of a party or the party's representative, that material qualifies as opinion work product.").

38. *Id.* at 566; *see also id.* at 565 (where disclosure statements are classified as opinion work product, it means "they almost never will have to be turned over to the defendant").

anticipation of litigation and is afforded only qualified immunity.[39] Fact work product may be discoverable if the party seeking it can show "a substantial need for the materials to prepare its case and cannot, without undue hardship, obtain their substantial equivalent by other means."[40]

Courts have differed as to whether a relator's disclosure statements constitute fact work product, opinion work product, or a combination of both. As explained by one court, the "inconsistency in the reported decisions finds a parallel in the practices of relators' counsel, who invest different levels of effort in preparing disclosure statements."[41] Some courts have been hesitant to extend attorney work product protection to a disclosure statement that merely recites factual information or that is devoid of mental impressions, opinions, or conclusions of counsel.[42] However, in *United States ex rel. Bagley v. TRW, Inc.*, the U.S. District Court for the Central District of California broadly held that a relator's entire disclosure statement was opinion work product protected by the attorney work product privilege and ruled it undiscoverable; the court relied on counsel's role in the "subjective and analytical process of culling, organizing, and summarizing the factual information presented in relator's disclosure statement."[43]

Generally, when ruling on whether a relator's disclosure statement is protected from disclosure as attorney work product, the courts have analyzed whether the statement constitutes fact or opinion work product, or both, and have required a showing by the defendant of substantial need in order for any portion that is opinion work to be produced.[44] The courts are split on whether a defendant's public disclosure bar defense—including the corollary issue of whether the relator is an "original source"—constitutes a substantial need sufficient to warrant disclosure.[45]

---

39. *See id.* at 559.

40. Fed. R. Civ. P. 26(b)(3)(A)(ii).

41. *Bagley*, 212 F.R.D. at 556.

42. *See, e.g.*, United States *ex rel.* Burns v. A.D. Roe Co., 904 F. Supp. 592, 594 (W.D. Ky. 1995) ("When the document on which discovery is sought contains a recitation of factual information provided by the client, the need for protection is minimal") (granting defendant's motion to compel discovery of disclosure statement); United States *ex rel.* Stone v. Rockwell Int'l Corp., 144 F.R.D. 396, 401 (D. Colo. 1992) ("Where, as here, the work product in question merely consists of a document reciting factual information provided by the client, the necessity for protection from discovery is weak, at best."); United States *ex rel.* Robinson v. Northrop Corp., 824 F. Supp. 830, 838–39 (N.D. Ill. 1993).

43. *See* United States *ex rel.* Bagley v. TRW, Inc., 212 F.R.D. 554, 563–64 (C.D. Cal. 2003).

44. *See* United States *ex rel.* Yannacopoulos v. Gen. Dynamics, 231 F.R.D. 378 (N.D. Ill. 2005) (summarizing the case law); *but see* United States *ex rel.* Burns v. A.D. Roe Co., 904 F. Supp. 592, 594 (W.D. Ky. 1995) ("The statement of material evidence does not contain any mental impressions, opinions or conclusions. It is simply a recitation of factual information.").

45. *Compare e.g.*, Bannon v. Edgewater Med. Ctr., No. 00 C 7036, 2005 WL 6783450, at *1 (N.D. Ill. Apr. 15, 2005) (finding a substantial need on the grounds that the disclosure statement "is the only way to determine whether Ms. Bannon's complaints are based upon public disclosures and whether

Given the varying case law, litigants and their counsel should be attentive to the law applicable in their relevant jurisdiction.

A related consideration is the extent to which work product protection applicable to a disclosure statement may be waived, thus making it discoverable. Courts have generally held that relators do not waive work product protection when turning over their disclosure statements to the government. This is based on the theory that there is a "common interest" or "joint prosecution" privilege between relators and the government.[46]

B. Safeguarding Privileged Information While Making Mandatory or Voluntary Disclosures

Mandatory or voluntary disclosures of misconduct to the government raise potential issues of waiver of attorney-client privilege if not handled properly. To the extent that a company discloses misconduct to the government, the company should take steps to protect investigatory materials subject to the attorney-client privilege.

For example, as discussed at greater length in Chapter 5, the Mandatory Disclosure Rule (MDR) in FAR 52.203-13 requires that certain federal contractors and subcontractors timely disclose to the government "credible evidence" that a principal, employee, agent, or subcontractor has committed either of the following in connection with the award, performance, or closeout of a government contract: (1) a violation of federal criminal law involving fraud, conflict of interest, bribery, or gratuity violations found in title 18 of the U.S. Code; or (2) a violation of the civil FCA.[47] Importantly, FAR 52.203-13 explicitly states that the obligations thereunder do not require a contractor "to waive its attorney-client privilege

---

Ms. Bannon is the original source of the disclosure"), United States *ex rel.* Stone v. Rockwell Int'l Corp., 144 F.R.D. 396, 401–02 (D. Colo. 1992) (finding a substantial need and undue hardship where trial was just three months away, making "it is imperative that the defendant be made aware of the facts supporting the plaintiff's position as quickly as possible"), *with e.g.*, United States *ex rel.* Carter v. Halliburton, 266 F.R.D. 130, 134 (E.D. Va. 2010) (finding no substantial need where defendant had the opportunity to question relator regarding the source of his knowledge during a deposition).

46. *See, e.g.*, United States *ex rel.* Fisher v. JPMorgan Chase Bank N.A., No. 4:16-CV-00395, 2020 WL 3265060, at *10 (E.D. Tex. June 17, 2020) (concluding that the common interest doctrine precluded any argument that relators waived the work product privilege by disclosing their written disclosure statements to the government); Schaefer v. Family Med. Ctrs. of S.C., LLC, No. 3:18-CV-02775-MBS, 2019 WL 2135675 (D.S.C. May 16, 2019) (granting government's motions to quash and for a protective order, finding relator could not waive the government's privileges, including the common interest privilege pertaining to the FCA action); United States *ex rel.* Purcell v. MWI Corp., 209 F.R.D. 21, 27 (D.D.C. 2002) ("a joint-prosecutorial privilege exists between the Government and the relator," but only in FCA cases in which the government intervenes).

47. 48 C.F.R. § 52.203-13(b)(3)(i).

or the protections afforded by the attorney work product doctrine" or restrict a contractor from "[c]onducting an internal investigation."[48]

The Fourth Circuit's decision in *In Re Fluor Intercontinental, Inc.* sheds light on the critical distinction between, on one hand, reciting facts and legal conclusions in a mandatory disclosure, and, on the other hand, revealing attorney-client communications.[49] In *Fluor*, the Fourth Circuit reversed a lower court's decision finding a waiver of attorney-client privilege in an MDR disclosure that recited facts and legal conclusions endorsed by counsel regarding the conduct of a fired employee.[50] Finding the district court's conclusion "clearly and indisputably incorrect," the Fourth Circuit ruled that no waiver occurred because the disclosure had not revealed any attorney-client communications.[51] The Fourth Circuit distinguished between "disclosures based on the advice of an attorney, on the one hand, and the underlying attorney-client communication itself, on the other."[52] The court explained that a publicly filed statement filed based on the advice of an attorney does not waive privilege or subject the underlying attorney-client communications regarding the submission of such statement to disclosure.[53] However, where the contents of the underlying attorney-client communication itself are disclosed in the statement, a waiver of such privilege results.[54] The court reasoned that the company's statements made in the disclosure at issue did "no more than describe Fluor's general conclusions about the propriety of [the employee's] conduct."[55] The court refused to infer waiver simply because Fluor's counsel had provided advice on the same topic. Importantly, the Fourth Circuit acknowledged that "requiring Fluor to produce privileged materials is particularly injurious here, where Fluor acted pursuant to a regulatory scheme mandating disclosure of potential wrongdoing. Government contractors should not fear waiving attorney-client privilege in these circumstances."[56] Nevertheless, *Fluor* is an important case for government contractors to consider when preparing potential disclosures.

As *Fluor* demonstrates, facts are not privileged, and thus a disclosure that merely conveys the facts learned during an internal investigation (or acknowledging the occurrence of an investigation) does not constitute a waiver of the privileges

---

48. *Id.* § 52.203-13(a).
49. *In re* Fluor Intercontinental, Inc., 803 F. App'x 697 (4th Cir. 2020).
50. *Id.*
51. *Id.* at 700.
52. *Id.* at 701.
53. *Id.*
54. *Id.*
55. *Id.* at 702.
56. *Id.* at 700.

associated with that investigation.[57] Although *Fluor* reaffirms this rule, companies and their counsel should nevertheless take care to analyze the breadth, scope, and source of the information they disclose to the government in connection with any disclosure, whether voluntary or mandatory. Steps should be taken to avoid any potential argument that the company has disclosed the mental impressions or legal conclusions of its lawyers to reduce the risks of waiver of privilege associated with that investigation (or more broadly, the subject matter of that investigation).

III. Evidence Regarding Materiality

As a result of the U.S. Supreme Court's 2016 decision in *Universal Health Services, Inc. v. United States ex rel. Escobar*[58] explaining that the FCA's materiality requirement is rigorous and demanding, involving a "holistic inquiry," with no one factor being dispositive, evidence relating to materiality has become a much more significant aspect of FCA litigation.

The FCA defines "material" as having a "natural tendency to influence, or be capable of influencing, the payment or receipt of money or property."[59] As the court explained in *Escobar*, materiality "look[s] to the effect on the likely or actual behavior of the recipient of the alleged misrepresentation."[60] Rather than articulating a bright-line rule for determining materiality, the court in *Escobar* set forth a rule-of-reason-type standard, explaining that "materiality cannot rest on a 'single fact or occurrence as always determinative.'"[61] Under *Escobar*, materiality "cannot be found where noncompliance is minor or insubstantial."[62] Also, when evaluating materiality, the court observed, the "Government's decision to expressly identify a provision as a condition of payment is relevant but not automatically dispositive."[63] Likewise, the court explained:

> [P]roof of materiality can include, but is not necessarily limited to, evidence that the defendant knows that the Government consistently refuses to pay claims in

57. *See also In re* Kellogg Brown & Root, Inc., 796 F.3d 137, 149 (D.C. Cir. 2015) (internal investigation conducted at direction of in-house counsel, pursuant to its Code of Business Conduct, was privileged).

58. Universal Health Servs., Inc. v. United States *ex rel.* Escobar, 579 U.S. 176, 192 (2016). In addition to addressing materiality, the Supreme Court's opinion held that the implied false certification theory of liability can be a basis for liability under the FCA under some circumstances. *Id.* at 1999–2001.

59. 31 U.S.C. § 3729(b)(4).

60. *Escobar*, 579 U.S. at 2002 (quoting 26 R. Lord, Williston on Contracts § 69:12, at 549 (4th ed. 2003)).

61. *Id.* at 2001.

62. *Id.* at 2003.

63. *Id.*

> the mine run of cases based on noncompliance with the particular statutory, regulatory, or contractual requirement. Conversely, if the Government pays a particular claim in full despite its actual knowledge that certain requirements were violated, that is very strong evidence that those requirements are not material. Or, if the Government regularly pays a particular type of claim in full despite actual knowledge that certain requirements were violated, and has signaled no change in position, that is strong evidence that the requirements are not material.[64]

Since *Escobar*, numerous lower courts have attempted to apply the Supreme Court's holistic analysis, giving rise to different—and sometimes disparate—approaches among the federal circuit courts of appeals.[65]

---

64. *Id.* at 2003–04.

65. *See, e.g.*, United States *ex rel.* Taylor v. Boyko, 39 F. 4th 177, 191–92 (4th Cir. 2002) (a single instance in which the Centers for Medicare & Medicaid Services (CMS) revoked a company's Medicare billing privileges for failure to comply with state corporate-licensing requirements doesn't amount to a "routine" denial of claims for noncompliance); United States *ex rel.* Int'l Bhd. of Elec. Workers Loc. Union No. 98 v. Fairfield Co., 5 F.4th 315, 342–47 (3d Cir. 2021) (false statements on payroll invoices misclassifying certain workers were material to the government's payment decision, because proper worker classification and accurate payroll certifications for purposes of Davis-Bacon law were express conditions of payment and the violations were not minor or insubstantial); United States *ex rel.* Foreman v. AECOM, 19 F.4th 85, 113–14 (2d Cir. 2021) (at the motion to dismiss stage, materiality not adequately alleged where "[d]espite knowledge of, and investigation into" the relator's allegations, the government had extended the contractor's contract and did not disallow any charged costs"); United States *ex rel.* Bibby v. Mortg. Invs. Corp., 987 F.3d 1340, 1350–52 (11th Cir. 2021) (when the law required the Department of Veterans Affairs (VA) to continue to pay lenders despite lender fraud, the VA's continued payment in the face of knowledge that lenders were improperly charging veterans closing fees did not support summary judgment for defendant on materiality), *cert. denied sub nom.* Mortg. Invs. Corp. v. United States *ex rel.* Bibby, 141 S. Ct. 2632 (2021); United States *ex rel.* Janssen v. Lawrence Mem'l Hosp., 949 F.3d 533, 541–42 (10th Cir. 2020) (CMS's inaction for years after being informed of the relator's detailed allegations that a hospital falsified patient arrival times and committed other frauds to increase Medicare reimbursement "suggests immateriality"), *cert. denied*, 141 S. Ct. 376 (2020); United States *ex rel.* Rose v. Stephens Inst., 909 F.3d 1012, 1018–22 (9th Cir. 2018) (a reasonable trier of fact could find that defendant art school's violations of the incentive compensation ban to recruit students were material to the Department of Education's payment of financial aid to students in light of evidence that other schools had paid fines and faced other consequences for violating the incentive compensation ban), *cert. denied*, 139 S. Ct. 1464 (2019); United States *ex rel.* McBride v. Halliburton Co., 848 F.3d 1027, 1034 (D.C. Cir. 2017) ("the DCAA investigated [the relator's] allegations and did not disallow any charged costs. . . . This is very strong evidence that the requirements allegedly violated . . . are not material" (internal quotation marks omitted)); United States *ex rel.* Harman v. Trinity Indus. Inc., 872 F.3d 645, 660–68 (5th Cir. 2017) (when the Federal Highway Administration had knowledge of the relator's allegations, but nevertheless approved guard end rail terminals for federal reimbursement and continued to approve them after extensive testing following trial, the manufacturer's alleged misstatements were not material, and other evidence could not overcome that "very strong evidence"); United States *ex rel.* Miller v. Weston Educ., Inc. 840 F.3d 494, 503–05 (8th Cir. 2016) (where the government sometimes terminates universities that falsify student attendance and grade records to render students eligible for federal financial aid, representations as to student attendance and grades are "material" to payment);

The Supreme Court has repeatedly declined petitions for certiorari asking it to clarify questions arising from *Escobar*,[66] including the extent to which the FCA's materiality requirement applies to fraudulent inducement claims,[67] the weight that should be attached to a change in the government's payment behavior,[68] and whether a plaintiff can establish materiality when the evidence shows that while the government cares about compliance, it nevertheless continues to pay claims even after learning of violations.[69] In the absence of consensus among the circuits regarding the materiality standard, when determining what evidence to seek to prove or disprove materiality, FCA litigants are well advised to consult the case law in the relevant jurisdiction. Practitioners should also consider what steps may be necessary to obtain information from the government or third parties related to whether an alleged noncompliance is minor or insubstantial, whether the government identified a provision as a condition of payment, and the government's response to similar misrepresentations or noncompliance.

IV. Statistical Evidence to Prove Falsity or Damages

Plaintiffs and defendants are increasingly using statistical sampling in FCA cases, particularly in health care cases involving large volumes of claims. Statistical sampling, which involves collecting and analyzing data from a subset of a population of interest and then projecting those results (i.e., extrapolating) across the population, has been accepted by the courts in areas such as antitrust and employment discrimination. Its use in FCA cases is not yet accepted by all courts and continues to generate litigation.

The Supreme Court has not offered any categorical rule concerning the use of statistical evidence. However, it has explained that a "statistical sample, like all evidence, is a means to establish or defend against liability. Its permissibility turns not on the form a proceeding takes—be it a class or individual action—but on the

---

United States v. Sanford-Brown, Ltd., 840 F.3d 445, 447–48 (7th Cir. 2016) (relator failed to establish materiality, because the record showed that federal agencies had examined the defendant multiple times and concluded that neither administrative penalties nor termination were warranted).

66. *See, e.g.*, United States *ex rel.* Foreman v. AECOM, 142 S. Ct. 2679 (2022) (denying certiorari); United States *ex rel.* Janssen v. Lawrence Mem'l Hosp., 141 S. Ct. 376 (2020) (denying certiorari); Stephens Inst. v. United States *ex rel.* Rose, 139 S. Ct. 1464 (2019) (denying certiorari); United States *ex rel.* Harman v. Trinity Indus., Inc., 139 S. Ct. 784 (2019) (denying certiorari).

67. *Foreman*, 2022 WL 1003990, Mar. 29, 2022 (petition for writ of certiorari), *cert. denied*, 142 S. Ct. 2679 (2022).

68. *Janssen*, 2020 WL 5369713, Aug. 27, 2020 (petition for writ of certiorari), *cert. denied*, 141 S. Ct. 376 (2020).

69. *Stephens Inst.*, 2019 WL 991119, Feb. 25, 2019 (petition for writ of certiorari), *cert. denied*, 139 S. Ct. 1464 (2019).

degree to which the evidence is reliable in proving or disproving the elements of the relevant cause of action."[70]

In recent years, the government and relators have increasingly attempted to use statistical sampling to prove not only damages but also liability in FCA cases, principally in health care cases with voluminous claims data. In some FCA cases, district courts have declined to allow a statistical sample as evidence of liability.[71] However, in other FCA cases, courts have permitted statistical sampling to prove liability.[72] For example, in *United States ex rel. Martin v. Life Care Centers*, the U.S. District Court for the Eastern District of Tennessee held that, on summary judgment, the use of statistical sampling was a "legally viable mechanism which the Government may employ in attempting to prove the FCA claims in this action."[73] The government had proposed using a random sample of claims involving 400 patients to estimate the total number of fraudulent claims submitted by the defendant, a skilled nursing facility, for noncovered services, extrapolating to a total population of more than 150,000 claims.[74] The court ruled that the "purpose of the FCA as well as the development and expansion of government programs as to which it may be employed support the use of statistical sampling in complex FCA actions where a claim-by-claim review is impracticable."[75] The court reasoned that if statistical sampling were never permissible, potential perpetrators of fraud would

70. Tyson Foods, Inc. v. Bouaphakeo, 577 U.S. 442, 454–55 (2016).

71. *See, e.g.*, United States *ex rel.* El-Amin v. George Washington Univ., 533 F. Supp. 2d 12, 31 n.9 (D.D.C. 2008) (requiring that the relator identify the "exact Medicare claims that were allegedly false" and details as to each claim); United States *ex rel.* Hockett v. Columbia/HCA Healthcare Corp., 498 F. Supp. 2d 25, 66 (D.D.C. 2007) ("it is all the more imperative for relator to produce real evidence to support her contention that patients were actually held longer than necessary"); United States *ex rel.* Trim v. McKean, 31 F. Supp. 2d 1308, 1314 (W.D. Okla. 1998) (finding that audits of the defendant's billing practices were not a "reliable or accurate representation of" all claims submitted by the defendant and "will not be used to find a percentage of false claims from *all* claims").

72. *See* United States v. Cabrera-Diaz, 106 F. Supp. 2d 234, 240 (D.P.R. 2000); United States v. Robinson, No. 13-CV-27-GFVT, 2015 WL 1479396, at *10–*11 (E.D. Ky. Mar. 31, 2015) ("statistical sampling methods and extrapolation have been accepted in the Sixth Circuit and in other jurisdictions as reliable and acceptable evidence in determining facts related to FCA claims as well as other adjudicative facts"); United States *ex rel.* Schmuckley v. Rite Aid Corp., No. 212CV01699KJMEFB, 2020 WL 3970201, at *8 (E.D. Cal. July 14, 2020) ("statistical sampling is a viable evidentiary tool for organizing voluminous information and then arguing for the drawing of reasonable inferences with respect to that information"); United States v. Krizek, 111 F.3d 934, 941 (D.C. Cir. 1997) (defendants were bound by an agreement to proceed to trial on a representative sample of claims to determine liability for more than 8,000 claims).

73. 114 F. Supp. 3d 549, 571 (E.D. Tenn. 2014).

74. *Id.* at 556.

75. *Id.* at 571.

be emboldened, undermining the FCA.[76] The court explained, however, that the evidentiary weight of a statistical sample and its application must be weighed by the fact finder.[77]

Other district courts have followed *Life Care*'s reasoning to hold that statistical sampling is permissible to raise a triable issue of fact to survive summary judgment, but that it is not a substitute for fact-finding altogether.[78] In *United States v. Robinson*, for example, the court rejected the argument that the government "must present individualized proof of each FCA element as to every single claim for Medicare payment at issue," observing that requiring such a claim-by-claim review "would be virtually impossible," thus preventing the prosecution of fraud cases.[79] As one court observed, the "takeaway" from these cases "is that statistical sampling is a viable evidentiary tool for organizing voluminous information and then arguing for the drawing of reasonable inferences with respect to that information. It is not, however, a tool that will conclusively resolve questions of fact or alleviate a plaintiff's burden of proof under the FCA."[80] Also, in cases when statistical sampling is allowed, the relator "is first required to identify and demonstrate the falsity of a smaller sample of individual claims."[81]

Parties may not be able to use interlocutory appeals to challenge a district court's decision on whether to allow statistical sampling. In *United States ex rel. Michaels v. Agape Senior Community, Inc.*, the Fourth Circuit held that the district court's refusal to allow statistical sampling to determine liability and damages in an FCA case was evidentiary in nature and not a pure question of law.[82]

---

76. *Id.*; *see also* United States v. Rogan, 517 F.3d 449, 453 (7th Cir. 2008) (stating in dictum that "[s]tatistical analysis should suffice" and that the district court was not required to address each of the relator's 1,812 claim forms).

77. *Life Care Centers of America, Inc.*, 114 F. Supp. 3d at 560, 572.

78. *See, e.g.*, *Schmuckley*, 2020 WL 3970201, at *7–*10 (holding that plaintiffs' proposed use of statistical sampling is allowable to prove falsity); *Robinson*, 2015 WL 1479396, at *10–*11 (rejecting argument that use of samples to extrapolate liability and damages was improper); *see also* United States v. Mariner Health Care, Inc., 552 F. Supp. 3d 938, 947 (N.D. Cal. 2021) (relator "is not categorically precluded from using a statistical analysis to allege an FCA claim" sufficient to overcome a motion to dismiss).

79. United States v. Robinson, No. 13-CV-27-GFVT, 2015 WL 1479396, at *10 (E.D. Ky. Mar. 31, 2015).

80. United States *ex rel.* Schmuckley v. Rite Aid Corp., No. 212CV01699KJMEFB, 2020 WL 3970201, at *8 (E.D. Cal. July 14, 2020).

81. United States v. Long Grove Manor, Inc., No. 10 C 368, 2019 WL 2774149, at *5 (N.D. Ill. July 2, 2019).

82. 848 F.3d 330, 340–41 (4th Cir. 2017).

At the trial court level, however, parties can challenge sampling through motions in limine and *Daubert*[83] challenges to expert testimony. In *United States ex rel. Ruckh v. Genoa Healthcare, LLC*, for example, while the court rejected the argument that sampling could never be used to establish liability in an FCA case, it noted that the defendant could move to exclude sampling evidence through a *Daubert* challenge for "defects in method, among other evidentiary defects."[84] In *United States ex. rel. Loughren v. UnumProvident Corp.*, the defendant did just that, successfully excluding a statistician's expert testimony on the ground that the expert's use of overlapping cohorts rendered his sampling methodology unreliable.[85]

V. Expert Testimony on Falsity

A. Objective versus Subjective Falsity

The question of the extent to which a statement of opinion or judgment can render a claim false under the FCA has been extensively litigated in recent years in health care fraud cases and is now the subject of a circuit split, although the majority of appellate courts to address the question have answered this question affirmatively. In *United States v. AseraCare Inc.*,[86] the Eleventh Circuit held that when a hospice provider submits a claim representing that a patient is terminally ill, "the claim cannot be 'false'—and thus cannot trigger FCA liability—if the underlying clinical judgment does not reflect an objective falsehood."[87] The court further held that a "reasonable difference of opinion among physicians reviewing medical documentation *ex post* is not sufficient on its own to suggest that those judgments—or any claims based on them—are false under the FCA."[88]

However, in *United States ex rel. Druding v. Care Alternatives*,[89] the Third Circuit held that "a physician's judgment may be scrutinized and considered 'false.'"[90] The court reasoned that "objectivity speaks to the element of *scienter*, not *falsity*" and that the elements of falsity and scienter must be analyzed separately.[91] And in

83. The admission of expert evidence is governed by Fed. R. Evid. 702, which codified the Supreme Court's holding in Daubert v. Merrell Dow Pharmaceuticals, Inc., 509 U.S. 579 (1993), and its progeny.

84. No. 8:11-CV-1303-T-23TBM, 2015 WL 1926417, at *4 (M.D. Fla. Apr. 28, 2015).

85. 604 F. Supp. 2d 259, 269 (D. Mass. 2009)

86. 938 F.3d 1278 (11th Cir. 2019).

87. *Id.* at 1296–97.

88. *Id.* at 1297.

89. 952 F.3d 89, 98–101 (3d Cir. 2020), *cert. denied*, 141 S. Ct. 1371 (2021).

90. *Id.* at 100–01.

91. *Id.* at 100.

United States ex rel. Polukoff v. St. Mark's Hospital, the Tenth Circuit similarly held that "a doctor's certification . . . that a procedure is 'reasonable and necessary' is 'false' under the FCA if the procedure was not reasonable and necessary under the government's definition of the phrase."[92] Likewise, the Ninth Circuit held in *Winter ex rel. United States v. Gardens Regional Hospital and Medical Center, Inc.* that "the FCA does not require a plaintiff to plead an 'objective falsehood'" and a "physician's certification that inpatient hospitalization was 'medically necessary' can be false or fraudulent for the same reasons any opinion can be false or fraudulent."[93] The Supreme Court has so far declined requests that it resolve the split among the circuits concerning objective falsity.[94]

In *United States ex rel. Marsteller v. Tilton*, the U.S. District Court for the Northern District of Alabama declined to extend *AseraCare* to a government contracts case involving allegations that a defense contractor fraudulently induced the Army to enter into a contract by failing to disclose criminal conduct as required by the MDR.[95] Citing *AseraCare*, the defendants argued that they could not be subject to FCA liability because their opinion as to whether the conduct needed to be reported was not an "objective falsity."[96] Noting that *AseraCare*'s procedural posture was "unique,"[97] the court reasoned that "[e]ven assuming *AseraCare*'s 'objective falsity' test applies beyond its factual and procedural context," it was distinguishable from this case because the evidence did not establish the existence of a mere difference of reasonable opinion as to whether the defendants had a reporting obligation under FAR 52.203-13.[98] Thus, the court found, *AseraCare* "does not render defendants immune from FCA liability whenever they must make subjective determinations."[99]

B. Use of Unpaid Witnesses with Compelling Knowledge about Defense Contracting and Other Specialized Industries

Parties to an FCA suit can often benefit from relying on witnesses who are not retained as experts and who have particularly strong experience in the industry or technology at issue, such as government and company employees with knowledge

92. 895 F.3d 730, 743 (10th Cir. 2018).

93. 953 F.3d 1108, 1119 (9th Cir. 2020), *cert. denied sub nom.* RollinsNelson LTC Corp. v. United States *ex rel.* Winters, 141 S. Ct. 1380 (2021).

94. *See* RollinsNelson LTC Corp. v. United States *ex rel.* Winters, 141 S. Ct. 1380 (Feb. 2021) (denying certiorari); Care Alternatives v. United States *ex rel.* Druding et al., 141 S. Ct. 1371 (Feb. 2021) (denying certiorari).

95. 556 F. Supp. 3d 1291, 1307 (N.D. Ala. 2021).

96. *Id.* at 1307.

97. *Id.* n.11.

98. *Id.* at 1307–08.

99. *Id.* at 1308.

of the underlying allegations, to provide the equivalent of "expert opinions." Such witnesses will not be subject to either the FRCP's requirements regarding the admission of expert testimony or the statutory prohibitions on former government employees serving as expert witnesses except by court order. Because they are not paid for their testimony, the opinions of such witnesses may come across as more credible than those of retained experts.

As courts have recognized, such hybrid fact/opinion witness testimony is permissible under FRE 701 and 702, although courts may restrict or limit the scope of such testimony in appropriate cases.[100] For example, in *United States ex rel. Watson v. Connecticut General Life Insurance Co.*, the court held that those portions of a former government employee's testimony that were based on his personal knowledge regarding the contract between the government and the defendant were admissible as fact and lay opinion testimony.[101] The court reasoned that the witness, who had provided declarations submitted by the defendant, was not an "expert witness" because he was not being paid and for the most part was testifying about matters "of which he had personal knowledge while working for the government."[102] The court acknowledged, however, that certain of the witness's statements that go beyond his personal knowledge might constitute expert testimony and held that, accordingly, the court would not rely upon them in deciding the pending motion for summary judgment.[103]

---

100. *See, e.g.*, Phoenix Restoration Grp., Inc. v. Liberty Mut. Grp. Inc., No. CV 18-2121 (BAH), 2020 WL 622152, at *4–*5 (D.D.C. Feb. 10, 2020).

101. 2003 WL 203568, at * 3–*4 & n.1 (E.D. Pa. Jan. 30, 2003).

102. *Id.* at *4.

103. *Id.* at *6.

CHAPTER 11

Remedies

BRIAN A. HILL AND ELIZABETH J. CAPPIELLO[1]

I. Introduction

Remedies under the False Claims Act (FCA) fall into six main categories: (1) treble damages for harm to the United States; (2) statutory penalties for violations against the United States; (3) double back pay, interest on the back pay, special damages, and reinstatement for relators facing employment-based retaliation; (4) plaintiff's costs, including, in the case of the relator, reasonable attorneys' fees and costs; (5) defendant's fees and costs; and, (6) relator's share of the government's recovery. This chapter will address each of these categories in turn.

In sum, the focus of the computation of the damages to the United States is ordinarily the actual loss suffered by the government, with offsets often made from either treble or single damages when the government has recovered some of its loss from the defendant or a third party. In addition, a defendant is liable for a mandatory penalty for each FCA violation (so-called statutory penalties), with each penalty currently set by statute to fall in the range of $12,537 to $25,076,[2] subject of course to any constitutional constraints.

In cases initiated by a relator that lead to a recovery for the United States, a defendant is liable for the relator's reasonable attorneys' fees and costs as well as the relator's "reasonable expenses necessarily incurred." Moreover, although the government rarely asserts this claim, defendant is also liable for the government's "costs" of bringing the civil action.

---

1. Brian A. Hill is a member and Elizabeth J. Cappiello is counsel at Miller & Chevalier. The authors would like to acknowledge Elizabeth Hadley, a 2023 JD candidate at Georgetown University Law Center, for her assistance with editing and updating this chapter.

2. 28 C.F.R. § 85.5(a). The penalty amounts are periodically adjusted to account for inflation.

On the flip side, the FCA also provides that the defendant may recover fees and costs when a relator's case is frivolous or vexatious or when the government proceeds with a case without substantial justification.

Finally, in a successful case, the relator is ordinarily entitled to 15 to 25 percent of the government's total recovery (treble damages plus penalties) if the government has pursued the action, and 25 to 30 percent of the government's total recovery when the government declines to intervene.

II. The United States' Damages

A. Burden of Proving Damages

The FCA places the burden of proving damages on the United States.[3] Because a relator "stands in the place of the government, he must assume the government's burden of proof as to damages in an FCA case."[4] Damages "must be proven with reasonable certainty," and the plaintiff therefore "must establish both that the fact of the damages is certain and that the amount of damages can be reasonably computed."[5] "Although 'speculation and guesswork' should not be the basis for ascertaining damages, damages need not be calculated by mathematical precision."[6] Instead, "where the defendant by his own wrong has prevented a more precise computation," "the jury may make a just and reasonable estimate of the damage based on relevant data, and render its verdict accordingly."[7] Courts have occasionally awarded nominal damages where proof of damages was lacking[8] and denied damages altogether where the plaintiff failed to prove any damage at all.[9] Relators have recently begun advancing statistical sampling as a methodology for computing and proving damages, and the decisions addressing that issue are dis-

---

3. 31 U.S.C. § 3731(d) ("In any action brought under section 3730, the United States shall be required to prove all essential elements of the cause of action, including damages, by a preponderance of the evidence.").

4. United States *ex rel.* Harrison v. Westinghouse Savannah River Co., 352 F.3d 908, 923 (4th Cir. 2003).

5. United States *ex rel.* Ervin & Assocs., Inc. v. Hamilton Sec. Grp., 370 F. Supp. 2d 18, 55 (D.D.C. 2005) (citation omitted); Morsell v. NortonLifeLock, Inc., 2023 WL 314506, at *73 (D.D.C. Jan. 19, 2023) (explaining that "treble damages imposed under the FCA are 'essentially punitive in nature' [and] [a]gainst that backdrop it is especially important to hold the United States to its burden of proving those damages rather than attempting through numerical guesswork").

6. United States v. Killough, 848 F.2d 1523, 1531 (11th Cir. 1988) (quoting United States v. Collyer Insulated Wire Co., 94 F. Supp. 493, 498–99 (D.R.I. 1950)).

7. Bigelow v. RKO Radio Pictures, Inc., 327 U.S. 251, 264 (1946).

8. *Collyer*, 94 F. Supp. at 498–99.

9. Ab-Tech Constr., Inc. v. United States, 31 Fed. Cl. 429, 434 (1994), *aff'd sub nom.* Ab-Tech Constr. v. United States, 57 F.3d 1084 (Fed. Cir. 1995), *abrogated on other grounds by* AEY, Inc. v. United States, 114 Fed. Cl. 619, 629 n.10 (2014).

cussed separately in Chapter 10. Although defendants frequently assert failure to mitigate damages as an affirmative defense, several recent decisions have held that the United States has "no duty to mitigate damages" in FCA actions.[10]

B. Causation Issues Related to Damages

In order for a plaintiff to recover actual damages, they must prove that "the Defendant caused the Government to pay claims 'because of' the alleged false claim or statement."[11] The D.C., Third, Fifth, Seventh, and Tenth Circuits, as well as a district court in the Sixth Circuit, have all adopted a narrow "proximate causation" standard.[12]

As the D.C. Circuit put it, "[u]nder this standard 'the submitter of a false claim should be liable only for those damages that arise because of the *falsity* of the claim, *i.e.*, only for those damages that would not have come about if the defendant's misrepresentations had been true.'"[13] In other words, a plaintiff must "show that the specific misrepresentations made to" the government "were the direct and proximate cause of" the government's "losses and not merely the 'but for' cause of those

---

10. *See, e.g.*, United States *ex rel.* King v. Solvay S.A., 304 F.R.D. 507, 513–14 (S.D. Tex. 2015); United States v. United Techs. Corp., 950 F. Supp. 2d 949, 954 (S.D. Ohio 2013), *rev'd on other grounds*, 782 F.3d 718 (6th Cir. 2015).

11. United States *ex rel.* Fago v. M & T Mortg. Corp., 518 F. Supp. 2d 108, 120 (D.D.C. 2007) (quoting United States *ex rel.* Schwedt v. Plan. Rsch. Corp., 59 F.3d 196, 200 (D.C. Cir. 1995)).

12. United States v. Luce, 873 F.3d 999, 1014 (7th Cir. 2017) (overturning circuit precedent (to use the "but for" test) and requiring the use of the "proximate cause" test in order to align with the Third, Fifth, Tenth, and D.C. circuits that have "adopted the common-law understanding of foreseeable, or proximate, causation with respect to the imposition of liability and damages under the FCA"); United States *ex rel.* Sikkenga v. Regence Bluecross Blueshield of Utah, 472 F.3d 702, 714–15 (10th Cir. 2006) (the proximate cause test is useful "to determine whether there is a sufficient nexus between the conduct of the party and the ultimate presentation of the false claim to support liability under the FCA"), *abrogated on other grounds by* Cochise Consultancy, Inc. v. United States *ex rel.* Hunt, 139 S. Ct. 1507 (2019); United States v. Miller, 645 F.2d 473, 475–76 (5th Cir. 1981) ("The language of the statute clearly requires that before the United States may recover double damages, it must demonstrate the element of causation between the false statements and the loss."); United States *ex rel.* Schwedt v. Plan. Rsch. Corp., 59 F.3d 196, 200 (D.C. Cir. 1995) ("several circuits . . . have concluded that the [FCA] does not contemplate liability for all damages that would not have arisen 'but for' the false statement. Surely, we agree" (citing United States v. Hibbs, 568 F.2d 347, 351 (3d Cir. 1977), and United States v. Miller, 645 F.2d 473, 475–76 (5th Cir. 1981)) (citations omitted)); United States v. Hibbs, 568 F.2d 347, 349 (3d Cir. 1977) ("We conclude that a causal connection must be shown between loss and fraudulent conduct and that a broad 'but for' test is not in compliance with the statute"); United States v. Quicken Loans Inc., 239 F. Supp. 3d 1014, 1042 (E.D. Mich. 2017) ("The use of foreseeability for proximate cause is consistent with its application to the 'causes to be presented' element of a presentment claim under the False Claims Act"); United States *ex rel.* Fago v. M & T Mortg. Corp., 518 F. Supp. 2d 108, 120 (D.D.C. 2007) ("This Circuit has adopted the proximate causation standard for actual damages in FCA cases which has been adopted by the Third and Fifth Circuits.").

13. *Fago*, 518 F. Supp. 2d at 120 (quoting *Schwedt*, 59 F.3d at 200).

losses."[14] "Thus, if the subject matter of the alleged misrepresentation is unrelated to the ultimate reason for the" government's loss, a plaintiff "cannot recover any damages on behalf of the Government."[15] Another district court applied the proximate cause standard to hold that allegations of damages "must support an inference that it was reasonably foreseeable that the false claim would result in" loss to the government.[16]

C. Measures of Damages

The FCA provides that a person who violates the Act "is liable to the United States Government for . . . 3 times the amount of damages which the Government sustains because of the act of that person."[17] The statute does not contain a "set formula for determining the government's actual damages."[18] The Senate Judiciary Committee has explained that, "[n]o single rule can be, or should be, stated for the determination of damages under the" FCA.[19] Instead, "the courts should remain free to fashion measures of damages on a case-by-case basis."[20]

Courts have used a variety of ways of measuring FCA damages, typically borrowed from the law of contracts or the law of damages generally.[21] "Ordinarily the measure of the Government's damages would be the amount that it paid out by reason of the false statements over and above what it would have paid if the claims had been truthful."[22]

1. Government's Actual Loss

The United States' actual loss is the touchstone for measuring FCA damages; any award of treble damages requires proof of, and must be based on, the "actual damages" suffered by the United States.[23] "When the government gets what it paid for despite a contractor's misstatements, it has suffered no 'actual damages'" and no

14. *Id.* at 122.

15. *Id.*

16. *Quicken Loans*, 239 F. Supp. 3d at 1042.

17. 31 U.S.C. § 3729(a)(1).

18. United States v. Killough, 848 F.2d 1523, 1532 (11th Cir. 1988) (citing S. Rep. No. 96-615, at 4).

19. S. Rep. No. 96-615, at 4 (1980) (reporting on S. 1981, the predecessor to S. 1562, the bill that passed six years later).

20. *Id.*

21. *See, e.g.*, United States v. Bornstein, 423 U.S. 303, 316 n.13 (1976) (citing C. McCormick, Law of Damages § 42, at 137 (1935) in discussion of appropriate damages); Com. Contractors, Inc. v. United States, 154 F.3d 1357, 1372 (Fed. Cir. 1998) (citing Restatement (Second) of Contracts § 347 (1981) in discussion of appropriate damages).

22. United States v. Woodbury, 359 F.2d 370, 379 (9th Cir. 1966).

23. *Bornstein*, 423 U.S. at 316 n.13; *Killough*, 848 F.2d at 1532; United States *ex rel.* Compton v. Midwest Specialties, Inc., 142 F.3d 296, 304 (6th Cir. 1998); United States v. Advance Tool Co., 902 F. Supp. 1011, 1017 (W.D. Mo. 1995), *aff'd*, 86 F.3d 1159 (8th Cir. 1996); Ab-Tech Constr., Inc. v.

damage award is appropriate.[24] Thus, in *United States ex rel. Marsteller v. MD Helicopters, Inc.*,[25] the court instructed the jury to evaluate first whether the contractor's "allegedly fraudulent conduct completely compromised the purpose" of the contracts at issue, which meant the government was likely entitled to the full value of the contracts. If, however, the jury found that that the products delivered "nevertheless conferred benefits of value to the U.S. government, this value would be subtracted from the . . . contract prices to find the actual damages amount.[26]

There is no single method for measuring the government's actual loss. Perhaps the easiest case is when the fraud relates to the quality or quantity of the goods or services delivered under the contract and the market value of the nonconforming or undelivered goods or services can be determined. In such situations, courts typically apply benefit-of-the-bargain damages, measured as the difference between the market value of the goods or services the government bargained for and the market value of the goods or services actually received.[27] Alternatively, courts will compare the contract price to the market value of the goods or services actually provided.[28]

In other instances, it is essentially impossible to prove the market value of nonconforming goods or services. When that occurs, some courts allow damages to be computed based on the cost of curing the defect, provided that cost is not disproportionate to the likely diminution in value caused by the defect.[29]

Damages can be difficult to determine when the false claims relate to a collateral aspect of the contract, such as compliance with organizational conflict of interest rules or with employee wage requirements. In these cases, courts often set damages equal to the market value of the contract performance that should have been delivered minus that of the actual contract performance. For example, where a contractor underpays its employees in violation of the Davis-Bacon Act, "[a]ctual damages are the difference in value between what the government bargained for

---

United States, 31 Fed. Cl. 429, 434 (1994), *aff'd sub nom.* Ab-Tech Constr. v. United States, 57 F.3d 1084 (Fed. Cir. 1995).

24. United States v. United Techs. Corp., 782 F.3d 718, 731 (6th Cir. 2015).

25. 2021 WL 4409093, at *8 (N.D. Ala. Sept. 27, 2021).

26. *Id.* at *1.

27. *See, e.g.*, United States v. Bornstein, 423 U.S. 303, 316 n.13 (1976).

28. *See, e.g.*, United States v. Midwest Specialties, No. 3:91CV7095, 1995 WL 811966 (N.D. Ohio Sept. 27, 1995).

29. *See, e.g.*, Com. Contractors, Inc. v. United States, 154 F.3d 1357, 1371–75 (Fed. Cir. 1998) (allowing several elements of damages based on the government's replacement or repair costs, but rejecting one as being disproportionate to the government's likely loss since the government failed to show that the defect significantly affected the structural integrity of the construction project); *see also* United States *ex rel.* Roby v. Boeing Co., 302 F.3d 637, 648 n.9 (6th Cir. 2002) (noting how *Commercial Contractors* would apply if the actual loss in value was indeterminable). *But see* United States v. Aerodex, Inc., 469 F.2d 1003, 1011 (5th Cir. 1972) (repair costs were unallowable consequential damages) (discussed later).

and what the government received," which is the additional amount of wages the contractor would have paid to be compliant with the Davis-Bacon Act.[30] Likewise, where a contractor engaged in undisclosed organizational conflicts of interest, a court held that the proper measure of damages was the amount the government paid for the contractor's services "over and above what the services the company actually delivered were worth to the government."[31] That amount might be very little or nothing if the government got what it paid for, or it might be the entire amount paid to the contractor if the services were "completely compromised" and thus worthless.[32] The court "recognize[d] the difficulty . . . in calculating the value of services tainted by potential conflict" in these kinds of cases.[33]

A similar approach is often utilized when the fraud relates to the pricing or negotiation of the contract, such as where a contractor has violated the Truth in Negotiations Act. Damages in cases involving misrepresentations of cost or pricing are typically the amount actually paid by the government minus the market value of the goods or services (i.e., the price the government would have agreed to were it not for the fraud).[34] Market value might be determined through sales of comparable goods or services, government price estimates of the goods or services, or expert analysis.[35]

---

30. United States *ex rel.* Wall v. Circle C Constr., LLC, 813 F.3d 616, 617 (6th Cir. 2016) ("Here, the government bargained for two things: the buildings, and payment of Davis–Bacon wages. It got the buildings but not quite all of the wages. The shortfall was $9,916. That amount is the government's actual damages.").

31. United States v. Sci. Applications Int'l Corp., 626 F.3d 1257, 1279 (D.C. Cir. 2010).

32. *Id.* at 1279–80.

33. *Id.* at 1280. *See also* United States *ex rel.* Davis v. District of Columbia, 679 F.3d 832, 839–40 (D.C. Cir. 2012) ("In this case, Davis does not allege that any services paid for were not provided. The sole defect Davis claims is the failure to maintain documentation for those services. Unlike the contractor's undisclosed conflicts in *Science Applications,* the defect in this case in no way calls into question the value of the medical care provided by DCPS."); United States *ex rel.* Harrison v. Westinghouse Savannah River Co., 352 F.3d 908, 922–23 (4th Cir. 2003) (finding damages were equal to "how much more the government paid [the defendant] to perform the subcontract than it would have paid another firm absent the false no-OCI certification," but that the relator presented no evidence of this amount); United States v. Advance Tool Co., 902 F. Supp. 1011, 1017 (W.D. Mo. 1995) (the court was "unable to award actual damages" because the plaintiff provided no evidence about the utility, or lack thereof, of the nonconforming tools), *aff'd,* 86 F.3d 1159 (8th Cir. 1996); Ab-Tech Constr., Inc. v. United States, 31 Fed. Cl. 429, 434 (1994), *aff'd sub nom.* Ab-Tech Constr. v. United States, 57 F.3d 1084 (Fed. Cir. 1995).

34. *See, e.g.,* United States v. Erhlich, 643 F.2d 634, 639 (9th Cir. 1981) (calculating damages using the amount by which the defendant overstated costs where excess payments from the government resulted from falsification of construction costs).

35. *See, e.g.,* United States v. United Techs. Corp., 782 F.3d 718, 734 (6th Cir. 2015) (determining market value based on competitor's prices); United States v. Killough, 848 F.2d 1523, 1531 (11th Cir. 1988) (competitor and expert testimony sufficiently evidenced fair market value).

In kickback cases, some courts calculate damages based on the government's actual loss, and the amount the contractor pays in kickbacks might be "circumstantial evidence" of the harm to the government but is "neither a floor nor a conclusive presumption of the measure of damages."[36] Other courts have found that the damages in kickback cases equals the full amount of the claims paid by the government.[37]

2. Damages Are Not Simply the Amounts Paid on False Claims

Whatever type of fraud is involved, it is clear that "actual damages" in procurement cases are not simply the entire amount of the false claims paid by the government, without consideration of the value the government actually received in return. Of course, if the value of the goods or services actually provided is zero, then damages might equal the entire amount paid by the government.[38] Although the government and relators sometimes have argued that damages equal the entire amount paid by the government even when the goods or services delivered might have value, courts have usually rejected these attempts.[39]

---

36. *Killough*, 848 F.2d at 1532; *see also* Kellogg Brown & Root Servs., Inc. v. United States, 728 F.3d 1348, 1367 (Fed. Cir. 2013).

37. United States v. Rogan, 517 F.3d 449, 453 (7th Cir. 2008) (value of services provided to Medicare and Medicaid patients in violation of anti-kickback law irrelevant to damages analysis, thus damages equaled the full amount of the claims paid); United States *ex rel.* Wheeler v. Union Treatment Ctrs., LLC, 2019 WL 571349, at *9 (Feb. 12, 2019 W.D. Tex.); United States v. Cameron-Ehlen Grp., Inc., 2023 WL 36174 (Jan. 4, 2023 D. Minn.).

38. *See, e.g.*, United States v. TDC Mgmt. Corp., 288 F.3d 421, 427–28 (D.C. Cir. 2002); United States *ex rel.* Compton v. Midwest Specialties, Inc., 142 F.3d 296, 304–05 (6th Cir. 1998).

39. *See, e.g.*, United States *ex rel.* Wall v. Circle C Constr., LLC, 813 F.3d 616, 617–18 (6th Cir. 2016); United States v. Sci. Applications Int'l Corp., 626 F.3d 1257, 1278–79 (D.C. Cir. 2010) ("automatic equation of the government's payments with its damages is mistaken"; "the full value of payments made to the defendant" constitute actual damages "only where the government proves that it received no value from the product delivered"); United States *ex rel.* Harrison v. Westinghouse Savannah River Co., 352 F.3d 908, 922–23 (4th Cir. 2003); *Advance Tool Co.*, 902 F. Supp. at 1017; *Ab-Tech Constr.*, 31 Fed. Cl. at 434. *But see* Young-Montenay, Inc. v. United States, 15 F.3d 1040 (Fed. Cir. 1994) (discussed later). Some courts have treated the damages analysis differently in non-procurement contexts where the government receives nothing in return, such as under grant programs or programs designed to benefit third parties. *See, e.g.*, United States *ex rel.* Longhi v. Lithium Power Techs., Inc., 575 F.3d 458, 472–73 (5th Cir. 2009) (finding in a Small Business Innovation Research grant case, "where there is no tangible benefit to the government and the intangible benefit is impossible to calculate, it is appropriate to value damages in the amount the government actually paid to the Defendants"); United States v. Sound Sols. Windows & Doors, Inc., No. 09 C 6948, 2017 WL 9517514, at *4 (N.D. Ill. May 11, 2017) (calculating damages at the full amount paid by the government for subcontractor work, despite completion of the work, where a contractor falsely claimed the subcontractor met MBE and DBE requirements), *report and recommendation adopted*, No. 09 C 6948, 2017 WL 6723765 (N.D. Ill. Dec. 18, 2017); *Rogan*, 517 F.3d at 453 (value of services provided to Medicare and Medicaid patients in violation of anti-kickback law irrelevant to damages analysis,

For example, in *United States v. Advance Tool Co.*, the contractor was found to have violated the FCA by supplying goods to the government that did not conform with the contract terms.[40] The government argued it was entitled to damages (before trebling) in the amount it paid out on the false claims.[41] The court disagreed, finding that the actual damage to the government was less than the amount paid out on the false claims because the nonconforming goods still had value.[42] Thus, the proper measure of single damages was the difference between the market value of the goods received and the market value of those for which the government had contracted.[43] Because the government failed to prove the market value of the goods it received, "the Court [was] unable to award actual damages" and it received only an award of statutory penalties.[44]

An issue to watch is the extent to which the courts apply the "presumed loss rule" in the Small Business Act to FCA cases alleging that a defendant obtained a small business set-aside contract by misrepresenting its status as a small business concern. As a result of a 2010 amendment, the Small Business Act states that there is a presumption that the government suffers a loss of "the total amount expended on the contract . . . whenever it is established that a business concern other than a small business concern willfully sought and received the award by misrepresentation."[45] Courts are beginning to address the intersection of that provision with the FCA, including questions such as whether—and, if so, how—the presumed loss rule might apply in FCA damages cases,[46] and whether any such

---

thus damages equaled the full amount of the claims paid); United States *ex rel.* Benitez v. Galliano, LLC, No. 15-cv-01688, 2018 WL 2247279, at *11 (D. Nev. Jan. 26, 2018) (calculating damages at the full amount paid by the government under a Housing Assistance Payments contract). However, other courts have held that the value of the services provided is relevant even in these contexts. *See, e.g.*, United States *ex rel.* Davis v. District of Columbia, 679 F.3d 832, 839–40 (D.C. Cir. 2012).

40. 902 F. Supp. at 1016–17.

41. *Id.* at 1017.

42. *Id.*

43. *Id.*

44. *Id.*

45. 15 U.S.C. § 632(w)(1).

46. *Cf.* United States *ex rel.* Lardner v. Smith & Nephew Inc., No. 17-cv-02013, 2018 WL 7050835, at *5 (W.D. Tenn. Sept. 17, 2018) ("This presumption [under 15 U.S.C. § 632(w)(1)] helps establish that such a misrepresentation is material [to an FCA claim] because it suggests the government would not enter into a contract for what the United States Code considers a loss. Materiality is also present when the defendant 'knew or had reason to know that the recipient of the representation attaches importance to the specific matter'") (quoting Universal Health Servs., Inc. v. United States *ex rel.* Escobar, 579 U.S. 176, 193 (2016)); United States *ex rel.* Howard v. Caddell Constr. Co., Inc., No. 11-cv-270, 2021 WL 1206584, at *22 (E.D.N.C. Mar. 30, 2021) ("While [15 U.S.C. § 632(w)(1)] illustrates the importance of small business contracting to the government, and the extent of damages that may be recouped by the government in the event of a failure of compliance with small business

presumption can be rebutted by a showing that the goods or services in question had substantial value to the government. For example, in *United States ex rel. Savage v. Washington Closure Hanford LLC*,[47] an unreported opinion out of the Eastern District of Washington, the court found that the presumption of loss applied to the government's claimed damages arising out of a contractor's alleged willful misrepresentation of the status of several subcontractors. The court found that the presumption could be rebutted, but only in a fairly narrow set of circumstances, including "unintentional errors, technical malfunctions, [or] other similar situations that demonstrate that a misrepresentation of size was not affirmative, intentional, willful, or actionable under the False Claims Act."[48]

A few courts have found FCA damages that are greater than the amount the government paid out on the false claims. For example, in *United States ex rel. Roby v. Boeing Co.*, the United States paid Boeing $4.1 million to remanufacture a helicopter.[49] Because the contractor used a "defective flight-critical" part that led to the total destruction of the helicopter, the court found that the helicopter as delivered was worthless and that the proper measure of damages was the difference between the market value of a properly remanufactured helicopter and the market value of the delivered helicopter (zero).[50] In that case, the amount paid to the contractor was not a limitation on the amount of damages.[51]

---

requirements, the statute does not advance the analysis of materiality for purposes of a False Claims Act claim."). One case has addressed section 632(w)'s presumption in the criminal context when determining the government's loss as part of calculating the sentencing range under the relevant sentencing guidelines. The court determined that "the *only* permissible means by which the presumption of loss may be rebutted would be through the introduction of evidence establishing that one of those circumstances enumerated in 13 C.F.R. § 121.108(d) ['unintentional errors, technical malfunctions, and other similar situations that demonstrate that a misrepresentation of size was not affirmative, intentional, willful or actionable under the False Claims Act'] is applicable." United States v. Singh, 195 F. Supp. 3d 25, 31 (D.D.C. 2016).

47. No. 10-cv-05051, 2017 WL 3667709, at *1–4 (E.D. Wash. Aug. 24, 2017).

48. *Id.* at *4 (quoting *Singh*, 195 F. Supp. at 30).

49. 302 F.3d at 639–40.

50. *Id.* at 647–49.

51. *Id.* There are several aspects of the *Roby* case that make it distinguishable from many other cases involving defective goods or services. First, because the contract at issue involved the remanufacture of a product, the market value of the item to be delivered was much higher than the contract amount. In cases where the contractor is producing an item in the first instance, the market value of that item will likely be close, if not equal, to the contract price. Second, the court, not surprisingly, seems to have been swayed by the fact that the helicopter had been completely destroyed by virtue of the defective component used by the contractor. If that defect had been discovered before the loss of the helicopter, it seems likely the court's damages analysis would have been different.

3. Prejudgment Interest

Whatever the proper measure of the government's actual loss in a particular case, prejudgment interest on that amount is generally not permitted under the FCA.[52]

4. Settlement Offsets

Because the FCA provides for joint and several liability without a right to contribution,[53] there are situations in which the government will have already received a significant recovery from one or more joint tortfeasors by the time a court is asked to assess damages against another party for the same FCA violations. Until recently, however, neither the Supreme Court nor the courts of appeals had explicitly decided the appropriate method to calculate settlement credits under the FCA.[54] In *United States v. Honeywell International Inc.*, the U.S. Court of Appeals for the D.C. Circuit addressed this issue and held that, as a matter of federal common law, "*pro tanto* is the settlement offset rule that best coheres with the FCA and the precedents interpreting it" and that "applying this rule will generally promote judicial economy."[55] The pro tanto approach involves simply reducing the amount of a party's liability for damages by the amount of settlement(s) or judgment(s) already paid by the joint tortfeasor(s).[56]

---

52. *See, e.g.*, Chapman L. Firm, LPA v. United States, 113 Fed. Cl. 555, 608 n.55 (2013) (citing cases), *aff'd*, 583 F. App'x 915 (Fed. Cir. 2014); Peterson v. Weinberger, 508 F.2d 45, 55 (5th Cir. 1975); *see also* Cook Cnty. v. United States *ex rel.* Chandler, 538 U.S. 119, 120 (2003) ("FCA has no separate provision for prejudgment interest."). *But see* United States v. Coop. Grain & Supply Co., 476 F.2d 47, 62 (8th Cir. 1973) (allowing prejudgment interest pre-*Chandler*).

53. United States v. Honeywell Int'l, Inc., 47 F.4th 805, 810 (D.C. Cir. 2022).

54. In *Bornstein*, the Supreme Court applied the *pro tanto* rule to calculating settlement offsets, but the rule was applied without comment and the Court was not asked to decide between the *pro tanto* rule and proportionate share approach. United States v. Bornstein, 423 U.S. 303, 314 (1976); *see also Honeywell*, 47 F.4th at 817.

55. 47 F.4th at 819. In that case, the government sued Honeywell, seeking approximately $11.5 million in damages, trebled to approximately $35 million, for alleged fraudulent misrepresentations relating to bulletproof vests. While the suit was ongoing, the government settled related lawsuits with the manufacturer of the vests and foreign suppliers for a total of $36 million. Honeywell moved for summary judgment on the question of damages, arguing that the court should apply an offset in the amount of all funds received in the other cases—which would leave Honeywell facing only civil penalties. The government argued that Honeywell was still responsible for its proportionate share of damages regardless of the amount of the settlements in the other lawsuits. The district court adopted the proportionate share approach but certified the question for interlocutory review, where the D.C. Circuit adopted the defendant's argument.

56. *Honeywell*, 47 F.4th at 811.

5. Damages for Premature Payments

The unavailability of prejudgment interest does not mean that interest cannot be the proper measure of the government's actual damages where the government suffered a temporary loss of use of its funds. This situation often arises when a contractor submits a false progress payment to obtain government funds prematurely, ultimately performs the contract, and later becomes entitled to the full contract price, including the progress payments. Courts have reached different results in such cases, measuring damages sometimes as the entire amount prematurely paid, sometimes as the interest lost on the prematurely paid funds, and sometimes as nonexistent.

In *Young-Montenay, Inc. v. United States*, a contractor doctored a subcontractor's invoice and then used that invoice to bill the government for $49,000 more than what was eligible for payment at that time.[57] The court had no trouble finding the inflated progress payment request was a false claim.[58] As to damages, the contractor argued that "the only damage, if any, suffered by the government would be for the loss of interest on the extra $49,000," "limited to the period of time the government was deprived of the use of its funds due to early payment."[59] The court rejected that argument and measured the government's loss at the entire $49,000.[60] The court noted that the government was harmed not only by the loss of "the use of the overpaid money" but also because the early payment meant "the contractor had less incentive to complete the project in a timely or satisfactory manner" and "[i]n fact, the completion of the project was delayed over 1,180 days."[61]

In a similar case, however, *BMY-Combat Systems Division of Harsco Corp. v. United States*, the Court of Federal Claims measured damages by the interest that the United States lost on the money as a result of the premature payment.[62] "While *Young-Montenay* awarded the overstatement of the invoice as FCA damages, the court finds that in this case the interest on the premature contract payments is a more appropriate measure of damages."[63]

And some courts don't see any damage at all to the government when an invoice is paid prematurely. In *United States v. American Precision Products Corp.*, the court found no actual damages—not even interest—for premature progress

57. 15 F.3d 1040, 1041 (Fed. Cir. 1994).

58. *Id.* at 1042–43.

59. *Id.* at 1043 n.3.

60. *Id.* at 1043.

61. *Id.* at 1043 n.3.

62. 44 Fed. Cl. 141 (1998).

63. *Id.* at 150. In *BMY*, the government argued that the proper measure of damages was the interest on the prematurely paid funds.

payments to the extent that the contractor eventually delivered the goods: "as to an item for which plaintiff wrongfully paid in January, but for which it should rightfully have paid in April, had not the payment been made in January, plaintiff was not actually damaged, though defendant did incur the technical forfeiture [i.e., FCA statutory penalty] in that regard."[64]

6. Consequential Damages

Courts generally hold that consequential damages are not recoverable under the FCA. For example, in *United States v. Aerodex, Inc.*, a contractor was found to have violated the FCA by supplying aircraft engine bearings that did not conform with contract specifications.[65] The trial court agreed with the government that the nonconforming bearings "constituted a safety hazard" and needed to be replaced.[66] The trial court awarded $27,000 in damages for the money paid out on the claims for payment for the nonconforming bearings, plus another $160,919.18 for the United States' costs in removing and replacing the nonconforming bearings on the aircraft engines.[67] The Fifth Circuit reversed the award of damages for the United States' costs of removing and replacing the bearings, holding that the FCA did not provide for the recovery of consequential damages.[68]

In 1986, after *Aerodex*, Congress considered but rejected adding a consequential damages provision to the FCA.[69] The change from a double damages to a "treble damages provision was, in a way, adopted by Congress as a substitute for consequential damages."[70]

7. Damages for Reverse False Claims

The FCA's "reverse false claims" provision imposes liability on anyone who "knowingly makes, uses, or causes to be made or used, a false record or statement material to an obligation to pay or transmit money or property to the Government, or knowingly conceals or knowingly and improperly avoids or decreases an obligation to pay or transmit money or property to the Government."[71] Damages in the

---

64. 115 F. Supp. 823, 828 (D.N.J. 1953).

65. 469 F.2d 1003, 1005 (5th Cir. 1972).

66. United States v. Aerodex, Inc., 327 F. Supp. 1027, 1030–31 (S.D. Fla. 1970), *rev'd*, 469 F.2d 1003 (5th Cir. 1972).

67. *Aerodex*, 469 F.2d at 1010.

68. *Id.* at 1011.

69. *See* S. 1562, 99th Cong. (1986); S. Rep. No. 99-345, at 19 (1986); H.R. Rep. No. 99-660, at 20 (1986).

70. Cook Cnty. v. United States *ex rel.* Chandler, 538 U.S. 119, 131 n.9 (2003); *see also* Sanders v. Allison Engine Co., 703 F.3d 930, 947 (6th Cir. 2012) (citing *Chandler*).

71. 31 U.S.C. § 3729(a)(1)(G).

reverse false claims context typically "consist of the difference between what the defendant should have paid the government and what the defendant actually paid the government."[72] For example, when a contractor fails to return a government overpayment, damages are the amount of the overpayment.[73]

A more complex case is presented where there is a false statement of the value of property owed to the government that the contractor retained in connection with the contract. In *United States v. Pemco Aeroplex, Inc.*, as part of its work as an aircraft maintenance contractor for the Air Force, the defendant ended up in possession of five aircraft wings.[74] The defendant informed the government of this fact and requested instructions on how to dispose of the wings. However, when informing the government of its possession of the aircraft wings, the defendant allegedly knowingly used improper stock numbers that referenced older, obsolete model wings that the government valued as scrap. Through this alleged scheme, the defendant was able to purchase the wings from the government at scrap value—a total of $1,875—and then sell two of the wings shortly thereafter for $1.5 million.[75] In essence, the complaint accused the defendant of depriving the government of the full value of its wings and sought damages amounting to the total market value of the five wings (more than $2 million) less the amount the defendant actually paid for them, $1,875, trebled.[76] The Eleventh Circuit found that these allegations sufficiently alleged a reverse false claim cause of action.

In other reverse false claims situations, damages are imposed based not on money or property improperly retained but as a result of the defendant's conduct in avoiding the imposition of duties or penalties. In such cases, damages have been assessed in the amount of the duties or penalties the defendant avoided by failing to report an event to regulatory authorities.[77]

D. Trebling of Damages

1. Method of Trebling

If a defendant violates the FCA, it "is liable to the United States Government" for "3 times the amount of damages which the Government sustains because of the act of that person."[78] The Supreme Court has noted that although "the current version of

---

72. United States v. Bourseau, 531 F.3d 1159, 1172 (9th Cir. 2008).

73. *Id.*

74. 195 F.3d 1234 (11th Cir. 1999).

75. *Id.* at 1235–36.

76. *Id.*

77. *See, e.g.*, United States *ex rel.* Customs Fraud Investigations, LLC v. Victaulic Co., 839 F.3d 242 (3d Cir. 2016) (defendant's alleged failure to report incorrect country-of-origin markings on pipe fittings to avoid a ten percent *ad valorem* duty sufficiently alleged a reverse false claim cause of action).

78. 31 U.S.C. § 3729(a)(1).

the FCA imposes damages that are essentially punitive in nature,"[79] the FCA's treble damages also "have a compensatory side, serving remedial purposes in addition to punitive objectives."[80] The remedial purposes served by trebling include paying the relator's share of the recovery, compensating the government for investigative costs, prejudgment interest, and consequential damages that are otherwise not recoverable under the Act.[81] Treble damages also serve as a strong deterrent, motivation for voluntary disclosures, and incentive for relators to come forward.[82]

In *United States v. Bornstein*, the Supreme Court held that damages were to be multiplied before subtracting a compensatory payment received by the government—specifically, a settlement received from a third party.[83] *Bornstein* is frequently used to argue that the government's gross loss should be trebled before deductions for *any* value received by the government, not just the value of compensatory payments. The Seventh Circuit has held, however, in a mortgage fraud case in which the United States recovered the collateral backing the loan from the defendants, that although the FCA "does not specify either a gross or a net trebling approach," neither "does it signal a departure from the norm—and the norm is net trebling."[84] Thus, it reversed a district court decision that trebled mortgage insurance claims before deducting the value of the property received by the government, and required the lower court to recalculate damages using a "net trebling" approach.[85]

The Ninth and Fifth Circuits, however, appear to have reached the opposite conclusion in the mortgage loan context, and have endorsed the type of gross trebling approach regularly sought by plaintiffs.[86] In the procurement context, *Bornstein* itself suggests the net trebling approach is the right one (except, of course, when true compensatory payments like settlements are at issue). The Supreme

---

79. Vt. Agency of Nat. Res. v. United States *ex rel.* Stevens, 529 U.S. 765, 784 (2000).

80. Cook Cnty. v. United States *ex rel.* Chandler, 538 U.S. 119, 130 (2003).

81. *Id.* at 131.

82. *See, e.g.*, United States. v. Hill, 676 F. Supp. 1158, 1167 (N.D. Fl. 1987) (FCA's 1986 amendments "seek to deter Government fraud through the imposition of substantial forfeitures and treble damages"); Morse Diesel Int'l, Inc. v. United States, 79 Fed. Cl. 116, 126–28 (2007) (treble damages "compensate[e] the Government for costs and delays caused by fraud, as well as providing an incentive for voluntary disclosure of any fraudulent activities"); *see also* Robertson v. Bell Helicopter Textron, 32 F.3d 948, 951 (5th Cir. 1994) (purpose of FCA is to "discourage fraud" and to "encourage" whistleblowers to come forward).

83. United States v. Bornstein, 423 U.S. 303, 316 (1976).

84. United States v. Anchor Mortg. Corp., 711 F.3d 745, 749 (7th Cir. 2013).

85. *Id.* at 749–51.

86. United States v. Eghbal, 548 F.3d 1281, 1285 (9th Cir. 2008); United States v. Americus Mortg. Corp., No. 4:12-CV-2676, 2017 WL 4117347, at *3 (S.D. Tex. Sept. 14, 2017) ("It is well established in this circuit that the damages awarded by the jury are to be tripled *before* any subtractions to the award are made for compensatory payments previously received by the Government from any source.").

Court held that "[t]he Government's actual damages are equal to the difference between the market value of the [goods] it received and retained and the market value that the [goods] would have had if they had been of the specified quality."[87] This subtraction to account for value the government actually received through the fraudulent transaction was done before trebling.

2. Reduction for Voluntary Disclosure

Treble damages must be reduced to double damages if the court finds that the defendant (1) "furnished officials of the United States responsible for investigating false claims violations with all information known to such person about the violation within 30 days after the date on which the defendant first obtained the information"; (2) "fully cooperated with any Government investigation of such violation"; and (3) "at the time such person furnished the United States with the information about the violation, no criminal prosecution, civil action, or administrative action had commenced under this title with respect to such violation, and the person did not have actual knowledge of the existence of an investigation into such violation."[88] Thus, this provision only applies "in some of those (presumably few) cases involving defendants who provide information concerning the violation before they have knowledge that an investigation is underway,"[89] and is therefore rather difficult to successfully invoke as a practical matter.[90]

3. Informing the Jury That Damages Are Trebled

Although actual damages are determined by the jury, the "trebling of actual damages are for the Court to determine."[91] Defendants have occasionally sought to inform the jury of the statute's trebling feature, but courts generally have declined to do so, holding that "evidence of civil penalties and treble damages is not admissible at trial,"[92] because "[w]hatever slight incremental probative value such evidence might carry is substantially outweighed by the significant prejudicial effect it is likely to have."[93]

---

87. *Bornstein*, 423 U.S. at 316 n.13 (citations omitted).

88. 31 U.S.C. § 3729(a)(2).

89. Vt. Agency of Nat. Res. v. United States *ex rel.* Stevens, 529 U.S. 765, 785 n.16 (2000).

90. *See, e.g.*, United States *ex rel.* Ervin & Assocs. v. Hamilton Sec. Grp., 370 F. Supp. 2d 18, 48–50 (D.D.C. 2005).

91. United States *ex rel.* Laymon v. Bombardier Transp. (Holdings) USA, Inc., 656 F. Supp. 2d 540, 547 (W.D. Pa. 2009).

92. *Id.* at 548; United States *ex rel.* Scutellaro v. Capitol Supply, Inc., No. CV 10-1094 (BAH), 2017 WL 9889370, at *2 (D.D.C. Sept. 20, 2017); United States v. BlueWave Healthcare Consultants, Inc., No. 9:11-CV-1593-RMG, 2017 WL 11621328, at *1–2 (D.S.C. Nov. 20, 2017).

93. United States *ex rel.* Miller v. Bill Harbert Int'l Constr., Inc., CA No. 95-1231 RCL, 2007 WL 851868, at *2 (D.D.C. Mar. 14, 2007).

III. Civil Penalties

A. Penalties Are Independent from Actual Damages

Plaintiffs may recover statutory civil penalties under the FCA even if they cannot prove that the alleged false claims caused the government any actual damages.[94] If a contractor knowingly submits a false claim or knowingly makes a false statement material to payment of a false claim, that contractor has committed a violation of the FCA and is subject to penalties even if the claim is rejected—"its very submission is a basis for liability."[95] Civil penalties are "automatic and mandatory for each claim which is false."[96]

Penalties, which range from $12,537 to $25,076 per claim,[97] can be so substantial that some relators have chosen to forego damages (and the difficulties of proving them) and to seek only statutory penalties.[98]

B. Determining the Number of Penalties

1. Section 3729(a)(1)(A) and (a)(1)(B) Cases

Penalties may be assessed on "false claims" that violate 31 U.S.C. § 3729(a)(1)(A) and on "false statements" that violate 31 U.S.C. § 3729(a)(1)(B).[99] What triggers imposition of a penalty, however, is the single "causative act" of submitting a false document to the government—multiple penalties are not imposed when the document reflects or is supported by multiple false claims or statements. Thus, the courts have generally held that "when a fraudulent claim consists of multiple components, the submission of an aggregate claim, rather than its individual

---

94. *See* United States *ex rel.* Fago v. M & T Mortg. Corp., 518 F. Supp. 2d 108, 120 (D.D.C. 2007).

95. United States *ex rel.* Schwedt v. Plan. Rsch. Corp., 59 F.3d 196, 199 (D.C. Cir. 1995).

96. S. Rep. No. 345, 99th Cong., 2d Sess. 8 (1986), *reprinted in* 1986 U.S.C.C.A.N. 5266, 5273, although some courts have concluded that they have discretion to refuse to impose penalties when they are excessive in relation to the harm. *See, e.g.*, United States v. Cabrera-Diaz, 106 F. Supp. 2d 234, 242 (D.P.R. 2000), citing United States v. Halper, 490 U.S. 435 (1989), *abrogated by* Hudson v. United States, 522 U.S. 93 (1997).

97. *See* 28 C.F.R. 85.5(a) (May 9, 2022).

98. *See* United States *ex rel.* Bunk v. Gosselin World Wide Moving, N.V., 741 F.3d 390, 404 (4th Cir. 2013) ("holding that relators seeking solely civil penalties enjoy standing to sue").

99. United States *ex rel.* Int'l Bhd. of Elec. Workers Loc. Union No. 98 v. Fairfield Co., 5 F.4th 315, 342, n.25 (3d Cir. 2021) (Post-FERA, the FCA imposes a civil penalty on any person who "knowingly makes, uses, or causes to be made or used, *a false record or statement* material to a false or fraudulent claim. 31 U.S.C. § 3729(a)(1)(B) (emphasis added)"). See *also* United States v. Saavedra, 661 F. App'x 37, 45–46 (2d Cir. 2016) ("[N]othing in the [FCA] requires the court to impose penalties based on the number of false *claims* under § 3729(a)(1)(A), instead of the number of false *statements* under § 3729(a)(1)(B).").

components, is the act that creates liability under the False Claims Act."[100] And this principle has also been applied to cases involving alleged false statements: a penalty is imposed on each false document submitted to the government in order to get a false claim paid, rather than on each of the multiple false representations that might underlie or be found within that false document. For example, in *U.S. ex rel. Koch v. Koch Industries*, the court imposed a single penalty for each false monthly royalty report submitted to the government in connection with a single oil lease, rejecting plaintiffs' request for penalties on each of "hundreds of run tickets each month for separate crude oil purchase transactions on federal and Indian leases."[101] As one district court has stated, "[w]here statutory penalties are at issue, defendants are liable for only one penalty on each . . . false statement in support of [a false] claim, even if those submissions contain multiple falsehoods."[102]

A second important principle that emerges from the case law is that the number of penalties in FCA cases is based on the number of statutory violations *by the defendant* and not on the number of false statements or false claims made by any third party who may have sought reimbursement from the government for defendant's false billings. As the Supreme Court held in *United States v. Borstein*, when determining the number of penalties to impose on a government subcontractor

100. Chapman L. Firm, LPA v. United States, 113 Fed. Cl. 555, 604–05 (2013), *aff'd*, 583 F. App'x 915 (Fed. Cir. 2014). *See also* United States v. Bornstein, 423 U.S. 303 (1976) (21 boxes of falsely marked items sent in three separately invoiced shipments, constituted only three violations of the False Claims Act); United States *ex rel.* Marcus v. Hess, 317 U.S. 537, 552 (1943) (under earlier version of the FCA, assessing a single forfeiture for each project for which a collusive bid was entered even though the bids included additional false forms); United States v. Krizek, 111 F.3d 934, 938–40 (D.C. Cir. 1997) (assessing penalties based on number of false health care claim forms submitted, not the 8,000 false codes within those forms); United States *ex rel.* Maxwell v. Kerr-McGee Oil & Gas Corp., No. 04-CV-01224-MSK-CBS, 2010 WL 3730894, at *3–6 (D. Colo. Sept. 16, 2010) (imposing penalties related to 48 monthly royalty reports, not the 1,403 allegedly separate false claims within the monthly reports); Miller v. United States, 550 F.2d 17, 23–24 (Ct. Cl. 1977) (under an earlier version of the FCA, rejecting an argument that a contractor had asserted sixteen false claims, eleven constituting invoices used in calculating five false monthly billings, because "the invoices are like tally sheets used in calculating a final figure to present to the Government; they are not the claim itself"); United States v. Woodbury, 359 F.2d 370, 378 (9th Cir. 1966) (under an earlier version of the FCA, rejecting the argument that a penalty could be assessed for each document that was attached to fraudulent applications for payment); United States v. Grannis, 172 F.2d 507, 515 (4th Cir. 1947) (under an earlier version of the law, assessing ten forfeitures against defendant for each of ten fraudulent vouchers even though the vouchers listed 130 items), *cert. denied*, 337 U.S. 918, 69 S. Ct. 1160, 93 L. Ed. 1727 (1949).

101. U.S. *ex rel.* Koch v. Koch Indus., Inc., 57 F. Supp. 2d 1122, 1125 (N.D. Okla. 1999) ("[P]enalties should not be imposed on the run tickets, tank tables and meter correction calculations at issue in this case because . . . those records are used only to support the allegedly false statements made in the MMS-2014's, Osage Royalty Reports and monthly check stubs.").

102. United States *ex rel.* Capella v. United Techs. Corp., No. 3:94-CV-2063 (EBB), 1999 WL 464536, at *11 (D. Conn. June 3, 1999).

who bills a government prime contractor, what is important is how many false statements or false claims the *defendant-subcontractor* submitted to the prime, not how many false statements or false claims the prime contractor might have submitted to the government. *Bornstein* involved a government subcontractor, United National Labs, who had billed a prime government contractor, Model Engineering & Manufacturing Corp., for three shipments of radio kits using three false invoices. Model, in turn, had has used 35 invoices to bill the government for these shipments. The government had sued United, the subcontractor, under the FCA to recover damages and penalties. The Supreme Court held that it was United's three false invoices that triggered FCA penalties rather than Model's 35 false bills:

> If United had committed one act which caused Model to file a false claim, it would clearly be liable for a single forfeiture. If, as a result of the same act by United, Model had filed three false claims, United would still have committed only one act that caused the filing of false claims, and thus, under the language of the statute, would again be liable for only one forfeiture. If, on the other hand, United had committed three separate such causative acts, United would be liable for three forfeitures, even if Model had filed only one false claim. The Act, in short, penalizes a person for his own acts, not for the acts of someone else. . . .
>
> A correct application of the statutory language requires . . . that the focus in each case be upon the specific conduct of the person from whom the Government seeks to collect the statutory forfeitures.[103]

Understanding what constitutes an FCA claim can become complicated when a defendant submits more than one type of request for payment of government funds. For example, the Fourth Circuit, in *United States ex rel. Drakeford v. Tuomey*, affirmed the district court's conclusion that the defendant had submitted 21,730 separate false claims under the Medicare program, resulting in total penalties of nearly $120 million.[104] The case involved alleged violations of the anti-referral statute (known as the Stark Law) by Tuomey Healthcare System, a small, rural, nonprofit hospital chain. Toumey had submitted at least two different types of requests for government funds, giving rise to a dispute about which of the two types of claims in the case triggered FCA penalties. One was a standard reimbursement

103. United States v. Bornstein, 423 U.S. 303, 312–13 (1976); *see also* Miller v. United States, 550 F.2d 17, 23–24 and n.11 (Ct. Cl. 1977) (rejecting government request for penalties on both consolidated billings and invoices as "a miscarriage of justice" because "the invoices are like tally sheets used in calculating a final figure to present to the Government."); *and compare* United States v. Erhlich, 643 F.2d 634, 637–38 (9th Cir. 1981) (imposing 76 penalties for monthly invoices) *with id.* at 639–49 (Canby, J. concurring in part and dissenting in part) (arguing that only two penalties for two false statements were appropriate under *Bornstein* for defendant's "own causative acts").

104. 792 F.3d 364, 386 (4th Cir. 2015).

form "used by hospitals to submit a claim for reimbursement to Medicare" for specific medical services rendered by the hospital.[105] The second type of submission was a cost report that constitutes "the final claim that a provider submits . . . for items and services rendered to Medicare beneficiaries" and that represents a truing up of previous "interim payments" made on a larger set of individual services.[106] The difference in liability for FCA penalties between the two was huge, as Tuomey had submitted 21,730 reimbursement forms and only four cost reports.

Tuomey argued that penalties should be assessed on the four cost reports only, citing earlier cases that calculated the number of penalties based on such reports.[107] The court, however, distinguished those cases by noting that the allegations there were not that the "forms themselves were . . . fraudulent. . . . [Rather], the fraud was consummated only when the cost report was submitted."[108] In *United States ex rel. Hockett v. Columbia/HCA Healthcare Corp.*, for instance, the underlying scheme involved improperly inflating costs that went into the cost reports themselves, not the individual reimbursement forms.[109] The court in that case refused to find that each of the 66 reimbursement forms submitted was a false claim because there was "no evidence that the forms billed the government for services that were not actually rendered or necessary. As to each [form], the government got what it paid for."[110] It was the "cost report that contained the false statements, did the damage, and completed the fraud."[111]

In contrast, in *Toumey*, the underlying fraudulent scheme was a violation of the Stark Law, which rendered "all services provided in violation of that law . . . medically unnecessary."[112] Thus, the court explained, "each time Tuomey submitted to Medicare a . . . form asking for reimbursement for a prohibited referral, it was knowingly asking the government to pay an amount that, by law, it could not pay. Consequently, . . . the district court did not err in finding that each [of the 21,730] . . . form[s] constituted a separate claim."[113] The key, then, is determining which claims violate the FCA in any particular case and using that as the basis for computing the number of penalties.

---

105. *Id.* at 385–86 & n.16.

106. *Id.* at 386 & n.17 (internal quotation marks omitted).

107. *See id.* at 386 (citing United States *ex rel.* Hockett v. Columbia/HCA Healthcare Corp., 498 F. Supp. 2d 25, 70–71 (D.D.C. 2007) and Visiting Nurse Ass'n of Brooklyn v. Thompson, 378 F. Supp. 2d 75, 99 (E.D.N.Y. 2004)).

108. *Id.*

109. 498 F. Supp. 2d at 32.

110. *Id.* at 71.

111. *Id.*

112. United States *ex rel.* Drakeford v. Tuomey, 792 F.3d 364, 386 (4th Cir. 2015).

113. *Id.*

2. Penalties May Be Imposed for FCA Violations Outside of the Section 3729(a)(1)(A) and (a)(1)(B) Contexts

Civil penalties are available in the reverse false claims context[114] and under the FCA's conspiracy provision.[115] A penalty for conspiracy is in addition to the penalties for any false claims that are submitted.[116] Civil penalties are generally considered unavailable for retaliation claims.[117]

C. Constitutional Limits on Penalties

In industries that generate high volumes of claims, the existence of penalties for each claim can raise significant liability concerns. Many courts have held that the Eighth Amendment's Excessive Fines Clause, as well as the Fifth Amendment's Due Process Clause, act as ceilings on runaway penalty assessments. The Excessive Fines Clause states that "[e]xcessive bail shall not be required, nor excessive fines imposed, nor cruel and unusual punishments inflicted."[118] In *United States ex rel. Bunk v. Gosselin World Wide Moving, N.V.*, the Fourth Circuit held that "[a] cumulative monetary penalty such as that imposed under the FCA will violate the Eighth Amendment proscription against excessive fines in the infrequent instance that it is 'grossly disproportional to the gravity of a defendant's offense.'"[119]

The Due Process Clause "imposes substantive limits beyond which penalties may not go."[120] It prohibits "'grossly excessive' monetary penalties that go beyond

---

114. *See* United States v. Bourseau, 531 F.3d 1159 (9th Cir. 2008) (assessing $31,000 in civil penalties for three cost reports that included nonexistent, nonallowed, and inflated costs); *see, generally*, United States *ex rel.* Customs Fraud Invs., LLC v. Victaulic Co., 839 F.3d 242, 253 (3d Cir. 2016).

115. 31 U.S.C. § 3729(a)(1)(C). *See* United States v. Bd. of Educ. of City of Union City, 697 F. Supp. 167, 176 (D.N.J. 1988) (finding that a conspiracy "is a separate violation of the Act and therefore entitles the United States to a separate statutory penalty").

116. 31 U.S.C. § 3729(a)(1)(C); *see also* Kelsoe v. Fed. Crop Ins. Corp., 724 F. Supp. 448, 453–54 (E.D. Tex. 1988); United States v. CFW Constr. Co., 649 F. Supp. 616, 618 (D.S.C. 1986); United States v. Uzzell, 648 F. Supp. 1362, 1368 (D.D.C. 1986).

117. *See* Leggins v. Orlando Hous. Auth., No. 6:13-CV-232-ORL-37, 2013 WL 937739, at *3 (M.D. Fla. Mar. 11, 2013).

118. U.S. Const. amend. VIII.

119. 741 F.3d 390, 408 (4th Cir. 2013) (quoting United States v. Bajakajian, 524 U.S. 321, 334 (1998), which held that fines are payments that are "punitive" in nature and that they are excessive where "grossly disproportional to the gravity of the defendant's offense"); United States v. Mackby, 261 F.3d 821, 829–31 (9th Cir. 2001) (holding that the Excessive Fines Clause analysis applies to FCA civil penalties). *But see* United States v. Rogan, 517 F.3d 449, 453–54 (7th Cir. 2008) (noting that "[i]t is far from clear that the Excessive Fines Clause applies to civil actions under the False Claims Act," and declining to rule on the issue).

120. Txo Prod. Corp. v. All. Res. Corp., 509 U.S. 443, 453–54 (1993) (quotation marks and citation omitted).

what is necessary to vindicate the government's 'legitimate interests in punishment and deterrence.'"[121] In *Tuomey*, the Fourth Circuit found the Excessive Fines Clause and Due Process analyses identical for purposes of assessing the constitutionality of penalties.[122] The Court noted that civil penalties are "completely punitive," and adopted the Supreme Court's guideposts when reviewing the constitutionality of punitive damages awards: "(1) the degree of reprehensibility of the defendant's misconduct; (2) the disparity between the actual or potential harm suffered by the plaintiff and the punitive damages award; and (3) the difference between the punitive damages awarded by the jury and the civil penalties authorized or imposed in comparable cases."[123] With regard to the disparity between the actual or potential harm suffered by the plaintiff and the total award, the court compared the actual damages assessed against Tuomey, nearly $40 million, to the civil penalty, nearly $120 million, and the portion of treble damages that could be considered punitive, nearly $67 million (after deducting the portion owed to the relator). The ratio of punitive to compensatory damages was approximately 3.6:1, which the court found to be just under the 4:1 ratio the Supreme Court had stated "might be close to the line of constitutional impropriety." As a result, the Fourth Circuit concluded that the damages plus penalty award was constitutional under the Excessive Fine and the Due Process Clauses. Because this type of ratio analysis becomes far more problematic when the government has suffered no actual damages, courts have greatly limited the amount of civil penalties imposed in such cases.[124]

The Supreme Court has not addressed whether the Excessive Fines Clause applies to nonintervened FCA qui tam actions.[125] The Eleventh Circuit recently held that it does, finding "damages and statutory penalties awarded in a non-intervened FCA qui tam action are subject to the Eighth Amendment's prohibition on excessive fines."[126] It further concluded that an FCA monetary award is a "fine

121. United States *ex rel.* Drakeford v. Tuomey, 792 F.3d 364, 387 (4th Cir. 2015) (quoting BMW of N. Am., Inc. v. Gore, 517 U.S. 559, 562 (1996)).

122. *Id.* at 388.

123. *Id.* (quoting State Farm Mut. Auto. Ins. Co. v. Campbell, 538 U.S. 408, 425 (2003)) (quotation marks omitted). The *Tuomey* Court also noted that, "[t]he fact . . . that Congress provided for treble damages and an automatic civil monetary penalty per false claim shows that Congress believed that making a false claim to the government is a serious offense." *Id.*

124. United States v. Cabrera-Diaz, 106 F. Supp. 2d 234, 242 (D.P.R. 2000) (finding civil penalty to be excessive because penalty was significantly greater than government's actual damages); United States v. Advance Tool Co., 902 F. Supp. 1011, 1018–19 (W.D. Mo. 1995) (finding civil penalty of $3.4 million to be unconstitutionally excessive when the government failed to prove actual damages; penalty reduced to $365,000).

125. Yates v. Pinellas Hematology & Oncology, P.A., 21 F.4th 1288, 1307 (11th Cir. 2021).

126. *Id.*

for the purposes of the Excessive Fines Clause."[127] Despite lack of intervention by the government, the court still concluded the monetary award is "imposed by the United States."[128]

IV. Relator's Personal Claim for Damages

Under the FCA, an "employee, contractor, or agent shall be entitled to all relief necessary to make that employee, contractor, or agent whole, if that employee, contractor, or agent" is retaliated against for engaging in whistleblowing activity.[129] Specifically, if a whistleblower can demonstrate retaliation they may receive "reinstatement with the same seniority status that [they] would have had but for the discrimination, 2 times the amount of back pay, interest on the back pay, and compensation for any special damages sustained as a result of the discrimination, including litigation costs and reasonable attorneys' fees."[130]

The FCA's direction to make whole a victim of retaliation heavily informs the damages analysis. For example, in *Wilkins v. St. Louis Housing Authority*, the plaintiff appealed the district court's method of calculating twice the plaintiff's back pay.[131] The district court had awarded back pay by taking the lost wages the plaintiff had suffered ($80,000), subtracting his mitigating income from his next job ($30,000), and doubled that amount (for a total of nearly $100,000). The plaintiff argued that the court should have doubled the lost wages amount and then subtracted the mitigation amount. The Eighth Circuit disagreed, noting that "[w]e feel confident that an award of nearly $100,000 completely compensates [plaintiff]."[132]

---

127. *Id.* at 1308.

128. *Id.*

129. 31 U.S.C. § 3730(h)(1).

130. *Id.* § 3730(h)(2).

131. 314 F.3d 927 (8th Cir. 2002).

132. *Id.* at 934; *see also* Harris v. Blue Ridge Health Servs., Inc., 388 F. Supp. 3d 633, 644 (M.D.N.C. 2019) ("The FCA's command that prevailing plaintiffs receive '2 times the amount of back pay,' then, refers to *net* back pay.") (emphasis in original); Miniex v. Houston Hous. Auth., No. CV 4:17-00624, 2019 WL 1675857, at *2 (S.D. Tex. Apr. 17, 2019) ("Back pay under 3730(h)(2) is the net loss [] suffered, which is [] lost wages less actual wages [] earned from third party sources before trial. For the statutory doubling of back pay, the net loss will be multiplied by two."), *amended*, 400 F. Supp. 3d 620 (S.D. Tex. 2019), *judgment entered*, No. CV 4:17-00624, 2019 WL 10892215 (S.D. Tex. Sept. 16, 2019). *But see* United States *ex rel.* Mooney v. Americare, Inc., 172 F. Supp. 3d 644, 646 (E.D.N.Y. 2016) ("to the extent the defendants are found liable to [relator] for retaliation under § 3730(h), her back pay damages will be doubled prior to subtracting any mitigation"); Neal v. Honeywell, Inc., 995 F. Supp. 889, 894–96 (N.D. Ill. 1998) ("The jury concluded that Neal was entitled to $50,000 in back pay less $10,000 earned in mitigation. Under the statute we double that $50,000 and subtract $10,000 for a beginning figure of $90,000.").

The amount of back pay permitted is calculated from the date of termination to the date of judgment.[133] Interest is calculated on net back pay before doubling.[134]

In addition to doubled back pay plus interest on the back page, a plaintiff may also seek "special damages," which include not only litigation costs and reasonable attorneys' fees but also damages for emotional distress.[135] However, the damages for emotional distress must be causally connected to the termination.[136] The Fourth Circuit has held that to receive more than nominal damages for emotional distress, a plaintiff must present "concrete evidence," not merely "conclusory allegations that [they] felt embarrassed, degraded, or devastated."[137] In this analysis, courts should consider "the need for medical, psychological, or psychiatric treatment, the presence of physical symptoms, loss of income, and impact on the plaintiff's conduct and lifestyle."[138]

Some courts have even recognized front pay as an allowed alternative to reinstatement when reinstatement is not practicable.[139] Punitive damages are generally not permitted.[140]

V. Plaintiff's Attorneys' Fees and Costs, and Relator's Expenses

A. Awards of Fees and Costs to Relator

The FCA provides that a prevailing relator shall be awarded "reasonable attorneys' fees and costs," regardless of whether the government intervened in the case.[141] The relator must affirmatively demand payment of fees—"without such a demand, the

133. *See* Molino v. Bast Servs., Inc., No. 08 C 4399, 2011 WL 841891, at *3 (N.D. Ill. Mar. 7, 2011).

134. *Neal*, 995 F. Supp. at 896–97.

135. *See* Hammond v. Northland Counseling Ctr., Inc., 218 F.3d 886, 892–93 (8th Cir. 2000) ("Damages for emotional distress caused by an employer's retaliatory conduct plainly fall within th[e] category of 'special damages.'").

136. *See id.* at 893 n.8 (noting that certain events occurring a year after the termination were "too attenuated").

137. Harris v. Blue Ridge Health Servs., Inc., 388 F. Supp. 3d 633, 645 (M.D.N.C. 2019) (quoting Doe v. Chao, 306 F.3d 170, 180 (4th Cir. 2002)).

138. *Id.*

139. Weihua Huang v. Rector & Visitors of Univ. of Virginia, No. 3:11-CV-00050, 2013 WL 865845, at *13 (W.D. Va. Mar. 7, 2013) (recognizing option of front pay but not awarding it due to 11th Amendment concerns); *cf. Hammond*, 218 F.3d at 892 (noting that the FCA does not explicitly authorize front pay).

140. *See* Leggins v. Orlando Hous. Auth., No. 6:13-CV-232-ORL-37, 2013 WL 937739, at *2–*3 (M.D. Fla. Mar. 11, 2013) ("Because Congress provided for punitive damages in one section of the False Claims Act, the Court presumes that the absence of punitive damages in the anti-retaliation section was intentional.").

141. 31 U.S.C. § 3730(d)(1)–(2).

defendant is under no obligation to pay."[142] In most cases, "[t]he starting point for determining a reasonable fee is the lodestar, which is the product of the number of hours billed and a reasonable hourly rate."[143] "[T]he party seeking compensation bears the burden of documenting its work."[144]

"A 'strong presumption' exists that a lodestar figure, without more, constitutes a reasonable fee award."[145] In only "rare" and "exceptional" cases will a fee applicant rebut this strong presumption against upward adjustments to the lodestar.[146] This requires "specific evidence" showing that "an adjustment is *necessary* to the determination of a reasonable fee."[147]

Further, some courts reduce the attorney fee award "in cases where a plaintiff prevails on only some of its claims."[148] "While a failure to prevail on related claims does not mandate a strict reduction in fee awards, it does serve as evidence that some discount may be appropriate."[149] Finally, "the fee shifting provisions of the [FCA] do not prohibit an attorney from receiving both statutory attorneys' fees and a contingency fee."[150]

Separately, the FCA provides that a successful relator may recover their "reasonable expenses which the court finds to have been necessarily incurred."[151]

Moreover, a defendant found liable for FCA violations is on the hook for the government's costs to bring the action.[152] While the government rarely seeks these

---

142. Gonter v. Hunt Valve Co., 510 F.3d 610, 614 (6th Cir. 2007).

143. *Id.* at 616 (citing Hensley v. Eckerhart, 461 U.S. 424, 434 (1983)); *see also* United States *ex rel.* Vuyyuru v. Jadhav, 555 F.3d 337, 356 (4th Cir. 2009).

144. *Gonter*, 510 F.3d at 617.

145. Miller v. Holzmann, 575 F. Supp. 2d 2, 45 (D.D.C. 2008) (citing City of Burlington v. Dague, 505 U.S. 557, 562 (1992)), *amended in part, vacated in part sub nom.* United States *ex rel.* Miller v. Bill Harbert Int'l Constr., Inc., 786 F. Supp. 2d 110 (D.D.C. 2011).

146. *Id.* Sometimes, fees may be adjusted to compensate for the delay in payment when litigation stretches over a longer period. *E.g.*, Schwarz v. Sec'y of Health & Human Servs., 73 F.3d 895, 908 (9th Cir. 1995) ("either current or historical prevailing rates may be used, [although] the use of current rates may be necessary to adjust for inflation if the fee amount would otherwise be unreasonable" (internal quotation marks omitted)); *Miller*, 575 F. Supp. 2d at 21 (exercising discretion "to compensate relator's counsel for delay in payment by applying current rates in calculating the lodestar").

147. *Id.* (quoting Blum v. Stenson, 465 U.S. 886, 898–99 (1984)) (internal quotations omitted).

148. United States *ex rel.* Maxwell v. Kerr-McGee Oil & Gas Corp., 793 F. Supp. 2d 1260, 1265 (D. Colo. 2011).

149. United States *ex rel.* Miller v. Bill Harbert Int'l Constr., Inc., 786 F. Supp. 2d 110, 121 (D.D.C. 2011). *But see* United States *ex rel.* Averback v. Pastor Med. Assocs. P.C., 224 F. Supp. 2d 342, 350 n.7 (D. Mass. 2002) (declining to base a fee award on the "degree of success obtained").

150. United States *ex rel.* Depace v. Cooper Health Sys., 940 F. Supp. 2d 208, 217 (D.N.J. 2013); *see also Maxwell*, 793 F. Supp. 2d at 1264 (holding that the existence of a contingent fee agreement between relator and their counsel "does not justify reducing the lodestar amount" of statutory attorneys' fees owed by the defendant under § 3730(d)(2)).

151. *See* 31 U.S.C. § 3730 (d)(1) and (2). *See also Maxwell*, 793 F. Supp. 2d at 1267 (finding that "reasonable expenses" under the FCA includes expert fees).

152. *See* 31 U.S.C. § 3729(a)(3).

costs during settlement discussions, courts have awarded costs to the government when it prevails in an FCA action.[153] Moreover, this provision has been cited by the government in justifying the imposition of statutory penalties that cover some or all of its costs of prosecuting the action.[154]

VI. Awards of Fees and Costs to Prevailing Defendant

In cases in which the government declines to intervene, the FCA permits a court to award "reasonable attorneys' fees and expenses" to a prevailing defendant if the court finds that the relator's claim was "clearly frivolous, clearly vexatious, or brought primarily for purposes of harassment."[155] At least one court has awarded defendant its attorneys' fees, finding that a relator's FCA claims were "clearly frivolous" when they were "groundless," "without foundation," and "unreasonable."[156] To recover fees, the defendant need not show that the relator brought their claims in subjective bad faith.[157] Section 3730(d)(4) governs "attorneys' fees and expenses," but not costs. Thus, even when the relatively high bar of that section is unmet, a prevailing defendant is nonetheless entitled to costs under FRCP 54(d)(1).[158]

The FCA provides that, if the United States intervenes in the case, then a prevailing defendant may look to 28 U.S.C. § 2412(d) for recovery of fees and expenses.[159] 28 U.S.C. § 2412(d) permits a defendant to recover these amounts from the government if the action was not "substantially justified" and if no special circumstances make an award of fees unjust.[160]

---

153. For examples of cases in which courts have awarded costs to the government, *see* United States v. Bli, No. 00-10484, 2006 WL 3333104, at *14 (E.D. Mich. Nov. 15, 2006); United States v. Irizarry-Colon, No. 05-1607 (JAF), 2006 WL 6911517, at *15 (D.P.R. June 9, 2006); United States v. Mic Dairy, Inc., No. 05-1613CCC, 2006 WL 8417225, at *8 (D.P.R. Sept. 19, 2006); United States v. Outland, CA No. 5:00-CV-123-J, 2001 WL 1793736, at *3 (W.D. Ky. Mar. 19, 2001); United States v. Cabrera-Diaz, 106 F. Supp. 2d 234, 243–44 (D.P.R. 2000); United States v. Entin, 750 F. Supp. 512, 520 (S.D. Fla. 1990).

154. United States v. Fliegler, 756 F. Supp. 688, 697 (E.D.N.Y. 1990).

155. 31 U.S.C. § 3730(d)(4); *see, e.g., In re* Natural Gas Royalties Qui Tam Litig., 845 F.3d 1010, 1024 (10th Cir. 2017).

156. *Natural Gas Royalties*, 845 F.3d at 1024.

157. United States *ex rel.* Grynberg v. Praxair, Inc., 389 F.3d 1038, 1058 (10th Cir. 2004).

158. *See, e.g.*, Assocs. Against Outlier Fraud v. Huron Consulting Grp., Inc., 817 F.3d 433, 437 (2d Cir. 2016) ("31 U.S.C. § 3730(d)(4) does not affect the award of costs under Rule 54(d)(1) to prevailing parties"); United States *ex rel.* Ritchie v. Lockheed Martin Corp., 558 F.3d 1161, 1172 (10th Cir. 2009); United States *ex rel.* Costner v. United States, 317 F.3d 889, 891 (8th Cir. 2003).

159. *See* 31 U.S.C.A. § 3730(g) ("In civil actions brought under this section by the United States, the provisions of section 2412(d) of title 28 shall apply.").

160. 28 U.S.C. § 2412(d) provides, in pertinent part:

> [A] court shall award to a prevailing party other than the United States fees and other expenses, in addition to any costs awarded pursuant to subsection (a), incurred by that party in any civil action (other than cases sounding in tort), including proceedings for judicial review of agency action, brought by or against the United States in any court

VII. Relator's Share

When the United States or the relator recovers in a qui tam action (and when the United States recovers through an "alternate remedy" as that term is used in the FCA[161]), a relator ordinarily is entitled to a share of the proceeds.[162] Specifically, a prevailing relator is entitled to a percentage of both the treble damages awarded and the penalties imposed.[163]

A. Intervened versus Nonintervened Cases

In intervened cases, a relator will receive at least 15 percent but no more than 25 percent "of the proceeds of the action or settlement of the claim."[164] If the government does not intervene, the relator is entitled to recover between 25 percent and 30 percent "of the proceeds of the action or settlement."[165] However, if relator "planned and initiated" the FCA violations, the court in its discretion may reduce the relator's share of the proceeds to zero, and if relator's action is "primarily" based on publicly disclosed material that did not originate with the relator, the court must reduce the relator's share to 10 percent in an intervened action.[166]

B. Computing the Relator's Share

"[D]etermination of the relator's share is left largely to the Court's informed discretion."[167] Where the government intervenes, the relator's share depends on "the extent to which the person substantially contributed to the prosecution of the action."[168] The minimum share is "usually considered a finder's fee" and is paid to

---

> having jurisdiction of that action, unless the court finds that the position of the United States was substantially justified or that special circumstances make an award unjust.

Id. § 2412(d)(1)(A).

161. *See* 31 U.S.C. § 3730(c)(5).

162. *See id.* § 3730(d).

163. *Id. See, e.g.*, United States *ex rel.* Ziebell v. Fox Valley Workforce Dev. Bd., Inc., 806 F.3d 946, 951 (7th Cir. 2015); United States *ex rel.* Zizic v. Q2Administrators, LLC, 728 F.3d 228, 231 (3d Cir. 2013) (finding a "successful relator is entitled to" a share "of the proceeds of the litigation, § 3730(d)(2), which include civil penalties and treble damages, § 3729(a)(1)"); United States *ex rel.* LaCorte v. Wagner, 185 F.3d 188, 190 (4th Cir. 1999) ("If the action is successful, the government and the original plaintiff split the damages and penalties.").

164. 31 U.S.C. § 3730(d)(1).

165. *Id.* § 3730(d)(2).

166. *Id.* § 3730 (d)(1) and (d)(3).

167. United States *ex rel.* Alderson v. Quorum Health Grp., Inc., 171 F. Supp. 2d 1323, 1331 (M.D. Fla. 2001).

168. 31 U.S.C. § 3730(d)(1).

the relator "even if that person does nothing more than file the action in federal court."[169]

Greater assistance by a relator results in greater rewards, with the maximum reward reserved for relators who "actively and uniquely assist the government in the prosecution of the case."[170] Courts often rely on factors set forth in the FCA's legislative history, which include the significance of the information provided by the relator to the government, whether the relator "carefully develop[ed] all the facts and supporting documentation necessary to make the case required by law," whether the relator continued to contribute to the result, and "[w]hether the information in the suit provided by the relator was previously known to the government."[171] The courts also look to the "Relator's Share Guidelines," published by DOJ. [172] Courts have also held that a relator may be entitled to the statutory maximum percentage if they suffered personal or professional hardship,[173] or encountered "formidable personal and legal difficulties," but nonetheless promptly disclosed the alleged fraud and "doggedly pursu[ed] his claim."[174]

C. Informing the Jury of the Relator's Share

Courts have held that it is appropriate for the jury to hear evidence of the relator's entitlement to a share of the proceeds of the action.[175]

169. United States *ex rel.* Johnson-Pochardt v. Rapid City Reg'l Hosp., 252 F. Supp. 2d 892, 897 (D.S.D. 2003) (citing *Alderson*, 171 F. Supp. 2d at 1331, 1332) (quotation marks omitted).

170. *Id.* (quoting United States *ex rel.* Burr v. Blue Cross & Blue Shield of Fla., Inc., 882 F. Supp. 166, 168 (M.D. Fla. 1995)) (internal quotation marks omitted).

171. *See, e.g., Alderson*, 171 F. Supp. 2d at 1332 (quoting 132 Cong. Rec. H9382-03 (Oct. 7, 1986) (statement of Rep. Berman); S. Rep. No. 99-345, at 28 (1986), *reprinted in* 1986 U.S.C.C.A.N. 5266, 5293)) (internal quotation marks omitted).

172. *See id.* at 1333–35 (listing as factors the DOJ considers, among others, whether the relator reported the fraud promptly, whether the complaint exposed a nationwide practice, whether the relator was an "excellent, credible witness" at a deposition or trial, the size of the recovery, whether "[t]he filing of the complaint had a substantial adverse impact on the relator," and whether the relator participated in the fraud).

173. *Burr*, 882 F. Supp. at 169.

174. United States *ex rel.* Alderson v. Quorum Health Grp., Inc., 171 F. Supp. 2d 1323, 1338 (M.D. Fla. 2001).

175. *See, e.g.*, United States *ex rel.* Miller v. Bill Harbet Int'l Constr., Inc., CA No. 95-1231 RCL, 2007 WL 851868, at *1 (D.D.C. Mar. 14, 2007) (denying relator's motion in limine to exclude evidence of relator's share in FCA settlement because "cooperation agreements . . . are probative of the witnesses' credibility and motivation in testifying"); United States *ex rel.* Koch v. Koch Indus., No. 91-cv-763, 1999 U.S. Dist. LEXIS 16622, at *10 (N.D. Okla. July 7, 1999) ("the Court will inform the jury that Plaintiffs will receive 25–30% of whatever amount the jury chooses to award to the United States and that the remaining 70–75% will be paid to the United States").

VIII. Other Remedies

The FCA does not foreclose equitable remedies such as an injunction to preserve a defendant's assets.[176] Moreover, it does not prevent the government from seeking contract or common law remedies along with FCA claims.[177]

176. *See* United States *ex rel.* Rahman v. Oncology Assocs., 198 F.3d 489, 492 (4th Cir. 1999) (upholding a prejudgment asset-freezing injunction in an FCA suit).

177. *See* United States v. Crumb, CA No. 15-0655-WS-N, 2016 WL 4480690, at *18 & n.27 (S.D. Ala. Aug. 24, 2016); United States *ex rel.* Roby v. Boeing Co., 184 F.R.D. 107, 112–13 (S.D. Ohio 1998) (concurring with government's assertion that "it may plead, in the alternative, common law claims for fraud, payment by mistake, unjust enrichment, and breach of contract along with its claim under the FCA").

CHAPTER 12

Other Consequences

MARK B. SWEET, KARA M. SACILOTTO, AND KEVIN J. MAYNARD[1]

The knowing submission of a false claim to the United States can have consequences beyond False Claims Act (FCA) liability. The knowing submission of a false claim can result in administrative sanctions, contractual actions, further civil suits, and even criminal prosecution of a company and the individuals who own or operate it.

I. Parallel Proceedings

While an investigation under the FCA is underway, the government may consider other enforcement actions against the target. In other words, the government can pursue "parallel proceedings," which are simultaneous actions against the same parties, whenever "an alleged offense or violation of federal law gives rise to the potential for criminal, civil, regulatory, and/or agency administrative" proceedings.[2]

The Department of Justice (DOJ) has a policy that its attorneys should consider and discuss the full range of potential remedies "from the moment of case intake."[3] Accordingly, qui tam complaints and mandatory disclosures under the Federal Acquisition Regulation (FAR) are routed to both the Civil and Criminal Divisions of DOJ for review. According to the Justice Manual, "[c]riminal attorneys handling corporate investigations should notify civil attorneys as early as permissible of conduct that might give rise to potential individual civil liability, even if criminal liability continues to be sought."[4] And, "if civil attorneys believe that an individual identified in the course of their corporate investigation should be subject to a criminal inquiry," DOJ policy requires the civil attorneys to refer the matter to criminal

1. Mark B. Sweet, Kara M. Sacilotto, and Kevin J. Maynard are partners at Wiley Rein.

2. U.S. DOJ, *Justice Manual*, Organizations and Functions Manual Ch. 27 at 1, https://www.justice.gov/jm/organization-and-functions-manual-27-parallel-proceedings.

3. U.S. DOJ, *Justice Manual*, 1-12.000, https://www.justice.gov/jm/jm-1-12000-coordination-parallel-criminal-civil-regulatory-and-administrative-proceedings (last updated May 2018).

4. *Id.*

prosecutors, "regardless of the current status of the civil corporate investigation."[5] This policy further requires government attorneys to "consider investigative strategies that maximize the Government's ability to share information among criminal, civil, and agency administrative teams to the fullest extent appropriate to the case and permissible by law, including the use of investigative means other than grand jury subpoenas for documents or witness testimony."[6] This approach encourages DOJ's civil attorneys to share with criminal prosecutors documents produced in response to a Civil Investigative Demand or in connection with a disclosure to the agency. It also encourages criminal prosecutors to obtain a court order under Federal Rule of Criminal Procedure 6(e) so that they can share evidence obtained through a grand jury subpoena with their civil or administrative counterparts.

Finally, "at every point between case intake and final resolution," the government's attorneys must assess the potential impact of their actions on these parallel proceedings.[7] A 2018 update to the Justice Manual cautions prosecutors to "remain mindful of their ethical obligation not to use criminal enforcement authority unfairly to extract, or to attempt to extract, additional civil or administrative monetary payments."[8] It also set a "goal of achieving an equitable result" by "avoid[ing] the unnecessary imposition of duplicative fines, penalties, and/or forfeiture against the company" related to the same misconduct.[9]

Nevertheless, settlement of an FCA case in and of itself is not a global resolution with the United States of all potential enforcement actions. The standard terms used by DOJ in an FCA settlement expressly reserve (i.e., do not release), among other things, criminal liability, tax liability, and the contracting or regulatory agency's administrative actions and enforcement rights (such as suspension and debarment). Additionally, DOJ's resolution of an FCA claim against a corporation does not mean that DOJ necessarily will resolve any related claims it may have against the corporation's officers, executives, or employees—any such claims are evaluated and resolved separately by DOJ.[10]

A. Criminal Prosecutions

The most serious collateral implication of the submission of a knowing false claim is a potential criminal charge. The Supreme Court has recognized that the

---

5. *Id.*

6. *Id.*

7. *Id.*

8. U.S. DOJ, *Justice Manual*, 1-12.100, https://www.justice.gov/jm/jm-1-12000-coordination-parallel-criminal-civil-regulatory-and-administrative-proceedings#1-12.100 (last updated May 2018).

9. *Id.*

10. DOJ policies for FCA settlement agreements are discussed in more detail in Chapter 13, Settlements under the False Claims Act.

government may conduct simultaneous civil and criminal proceedings without violating the Due Process Clause of the U.S. Constitution.

A primary obligation of the government when pursuing parallel civil and criminal actions is to act in good faith. For example, the government may not use a civil action solely to obtain evidence for a criminal prosecution or make misrepresentations to a defendant about the nature of its inquiry. Nevertheless, the government will sometimes wait to decide on whether to launch a criminal matter until it has obtained evidence and information from the civil investigation to assess the defendant's criminal culpability.

The conduct underlying a violation of the FCA can trigger a number of different criminal offenses. The most analogous criminal provisions are 18 U.S.C. § 287, which prohibits a knowing submission of a "false, fictitious, or fraudulent" claim to the United States, and 18 U.S.C. § 286, which prohibits a conspiracy to defraud the United States "by obtaining or aiding to obtain the payment or allowance" of such a claim. The elements of a criminal false claim are similar to a civil false claim, with the key difference being that under the criminal statute the defendant must submit the false claim to the United States with a specific intent to violate the law or a consciousness that what it is doing is wrong. A conviction under § 287 can result in a fine and prison sentence of up to five years, while a conspiracy charge under § 286 can result in a fine and a prison sentence of up to ten years.

Another analogous offense is the criminal charge of false statements under 18 U.S.C § 1001. Among other things, § 1001 prohibits knowingly and willfully making a materially false, fictitious, or fraudulent statement or making or using any false document knowing it to contain a false statement or entry "in any matter within the jurisdiction of the executive, legislative, or judicial branch of the Government of the United States." Like a criminal false claim, a conviction under § 1001 can result in a fine and imprisonment for up to five years or, for certain categories of offenses such as those involving terrorism, up to eight years.

Prosecutors often pursue other criminal charges against defendants in FCA cases—some of which carry even heavier penalties than a criminal false claim or statement. For example, some commonly pursued criminal charges against defendants who submit false claims are:

- Mail or wire fraud;[11]
- Major fraud against the United States;[12]
- Health care fraud;[13]

11. *See* 18 U.S.C. §§ 1341, 1343.
12. *See id.* § 1031.
13. *Id.* § 1347.

- False statements or representations in a health care program;[14]
- Kickbacks;[15] and
- Violations of the Food, Drug, and Cosmetic Act.[16]

Defending a criminal case and a civil case at the same time can be tricky. For instance, although invoking the Fifth Amendment can protect a defendant against self-incrimination, it can lead to an adverse inference in a parallel civil case. On the other hand, statements made in civil discovery, such as sworn interrogatories or deposition testimony, can be used as admissions in a criminal case. To avoid these complications, defendants—and sometimes prosecutors, if it is in their interest—will seek a stay of the civil suit until the criminal proceedings have concluded.

B. Actions against Corporate Owners and Executives

Whether it pursues a civil or criminal case, the government will focus on both corporate and individual wrongdoing. The FCA applies to any "person" who, inter alia, knowingly presents a false claim for payment or makes or uses a false statement or record material to payment of a false claims. For many years, the government focused its enforcement efforts on corporations, agreeing to settlements that involved a large payment from the company in exchange for releases not only for the corporation but also for corporate officers and other executives. In recent years, DOJ has emphasized that civil fraud investigations of corporations "should focus on individuals from the inception of the corporate investigation," and that "before finalizing a civil corporate resolution, the Department should carefully consider the liability of culpable individuals."[17] (This policy, most recently articulated in a memorandum by former Deputy Attorney General Sally Yates, is discussed in greater detail in Chapter 13 on settlements.)

As a result of this DOJ emphasis on prosecuting culpable individuals, it is possible that DOJ will name individual owners or executives of a company as co-defendants in any FCA case against the company or decide to pursue criminal actions against them. And, even if the company enters settlement discussions, the government may continue to pursue cases against the individuals. This may put the company in the uncomfortable position of having to choose between providing evidence against its current and former employees or relinquishing the opportunity

---

14. *Id.* § 1320a-7b.

15. *Id.* §§ 8701 *et seq.* (procurement); *id.* § 1320a-7b(b) (health care).

16. *See* 21 U.S.C. § 333.

17. U.S. DOJ, *Justice Manual*, 4-3.100, https://www.justice.gov/jm/jm-4-3000-compromising-and-closing#4-3.100 (last updated Nov. 2018).

to obtain "cooperation credit" from the government in order to reduce the amount of its civil settlement or avoid criminal prosecution. "To earn maximum cooperation credit," corporations must "identify[] all individuals substantially involved in or responsible for the misconduct."[18]

Finally, as a condition of settlement in a large FCA case, DOJ may insist that the company recoup money paid to culpable executives or rework employment agreements so that the company can more easily recoup money paid to culpable executives in the future.

C. State False Claims Acts

Because some programs are jointly administered or funded by the federal and state governments, a knowing submission of a false claim can also trigger liability under one or more state false claims laws. Most states have enacted their own false claims laws,[19] and many of these laws are modeled on the federal FCA, containing similar if not identical liability and qui tam provisions.[20] Participation in federal–state programs like Medicaid,[21] receipt of federal grant funds that flow through state governments, and entering into contracts for jointly funded infrastructure projects, consequently, may expose a company to FCA liability under both federal and state law.

As a practical matter, states often pursue their cases with the United States in the same action. If multiple states and the federal government initiate investigations separately, it may be in the parties' interest to consolidate the matters: for the government entities, consolidation spreads the cost and burden of investigating across multiple entities and encourages the coordination of investigative and litigative strategies and tactics; for the defendant, consolidation can minimize duplicative or competing requests for discovery. Furthermore, if the parties are interested

---

18. *Id.*

19. Even a few cities, such as New York, Chicago, and Philadelphia, have adopted false claims laws with qui tam provisions.

20. Some states' false claims laws are limited to fraud in health care programs and do not apply to fraud in procurement and other government programs. A handful of states' false claims laws do not permit whistleblower suits. A few states go beyond the federal FCA. The state of New York's FCA, for example, covers false tax claims, narrows defenses such as the public disclosure bar, and eases the burden for a whistleblower pleading fraud in a complaint. *See* N.Y. Fin. Law §§ 187 *et seq.*

21. The Deficit Reduction Act of 2005 incentivized states to establish robust false claims rules in connection with Medicaid claims. Under the law, states receive a 10 percent increase in their share of Medicaid claims recovery if they have false claims statutes that establish the same potential liability and penalties for false claims to Medicaid and are generally as effective in rewarding and facilitating qui tam suits as the federal FCA. Pub. L. No. 109–171, Feb. 8, 2006, 120 Stat. 4.

in resolving the case, consolidation can open the door for a global settlement agreement in which each jurisdiction shares in the recovery and the defendant gets closure.[22]

II. Suspension and Debarment

When faced with an FCA complaint, judgment, or settlement, a contractor may also find itself subject to additional actions from contracting agencies. In addition to potential contractual action, such as a termination of an affected contract for default, an agency may also pursue administrative action in the form of suspension or debarment from government contracting or, if the agency requires more information before reaching a determination whether to take action, a show cause notice or request for information from the agency suspension and debarment office.[23]

Under the FAR, it is the policy of the United States to solicit offers from, award contracts to, and generally only do business with contractors that are presently responsible.[24] The administrative remedies of suspension and debarment from government contracting are available to the United States to protect the public interest and the United States from contractors that are not presently responsible.[25] These remedies are not intended to be used as an additional form of punishment; they are intended for use only when necessary to protect the United States.[26]

Both corporate entities and individuals can be suspended, proposed for debarment, or debarred. In fact, the fraudulent conduct of a corporate contractor can

---

22. For a more detailed discussion of state false claims acts, *see* State False Claims Acts: A Practitioner's Guide to the False Claims Laws of the Various States (ABA Book Publishing 2014).

23. This section refers to suspension and debarment from procurement contracting, which is governed by FAR subpart 9.4. The Non-Procurement Common Rule, 2 C.F.R. part 180, governs suspension, proposed debarment, and debarment in connection with non-procurement actions, such as grants or cooperative agreements. Under both the FAR and the Non-Procurement Common Rule, suspension or debarment under one regime is treated with reciprocity. Thus, for example, a contractor debarred from procurement contracting pursuant to the FAR is also debarred for purposes of the Non-Procurement Common Rule. *See* FAR 9.401. Moreover, a contractor suspended, proposed for debarment, or debarred by one executive agency debarring official is deemed excluded from federal contracting by all other executive branch agencies. *See* FAR 9.406-1(c). Companies and individuals that participate in federal health care programs similarly can face exclusion under the Social Security Act. *See* 42 U.S.C § 1320a–7. The suspension and debarment process is addressed in detail in the separate Public Contract Law Section publication. *See* Frederic Levy & Michael Wagner, eds., The Practitioner's Guide to Suspension and Debarment (4th ed. 2018).

24. FAR 9.402(a).

25. *Id.*

26. FAR 9.402(b).

be "imputed" to officers, directors, employees, and others who "participated in, knew of, or had reason to know of the contractor's conduct" for purposes of determining whether the individual should be suspended, proposed for debarment, or debarred.[27] Similarly, the fraudulent conduct of an officer, director, shareholder, or employee, among others, can be imputed to the contractor entity "when the misconduct occurred in connection with the individual's performance of duties for or on behalf of the contractor" or the contractor knew, acquiesced, or approved of the individual's actions.[28] In the case of joint ventures, the misconduct of one person in the joint venture can be attributed to the other members of the joint venture if the conduct occurred in the performance of joint venture activities or with the knowledge, approval, or acquiescence of the other participating entities.[29] Furthermore, the scope of debarment usually will cover an entire contractor entity, including all divisions and organizational elements, unless the debarment is expressly limited by its terms to specific divisions or elements; affiliated entities may also be subsumed within the exclusion if they are specifically named and provided the opportunity to respond.[30]

Suspension, proposed debarment, and debarment result in the immediate exclusion of the contractor or individual from government contracting actions going forward. The exclusion is implemented government-wide by the public listing of the contractor or individual in the System for Award Management (SAM) database of excluded contractors and individuals.[31]

The effects of a SAM listing are numerous. For example, absent an agency head determining that there is a "compelling need" for such action, agencies are not to solicit offers from or award contracts to a contractor that is suspended, proposed for debarment, or debarred.[32] Likewise, absent a finding of "compelling need" by the agency head, agencies cannot consent to subcontracts with such contractors.[33] Finally, contractors that have been suspended, debarred, or proposed for debarment may not act as sureties.[34]

If a contractor has been found ineligible to receive contracts on the basis of statutory or regulatory procedures, and has an active exclusion record in SAM,

---

27. FAR 9.406-5(b).
28. FAR 9.406-5(a).
29. FAR 9.406-5(c).
30. FAR 9.406-1(b); *see also* Agility Def. & Gov't Servs. v. U.S. Dep't of Defense, 739 F.3d 586 (11th Cir. 2013) (affiliated entities could be suspended for more than 18 months based solely on their status as affiliates and the initiation of legal proceedings against the affiliates' parent).
31. FAR 9.404.
32. FAR 9.405(a), 9.405-2(a).
33. FAR 9.405(a).
34. FAR 9.405(d).

the agency may not solicit offers from, award contracts to, or consent to subcontracts with the contractor under the conditions and for the period set forth in the statute or regulation that led to the exclusion.[35]

With regard to contracts that have already been awarded and are being performed, the FAR does not require agencies to terminate contracts with contractors suspended, proposed for debarment, or debarred, although an agency could choose to take that course of action.[36] Nonetheless, absent the agency head issuing a written determination of "compelling circumstances," agencies are precluded from expanding work with an excluded contractor by extending the term of a contract or task order, exercising options, adding work, placing orders under Federal Supply Schedules or blanket purchase agreements, and, in the case of indefinite quantity contracts, placing orders above the guaranteed minimum.[37]

The grounds for suspension or debarment can encompass conduct that is the subject of a civil FCA proceeding. For example, a contracting officer "may" debar a company based on:

- A civil judgement for commission of fraud related to obtaining or performing a government contract, bribery, or making false statements;[38] or
- Evidence the contractor knowingly failed to timely disclose to the government a violation of the FCA or certain criminal laws, or significant overpayments.[39]

The FAR allows a debarring official to suspend a contractor based on adequate evidence of fraudulent conduct related to a government contract or subcontract.[40]

Moreover, the FAR includes "catchall" provisions that would cover conduct alleged to be fraudulent and allow a debarring official to debar or suspend a contractor for a cause "so serious or compelling in nature that it affects the present responsibility of the contractor."[41]

The procedures for addressing a notice of suspension or proposed debarment are set forth in FAR 9.407-3 (suspension) and FAR 9.406-3 (debarment). Generally,

35. FAR 9.405(b).
36. FAR 9.405-1(a).
37. *Id.*
38. FAR 9.406-2(a)(1) and (3).
39. FAR 9.406-2(b)(1)(vi).
40. *See* FAR 9.407-2(a)(1).
41. FAR 9.406-2(c) (cause for debarment); FAR 9.407-2(c) (cause for suspension). FAR 9.406-2, listing the causes for debarment, includes an additional "catchall" ground not identified specifically as a basis for suspension: a conviction or civil judgment for "[c]omission of any [non-enumerated] offense indicating a lack of business integrity or business honesty that seriously and directly affects the present responsibility of a government contractor or subcontractor." FAR 9.406-2(a)(5).

both provisions allow a contractor entity or individual that has received a notice of suspension or proposed debarment to respond in writing, in person, or through a representative within 30 days with information and argument in opposition to the suspension or proposed debarment.[42] In actions not based on a conviction or civil judgment, if there are genuine disputes over material facts, then the FAR affords contractors and individuals proposed for debarment the opportunity to appear before the agency and present and confront witnesses, and the debarring agency is required to transcribe the proceedings and prepare findings of fact in connection with a decision.[43] With regard to challenging a suspension, the procedures are slightly different because of the possibility of ongoing investigative or legal proceedings by the United States. Thus, when challenging a suspension, if a suspension is not based on an indictment and the contractor's submission in opposition raises genuine issues of material fact, DOJ must weigh in on whether further proceedings would prejudice pending or contemplated legal action.[44] If they will not, then similar rights to present and confront witnesses are available.[45]

Both FAR 9.406-3 and FAR 9.407-3 provide that agencies should establish procedures for addressing suspension and debarment that are as informal as practicable. As a practical matter, therefore, most suspension and debarment matters are handled more informally than the procedures outlined in the FAR, typically through the submission of written information and in-person meetings with agency debarring officials and their staff.

Whether in a more informal setting or formal proceedings, suspension and debarment are not intended as punishment and are intended to be used only when necessary to protect the government. Consequently, even if grounds for suspension or debarment exist, an agency debarring official is still required to determine whether it is necessary to exercise those remedies. To do so, the FAR instructs debarring officials to consider what are called "mitigating factors" that are set forth in FAR 9.406-1(a)(1)–(10). These factors are intended to assist the debarring official with determining whether the contractor or individual, despite grounds for suspension or debarment existing, is nonetheless presently responsible. Where grounds for suspension and debarment exist, the contractor or individual has the burden of proving present responsibility and that exclusion is not necessary.[46]

42. *See* FAR 9.406-3(c)(4), 9.407-3(c)(5).
43. FAR 9.406-3(b)(2), 9.406-3(d)(2)(i).
44. FAR 9.407-3(b)(2).
45. FAR 9.407-3(b)(2)(i)–(ii).
46. FAR 9.406-1(a).

A suspension or proposed debarment can terminate in a variety of ways. A suspension could lead to debarment of the contractor or individual.[47] A proposed debarment could be lifted by the debarring official after the fact-finding or consideration of mitigating factors discussed earlier or could become an actual debarment. Finally, an actual debarment could be reduced in length or terminated at the discretion of the debarring official.[48]

Although not discussed in detail in the FAR, another option is the entry and execution of an administrative agreement between the contractor (or an individual) and the agency in lieu of suspension or debarment.[49] These agreements generally include undertakings by the contractor entity or individual which, if fulfilled, protect the interests of the United States and allow the contractor or individual to continue with government contracting and be removed from the excluded parties list on SAM so long as the entity or individual complies with the terms of the administrative agreement.

III. Rescission or Nullification of Fraudulently Induced Contracts

A. Common Law Remedies for Fraudulent or Material Misrepresentations

Under principles of common law, a "fraudulent" or "material misrepresentation"[50] made in connection with the formation of a contract can render the contract void[51]

47. The standard period for debarment is no more than three years. FAR 9.406-4(a)(1). A suspension is intended to be temporary pending the completion of the investigation or legal proceedings. If legal proceedings are not initiated within 12 months of the notice of suspension, the suspension shall be terminated unless a DOJ Assistant Attorney General requests an extension. FAR 9.407-4(b). If an extension is requested, it may be granted for no longer than six months. The FAR provides for termination of a suspension after 18 months if no legal proceedings have been initiated. *Id.*

48. FAR 9.406-4(c).

49. *See, e.g.*, FAR 9.406-3(f) (referencing administrative agreements and the debarring officials' duty to post such agreements on the Federal Awardee Performance and Integrity Information System (FAPIIS)).

50. The Restatement defines a "misrepresentation" as "an assertion that is not in accord with the facts." RESTATEMENT (SECOND) OF CONTRACTS § 159 (1981). Similar to the definitions of "falsity" in the FCA, the Restatement further defines a misrepresentation as "fraudulent" if the maker either "knows or believes that the assertion is not in accord with the facts," "does not have the confidence that he states or implies in the truth of the assertion," or "knows that he does not have the basis that he states or implies for the assertion." *Id.* § 162.

51. *See id.* § 163, "When a Misrepresentation Prevents Formation of a Contract," cmt. a (explaining common law rule that a "misrepresentation as to the *character or essential terms* of a proposed contract," renders the contract void, where the misrepresentation "relates to the *very nature of the proposed contract itself* and not merely to one of its nonessential terms" (emphasis added)).

or voidable.[52] Applying these common law principles, a number of courts have held that "a Government contract tainted by fraud or wrongdoing is void *ab initio*."[53] Thus, for example, the U.S. Supreme Court in the seminal case *United States v. Mississippi Valley Generating Co.* held that a contract was unenforceable as a matter of public policy when "tainted by a conflict of interest."[54] The Court of Appeals for the Federal Circuit applied these same principles in *J.E.T.S., Inc. v. United States*, holding that a government contract awarded to a contractor who falsely certified its status as an eligible small business was "tainted from its inception by fraud" and therefore "void *ab initio*, like the government contracts held void because similarly tainted by a prohibited conflict of interest in *United States v. Mississippi Valley Generating Co.*"[55]

As the Federal Circuit explained in *Long Island Savings Bank, FSB v. United States*, "to prove that a government contract is 'tainted from its inception by fraud' and is thus 'void ab initio,' the government must prove that the contractor (a) obtained the contract by (b) knowingly (c) making a false statement."[56]

It is important to note, however, that "for a government contract to be tainted by fraud or wrong doing and thus void ab initio, the record must show some causal link between the fraud and the contract."[57] As stated by the Federal Circuit in *Godley v. United States*, "[i]llegal acts by a Government contracting agent do not alone taint a contract and invoke the void *ab initio* rule. Rather, the record must show some *causal link* between the illegality and the contract provisions. Determining whether illegality taints a contract involves questions of fact."[58] Thus, for example, the court in *J.E.T.S.* found that the contract was "tainted by fraud" and therefore

52. *See id.* § 164, "When a Misrepresentation Makes a Contract Voidable," cmt. a (explaining common law rule that a misrepresentation may render a contract voidable if "the misrepresentation must have been either fraudulent or material," "the misrepresentation must have induced the recipient to make the contract," and "the recipient must have been justified in relying on the misrepresentation").

53. Godley v. United States, 5 F.3d 1473, 1476 (Fed. Cir. 1993) (citing United States v. Miss. Valley Generating Co., 364 U.S. 520, 564 (1961); J.E.T.S., Inc. v. United States, 838 F.2d 1196, 1200 (Fed. Cir. 1988)).

54. *Miss. Valley*, 364 U.S. at 564–66.

55. 838 F.2d at 1200.

56. 503 F.3d 1234, 1246 (Fed. Cir. 2007); *see also* L.C. Gaskins Constr. Co., Inc., ASBCA No. 58550, 15-1 B.C.A. (CCH) ¶ 36059 (July 16, 2015) ("To prove that a government contract is 'tainted from its inception by fraud' and thus 'void ab initio,' requires proof of four elements: (1) there was a misrepresentation; (2) the misrepresentation must have been either fraudulent or material; (3) the misrepresentation must have induced the recipient to make the contract; and (4) the recipient must have been justified in relying on the misrepresentation.") (citing Servicios y Obras Isetan S.L., ASBCA No. 57584, 13 BCA ¶ 35,279).

57. *Long Island Savings*, 503 F.3d at 1250.

58. 5 F.3d at 1476 (emphasis added).

void *ab initio* where the contractor "obtained this contract by knowingly falsely stating that it was a small business. Had it stated the truth about its size, it would not have received the contract."[59] By contrast, in *Godley* the court could not determine that the illegal conduct (which involved bribery and conspiracy by a subcontractor) tainted the contract, where it was not clear that the "illegal conduct caused any unfavorable contract terms."[60] As a result, the Court of Appeals in *Godley* remanded the case for further fact-finding regarding the existence of a "causal link" between the fraud and the terms of the contract.[61] As the Court of Appeals for the Federal Circuit has more recently explained, to void a contract on the ground that it was obtained through fraud, the government must establish that the alleged fraud was "a *but-for cause* of the outcome,"[62] or that the fraud "materially affected" or "permeated"[63] the award of the contract.

In addition to the requirement for a causal link between the fraud and the terms of the contract, the Government's right to void a contract requires that the fraud have been committed *by the contractor*: "[T]he void-for-fraud rule does not extend to cases 'where a completely innocent contractor entered a contract with the [g]overnment which, despite illegal conduct by [another party], was nonetheless wholly untainted by fraud.'"[64]

59. J.E.T.S., Inc. v. United States, 838 F.2d 1196, 1200 (Fed. Cir. 1988); *see also, e.g., Miss. Valley*, 364 U.S. at 553 (noting that without illegal conduct, "no contract would have been made").

60. Godley v. United States., 5 F.3d 1473, 1476 (Fed. Cir. 1993).

61. *Id. See also, e.g.*, Appeal of Gutierrez, ASBCA No. 42984, 92-1 B.C.A. (CCH) ¶ 24633 (Dec. 10, 1991) (rejecting government's argument that contract was tainted by fraud and therefore void *ab initio*, where contractor's "conduct in controlling two bidders can hardly be termed fraudulent, rendering the contract void ab initio, when there is no statute, regulation, rule or contract clause that is being violated," and where "no effort has been made by the Government to prove that it relied on the alleged misrepresentation" in entering into contract).

62. Kellogg Brown & Root Servs., Inc. v. United States, 728 F.3d 1348, 1371–72 (Fed. Cir. 2013) (affirming lower court's determination that contractor was not liable for common law fraud as a result of kickbacks paid in connection with award of subcontract, where evidence at trial established that contractor would have awarded subcontract even without the participation of individuals who received kickbacks), *opinion corrected on denial of reh'g*, 563 F. App'x 769 (Fed. Cir. 2014); *see also* Appeals of -- Supreme Foodservice Gmbh, ASBCA No. 57884, 20-1 BCA (CCH) ¶ 37618 (May 28, 2020) (rejecting government's void *ab initio* claim where government had failed to establish "causal link" as required by *Godley* and *KBR*, and remarking that "[t]he lesson of *KBR* is that not every fraudulent or corrupt action gives rise to a void contract, even when there is bribery").

63. Oracle Am., Inc. v. United States, 975 F.3d 1279, 1295–96 (Fed. Cir. 2020) ("[C]onflicts of interest invalidate government contracts only if the conflicts materially affect the contracts. That is the way this court read the *Mississippi Valley* case in *Godley*. . . . In that case, we noted that the illegality in the *Mississippi Valley* case 'permeated the contract.'"), *cert. denied*, 142 S. Ct. 68 (2021).

64. Ameriserv Trust v. United States, 125 Fed. Cl. 733, 746 (2016) (citing *Godley*, 5 F.3d at 1475 n.2; United States v. Amdahl Corp., 786 F.2d 387, 395 (Fed. Cir. 1986) ("'[T]he binding stamp of nullity' should be imposed only . . . because of some action or statement *by the contractor* . . . , [but] if the contractor did not contribute to the mistake . . . the award should not be considered plainly or

Moreover, in order for the government to exercise its right to cancel a contract tainted by fraud, the government must act "within a reasonable time after discovery of the illegality."[65] According to the Federal Circuit's decision in *Godley*, assessing the reasonableness of the government's delay in asserting that a contract is voidable involves factual questions, such as whether the contractor "incurred expenses (or otherwise suffered prejudice) due to the delay, whether protection of legitimate public interests (including perhaps the investigation of [the contractor's] conduct) justified the delay, and whether the length of the delay bore a reasonable relationship to its asserted causes."[66]

Finally, even where the government establishes that a contract should be declared void under the doctrine of common law fraud, the courts and boards of contract appeals have generally been reluctant to require forfeiture of amounts paid under the contract.[67] Instead, courts and boards have more often applied the doctrine of common law fraud as a defense against contractor claims, and denied contractors recovery for claims under a contract that has been declared void as a result of fraud.[68]

---

palpably illegal.")); *see also, e.g.*, Gulf Grp. Gen. Enterprises Co. W.L.L. v. United States, 114 Fed. Cl. 258, 351 (2013) (holding that contract was not tainted by fraud where contractor "appears to have been an 'innocent contractor' that entered legitimately into a government contract, despite [another party's] improper and illegal conduct in other regards").

65. Godley v. United States, 5 F.3d 1473, 1476 (Fed. Cir. 1993) (citing ACME Process Equip. Co. v. United States, 347 F.2d 509, 516 (1965), *rev'd on other grounds*, 385 U.S. 138 (1966)).

66. *Godley*, 5 F.3d at 1476.

67. *See, e.g.*, Veridyne Corp. v. United States, 83 Fed. Cl. 575, 586 (2008) ("Forfeiture is an inappropriate remedy for common-law fraud except when a conflict of interest is perpetuated by a contractor involved in facilitating and maintaining a Government agent's conflict of interest or where an agent of the contractor obtains a contract through a conflict of interest."); Appeals of -- Hollymatic Corp., ASBCA No. 61920, 21-1 BCA (CCH) ¶ 37823 (Mar. 22, 2021) (holding that "[s]ince the contract has been determined to be void ab initio, there is no CDA contract in being," and as a result "we lack jurisdiction to order appellant to return the monies paid" under the contract); Appeals of -- ABS Dev. Corp., ASBCA No. 60022, 19-1 BCA ¶ 37234 (Jan. 7, 2019) (holding that because contract was void *ab initio*, "the government cannot assess liquidated damages"). *But see* K & R Eng'g Co. v. United States, 616 F.2d 469, 476–77 (Ct. Cl. 1980) (holding that government was entitled on its counterclaim to recover amounts previously paid under contract that was tainted by violation of criminal conflict of intertest laws, recognizing that "there are no federal decisions dealing with the right of the United States to recover money paid under a contract that subsequently is determined to have been illegal" and instead relying on state court decisions to hold that "a contractor who has participated in an illegal conflict-of-interest situation is not entitled to retain the amounts received under the tainted contract").

68. *See, e.g.*, Appeal of ORC Inc., ASBCA No. 49693, 97-1 BCA ¶ 28750 (Dec. 30, 1996) ("A contractor who is responsible for the conditions which render a contract void, as in the instant appeal, is not entitled to recovery on a claim."); J.E.T.S., Inc. v. United States, 838 F.2d 1196, 1200 (Fed. Cir. 1988) (affirming board's denial of contractor's claim for equitable adjustment in price where contractor had "obtained this contract by knowingly falsely stating that it was a small business," holding that

B. Doctrine of "First Material Breach"

In addition to the government's common law right to void a contract that is tainted by fraud, the common law doctrine of "first material breach" can also potentially excuse the government's obligations and serve as a defense against a contractor's claims under a contract tainted by fraud. As the Court of Appeals for the Federal Circuit explained in *Barron Bancshares, Inc. v. United States*:

> Under th[e] doctrine [of prior material breach], when a party to a contract is sued for breach, it may defend on the ground that there existed a legal excuse for its nonperformance at the time of the alleged breach. Faced with two parties to a contract, each of whom claims breach by the other, courts will "often . . . impose liability on the party that committed the first material breach." According to the Restatement, the doctrine of prior material breach is based on the principle that where performances are to be exchanged under an exchange of promises, each party is entitled to the assurance that he will not be called upon to perform his remaining duties . . . if there has already been an uncured material failure of performance by the other party.[69]

The court in *Long Island Savings Bank, FSB v. United States* applied these principles and held that a contractor's claim for damages was precluded by the doctrine of first material breach based on its finding that the contractor's "false certification [to the government] constitutes an uncured material failure of performance that precludes the plaintiffs' claim for damages."[70] The court noted that the government's obligations under the agreement were expressly conditioned on "receipt of a certificate 'signed by the [contractor] stating' that the 'representations and

---

fraud rendered contract void and therefore precluded contractor from recovering on claim, reasoning that "'to permit recovery of any further monies under the circumstances would be an affront to the integrity of the federal procurement process'" (quoting United States v. Mississippi Valley Generating Co., 364 U.S. 520, 564–65 (1961))); Dongbuk R&U Eng'g Co., Ltd., ASBCA No. 58300, 13 B.C.A. (CCH) ¶ 35389 (Aug. 13, 2013) (finding that contract was void *ab initio* as a result of contractor's "knowing misrepresentation" regarding employee licenses, and therefore holding that contractor was not entitled to recover on claim for payment, reasoning that "[t]he alleged rights [contractor] seeks to enforce (payment for work performed) spring directly from the contract, which is illegal and fraudulent. No tribunal of law will lend its assistance to carry out the terms of an illegally obtained contract. . . . The fact that the government received some benefit does not relieve [contractor] from the consequences of its fraud. When one has been guilty of fraud, one cannot recover in any form of action." (citations omitted)).

69. 366 F.3d 1360, 1380–81 (Fed. Cir. 2004) (quoting E. Allen Farnsworth, Farnsworth on Contracts § 8.15, at 439 (1990)) (citations omitted).

70. 503 F.3d at 1251–52.

warranties of [the contractor] . . . are true and substantially correct" and that the government had relied on the contractor's false certification.[71]

The Federal Circuit has recognized, however, that a government claim for prior material breach may be waived "through [the government's] continued performance of the contract."[72] Thus, the court in *Barron* found that the government had waived its claim of prior material breach where it continued to perform its obligations under the agreement for the full five-year term of the agreement.[73] According to the *Barron* court, "[i]n order to preserve its claim of a prior material breach giving rise to the right to terminate the contract, the government had to treat [the contractor] as if it had breached the contract."[74] By failing to do so and instead "continuing to perform, the government waived any claim with respect to a prior material breach or material misrepresentation by [the contractor]."[75]

Waiver of a claim for prior material breach will only occur, however, if the government actually knew of the breach, yet continued to perform. Thus, in *Laguna Construction Co., Inc. v. Carter*, the Federal Circuit refused to find a waiver based on the fact that the government continued to perform under a contract while investigating allegations that the contractor's employee was involved in a kickback scheme.[76] The court held that until the employee pleaded guilty to participating in the kickback scheme, "the government did not have a 'known right' that would have invoked the prior material breach rule."[77]

C. Agency Authority to Void or Rescind for Violations of Procurement Integrity Laws

In addition to these common law remedies, FAR 3.104-7(d)(2) authorizes the head of a contracting authority (HCA) who learns that a violation of the Procurement Integrity Act[78] has impacted a procurement that led to an award to "[e]ffect appropriate contractual remedies," including voiding or rescinding the contract. FAR 3.104-7(a) requires contracting officers to investigate possible or actual violations

71. *Id.* at 1246.

72. *Barron*, 366 F.3d at 1383.

73. *Id.*

74. *Id.* (citing 14 Williston on Contracts § 43:15 (4th ed. 2000) (explaining that faced with a material breach by the other party to a contract, one has the choice "to continue to perform under the contract or to cease to perform, and conduct indicating an intention to continue the contract . . . in effect waiv[es] the right to assert that the breach discharged any obligation to perform")).

75. *Id.*

76. 828 F.3d 1364 (Fed. Cir. 2016).

77. *Id.* at 1372.

78. 41 U.S.C. §§ 2102 *et seq.*

of the Act to see if they had an impact on the pending award or selection of the contractor, and, if they determine that they did, forward the information to the HCA.

In addition, FAR subpart 3.7 establishes policies and procedures for the government to exercise its discretionary authority to void or rescind contracts in the following circumstances:

> (1) There has been a final conviction[79] for bribery, conflict of interest, disclosure or receipt of contractor bid or proposal information or source selection information in exchange for a thing of value or to give anyone a competitive advantage in the award of a Federal agency procurement contract, or similar misconduct; or
>
> (2) There has been an agency head determination that contractor bid or proposal information or source selection information has been disclosed or received in exchange for a thing of value, or for the purpose of obtaining or giving anyone a competitive advantage in the award of a Federal agency procurement contract.[80]

Before exercising its authority to void or rescind a contract for one of the enumerated causes, the government must follow the procedures outlined in FAR 3.705, which require as follows:

- A final conviction involving one of the enumerated statutes must first be reported to the agency head or designee for consideration, in consultation with the Civil Division, Department of Justice.[81]
- After assessing the facts, "the agency head or designee may declare void and rescind contracts with respect to which a final conviction has been entered, and recover the amounts expended and the property transferred by the agency under the terms of the contracts involved."[82]
- Before voiding or rescinding a contract, the government must provide the contractor with a "notice of the proposed action to declare void and rescind the contract," and an opportunity to submit pertinent information before any final decision is made, including an opportunity for a hearing at which witnesses may be presented and any witness the agency presents may be confronted.[83]

---

79. For purposes of these rules, a "final conviction" is defined to include "a conviction, whether entered on a verdict or plea, including a plea of nolo contendere, for which a sentence has been imposed." FAR 3.702.

80. FAR 3.700(a).

81. FAR 3.705(a).

82. FAR 3.705(b).

83. FAR 3.705(c).

- "If the agency head or designee decides to declare void and rescind the contracts involved," a written decision must be issued, which states "the amounts due and property to be returned to the agency," and "reflects consideration of the fair value of any tangible benefits received and retained by the agency."[84]

IV. Other Contractual and Administrative Remedies

The United States has several, additional contractual and administrative remedies it can pursue against a contractor that has submitted fraudulent claims. If a contractor brings a claim against the United States in the Court of Federal Claims, the United States can assert, as part of a counterclaim, a "special plea in fraud" under the Forfeiture of Fraudulent Claims Act (FFCA).[85] The government's right to assert this counterclaim, which courts have described as a condition of the government's "consent to be sued waive[r of] its sovereign immunity" in connection with contractor claims, can result in forfeiture of the entire amount of the claim against the United States. [86] Specifically, the FFCA requires a claim to "be forfeited to the United States by any person who corruptly practices or attempts to practice any fraud against the United States in the proof, statement, establishment, or allowance thereof."[87]

The elements of a counterclaim and the burden of proof under the FFCA are more stringent than under the FCA. The government must show that the contractor knowingly submitted a false claim with an intent to defraud the government, and the government must establish these elements by clear and convincing evidence. If part of a contract claim is fraudulent and submitted knowingly, all claims under that contract can be forfeited.

The anti-fraud provision of the Contract Disputes Act[88] provides another potential remedy for the United States in cases of fraud. "If a contractor is unable to support any part of the contractor's claim and . . . the inability is attributable to a misrepresentation of fact or fraud by the contractor, then the contractor is liable

84. *Id.*

85. *See* 28 U.S.C. § 2514.

86. *See* Kamen Soap Products Co. v. United States, 129 Ct. Cl. 619, 124 F. Supp. 608 (1954) ("It will be noted that this statute [the Forfeiture of Fraudulent Claims Act] goes further than merely banning fraudulent claims. It provides for a forfeiture of the claim if any fraud is practiced or attempted to be practiced in proving, establishing or allowing a claim. This is one of the conditions on which the Government gives its consent to be sued and waives its otherwise sovereign immunity."); *accord* Morse Diesel Int'l, Inc. v. United States, 74 Fed. Cl. 601, 635 (2007).

87. *Id.*

88. 41 U.S.C. §§ 7101 *et seq.*

to the Federal Government for . . . the unsupported part of the claim plus all of the Federal Government's costs attributable to reviewing the unsupported part of the claim."[89] A "misrepresentation of fact" means a "false statement of substantive fact, or conduct that leads to a belief of a substantive fact material to proper understanding of the matter in hand, made with intent to deceive or mislead."[90] Like the FCA, the government must prove its case by a preponderance of the evidence. As one recent case demonstrates, the government can recover substantial dollars under this provision and successfully combine it with affirmative claims under the FCA and counterclaims under the FFCA to enhance the government's recovery.[91]

In small-dollar cases, the government can use the Program Fraud Civil Remedies Act (PFCRA) as an administrative process to remedy false claims.[92] This statute, which is limited to claims up to $150,000,[93] imposes assessments of up to twice the amount of the fraudulent claim and penalties of up to $5,000 for each false statement.[94] The statute charges agency officials with the initial task of investigating allegations of liability.[95] If the reviewing official determines that there is adequate evidence of liability, the agency refers the matter to DOJ, which must approve the reviewing official's findings before the matter is referred to an Administrative Law Judge or other presiding officer for a hearing.[96]

The government can pursue penalties under the PFCRA "in addition to any other remedy that may be prescribed by law."[97] Assessments under the PFCRA "may provide the authority with grounds for commencing any administrative or contractual action against such person which is authorized by law," though a determination of liability under the PFCRA is not a conclusive determination of a contractor's responsibility for purposes of suspension or debarment.[98]

V. Impact on Responsibility Determinations

In addition to creating a risk of suspension or debarment, FCA proceedings can potentially impact an individual agency's evaluation of a contractor's "responsibility."

---

89. *Id.* § 7103(c).
90. *Id.* § 7101(9).
91. *See* Daewoo Eng'g & Constr. Co. v. United States, 557 F.3d 1332, 1341 (Fed. Cir. 2009) (upholding $51 million penalty under Contract Disputes Act, additional $13 million forfeiture under Forfeiture of Fraudulent Claims Act, and $10,000 penalty under the FCA).
92. 31 U.S.C. §§ 3801 *et seq.*
93. *Id.* § 3803(c).
94. *Id.* § 3802(a).
95. *Id.* § 3803(a).
96. *Id.* § 3803(a)–(b).
97. *Id.* § 3802(a).
98. *Id.* § 3802(b).

Under FAR subpart 9.1, government agencies may purchase from, and enter into contracts with, "responsible prospective contractors only."[99] As a result, contracting officers must "make[] an affirmative determination of responsibility" before every contract award.[100] A determination that a prospective contractor is "responsible" requires contracting officers to consider a number of different factors, including whether the contractor possesses "a satisfactory record of integrity and business ethics."[101]

One source of information that contracting officers are required to consult in determining whether an offeror is "responsible" is the Federal Awardee Performance and Integrity Information System (FAPIIS) database.[102] In addition to containing information regarding any prior determinations that the contractor was not responsible, FAPIIS also contains information that would show whether the contractor or any of its principals[103] has, within the past five years, been the subject of the following types of "proceedings":

> (i) In a criminal proceeding, a conviction.
>
> (ii) In a civil proceeding, a finding of fault and liability that results in the payment of a monetary fine, penalty, reimbursement, restitution, or damages of $5,000 or more.
>
> (iii) In an administrative proceeding, a finding of fault and liability that results in—
>
> (A) The payment of a monetary fine or penalty of $5,000 or more; or
>
> (B) The payment of a reimbursement, restitution, or damages in excess of $100,000.
>
> (iv) In a criminal, civil, or administrative proceeding, a disposition of the matter by consent or compromise with an acknowledgment of fault by the Contractor if the proceeding could have led to any of the outcomes specified in paragraphs (c)(1)(i), (c)(1)(ii), or (c)(1)(iii) of this provision.[104]

---

99. FAR 9.103(a).

100. FAR 9.103(b).

101. FAR 9.104-1.

102. *See* FAR 9.104-6(a), (b).

103. For purposes of this clause, "principal" is defined as "an officer, director, owner, partner, or a person having primary management or supervisory responsibilities within a business entity (e.g., general manager; plant manager; head of a division or business segment; and similar positions)." FAR 52.209-7(a).

104. FAR 52.209-7(c). The clause at FAR 52.209-7, "Information Regarding Responsibility Matters," is required in all solicitations where the resultant contract value is expected to exceed $600,000. FAR 9.104-7(b). Pursuant to this clause, any contractor with more than $10 million in federal contracts or grants must represent that the information in FAPIIS is "current, accurate, and complete as of the date of submission of [the] offer." FAR 52.209-7(c). In addition, contractors must update the

Notably, however, the fact that a contractor has been subject to one of the identified proceedings (including a settlement under the FCA) does not automatically result in a determination that the contractor lacks responsibility or a satisfactory record of integrity or business ethics. Instead, the FAR requires that, unless the contractor has already been suspended or debarred, the contracting officer must first "request such additional information from the offeror as the offeror deems necessary in order to demonstrate the offeror's responsibility to the contracting officer."[105]

VI. Private Causes of Action

A party subject to an FCA investigation or litigation can face collateral consequences from private rights of action as well. For example, in one recent case, a company that paid $9 million to resolve FCA allegations that it sold defective earplugs to the U.S. military subsequently faced billions of dollars in exposure as a result of hundreds of thousands of personal injury suits by U.S. service members who alleged hearing damage caused by the defective earplugs.[106] Additionally, if a company's FCA violations lead to financial consequences for its prime contractors or other business partners, those entities may seek indemnification under their agreements with the company. Lawsuits from lenders, shareholders, and other investors, as well as insurers, are also possible. Settlements with the government do not ordinarily provide a release for claims that might be asserted by private parties, such as claims for personal injury, property, or other damages arising from the misconduct.

---

information reported in FAPIIS throughout the performance of the contract, pursuant to the clause at FAR 52.209-9, "Updates of Publicly Available Information Regarding Responsibility Matters."

105. FAR 9.104-6(c); *cf.* Matter of: Dyncorp Int'l LLC, B-411465 (Aug. 4, 2015) (rejecting protester's argument that pending FCA cases demonstrated that contractor lacked "satisfactory record of integrity and business ethics to justify an affirmative responsibility determination," where GAO found that contracting officer was aware of and reasonably considered the pending FCA cases and nevertheless determined that awardee was "responsible").

106. *See* U.S. DOJ, *3M Company Agrees to Pay $9.1 Million to Resolve Allegations That It Supplied the United States with Defective Dual-Ended Combat Arms Earplugs* (July 26, 2018), https://www.justice.gov/opa/pr/3m-company-agrees-pay-91-million-resolve-allegations-it-supplied-united-states-defective-dual; Austen Hufford, *3M Earplugs Fight Stems from Self-Made Legal Battle*, Wall St. J. (July 18, 2022), https://www.wsj.com/articles/3m-earplugs-fight-stems-from-self-made-legal-battle-11658156756?mod=article_inline.

CHAPTER 13

Settlements under the False Claims Act

SUSAN GOUINLOCK, LAURENCE FREEDMAN,
AND STEPHEN D. ALTMAN[1]

I. Introduction

A large percentage of False Claims Act (FCA) cases are ultimately resolved by settlement. In this chapter, we discuss the parties' respective incentives to settle, their roles in the resolution of FCA cases, the settlement processes, and Department of Justice (DOJ) policies and procedures that shape those processes.

For purposes of settlement, there are four types of FCA cases, and the settlement process differs in each: (1) DOJ can instigate and file an action under the FCA, in which case there is no relator; (2) a private individual (a relator) can file a case under the qui tam provisions of the FCA, and the DOJ can intervene in the qui tam and take over prosecution of the case; (3) DOJ can intervene in some but not all claims in the qui tam, in which case settlement of the declined claims will involve a larger role for the relator; and (4) DOJ can decline to get involved in the case and allow the relator and the relator's legal team to proceed with litigation and settlement.

II. Incentives to Settle

A. The Defendant's[2] Incentives to Settle

There is much about the FCA that encourages pre-trial settlement. Depending on the parties' respective assessments of litigation risk and the proposed payment amount, settlement is often an attractive option to resolve uncertainty and risk.

1. Susan Gouinlock is a partner at Wilbanks & Gouinlock. Laurence J. Freedman is a partner with Mintz. Stephen D. Altman is the principal of Altman Dispute Resolution Services.

2. This chapter uses the term "defendant" to reference both potential defendants and actual defendants in FCA lawsuits.

The parties may differ on how the law applies to the facts or about the facts themselves; but, for the FCA defendant, the stakes of proceeding to trial are often higher than for defendants in private litigation.

An FCA defendant who is found liable at trial is subject to civil monetary penalties for each false claim it submitted and damages equal to three times the government's actual damages. The trial court is required by FCA § 3729(a)(1) to assess a civil monetary penalty for every false claim identified by the jury. Such penalties are currently between $12,537 and $25,076 each.[3] That section of the FCA also mandates that the trial court triple the damages verdict ("treble damages"). In addition, the FCA has a fee shifting provision that requires the defendant to pay the relator's reasonable attorneys' fees and costs.[4] Finally, the defendant could face suspension or debarment from government programs if found liable at trial for violating the FCA, as opposed to settling without an admission of liability.

In contrast, DOJ often agrees to settlements without payment of civil monetary penalties and is willing to negotiate both the amount of damages and the multiplier to be applied to those damages (i.e., less than three times the damages). In addition, the earlier the settlement takes place during the case, the lower the defendant's exposure for the relator's reasonable attorneys' fees and costs.

Further, defendants have to worry about their reputations with their constituencies, whether that be shareholders, other investors, federal agencies, or private customers, and such bad press becomes more likely as the case heads toward trial. Ending financial and reputational uncertainty by ending a pending FCA suit can be valuable to a defendant facing allegations of defrauding the government, even if those allegations are poorly pleaded or are arguably not legally defensible.

B. The Government's and Relator's Incentives to Settle

For the government or a relator who is proceeding without the government in a declined case, there are also incentives to settle. DOJ and/or the U.S. Attorney's Office (USAO) have limited resources and can spread them more broadly if cases settle rather than proceed to trial. The impacted government agency makes a recommendation about whether a settlement is acceptable[5] and may seek deterrence

3. The Federal Civil Penalties Inflation Adjustment Act, as amended by the Federal Civil Penalties Inflation Adjustment Act Improvements Act of 2015 (28 U.S.C. § 2461), requires that civil monetary penalties be adjusted on an annual basis.

4. *See* 31 U.S.C. § 3730(d)(1) and (2).

5. This process is described, in part, in the Justice Manual, 4-4.110, which says that in "any False Claims Act matter, the USAO or Fraud Section attorneys will confer with the relevant agency during the investigative, litigation, and settlement phases of the matter. The Department's attorneys will

by setting an example of government enforcement of the FCA through quicker settlement of a case.[6] Certain DOJ priorities, set by the Attorney General, also play a role in whether the government wants to settle an FCA case and, if so, at what settlement amount. FCA litigation is complicated, often requiring costly expert testimony in addition to the substantial time and expense required of litigation counsel. Even if liability is eventually determined at trial, there may be limited resources to satisfy a judgment. Settlement can offer an opportunity to improve the chances of collection by the government or relator, and they can get paid sooner rather than later. The government may also benefit from the "precedent" of a settlement with respect to other similar FCA investigations. Accordingly, DOJ is concerned with the precedential value of the legal authority created for future FCA cases and settlement standards.

As to the relator, their counsel, who are ordinarily representing the relator on a contingent basis, will not get paid any fees and there is no federal recovery from which the relator can receive an award unless and until they prevail in the FCA case (with or without the government) through settlement or judgment. If the case is a small one, there is less to gain by going to trial. If the case is large or complex, the relator and their legal team have to balance their resources and the likelihood of victory against what the defendant is willing to pay in settlement. The relator's team, however, often worries less than the government about setting bad legal precedent and so may seek to push a less common or new legal theory rather than settling a case, especially earlier in the litigation. Unlike a commercial defendant, a relator may be highly motivated to push to trial, seeking to prove they were right about the defendant defrauding the government. Another factor in settling a declined qui tam is that the relator cannot settle without approval of the settlement by the government, and thus might face constraints on the terms or structure of a settlement.[7]

---

solicit the agency's views on the False Claims Act matter, including, for example, on the falsity and materiality aspects of any alleged violations of the relevant agency requirements, in order to assist the Department in determining whether the elements of the False Claims Act can be established." DOJ, *Justice Manual*, 4-4.110, https://www.justice.gov/jm/jm-4-4000-commercial-litigation#4-4.110 (last updated Dec. 2019).

6. By regulation, the Assistant Attorney General for the Civil Division has authority as to the decision to settle or litigate FCA actions, even in the event of disagreement among components of DOJ or between DOJ and its client-agency. DOJ Manual, 28 C.F.R. §§ 0.160, *et seq.*

7. A relator may settle their retaliation claim under FCA § 3730(h) separately from the qui tam settlement without approval from the government, because that claim does not belong to the government.

III. DOJ Policies, Practices, and Procedures Impacting Settlement

A. Criteria for Settlement

DOJ does not have written guidelines for settling FCA cases.[8] However, in 2003, then-Assistant Attorney General Robert McCallum provided the following written answer to a question from Senator Grassley concerning criteria for settling FCA cases:

> The Department will usually consider a presentation from the Defendant and from Relators regarding the facts and applicable law. Our touchstone for settling matters is the litigation risk in establishing the facts, proving the requisite scienter under the statute, and establishing good case precedents. In strong cases, any settlement is likely to be closer to the full triple damages as provided for in the statute. In cases where the litigation risk may be higher, a lower "multiple" to the single damages may be appropriate for the purpose of our settlement evaluation. In addition, we also take into account the financial capacity of the Defendant, particularly in the bankruptcy context.[9]

DOJ also has an obligation to use its prosecutorial discretion to ensure defendants are treated fairly in the settlement context. DOJ also must consider its obligation to serve its client agencies. Some agencies take greater roles than others in the prosecution of FCA cases. In every case, DOJ obtains a written recommendation from the client agency as to whether it should settle, but it is DOJ's decision—not the client agency's—whether to accept a settlement. Moreover, the money recovered does not always revert to the agency. Generally, single damages are provided to the agency, but the agency must determine whether it has an open appropriation through which it can use the money or the money must be turned over to a miscellaneous account in the Treasury. With the exception of certain cases with recoverable interest, amounts above single damages are placed in an account in the Treasury.

B. Authority Issues

Responsibility for settlement of an FCA case usually resides with the Civil Division of Main Justice in Washington, D.C., which has delegated that authority to

---

8. The Justice Manual has some litigation guidance in title 4 at 4-4.110-111, *see* 28 C.F.R. §§ 0.160, *et seq.*

9. *Confirmation Hearing on Nominations of Robert D. McCallum, Jr., to Be Assoc. Atty. Gen. & Peter D. Keisler to be Assist. Atty. Gen., Civil Div.: Hearing Before the Committee on the Judiciary, United States Senate*, 108th Cong. 85-91 (2003).

USAOs for cases in which the single damages are less than $10 million.[10] Many cases over that amount are handled jointly between the Civil Division and the USAOs, though some are litigated by the USAO. If, upon investigation, the single damages are determined to be more than $10 million, then the U.S. Attorney must obtain approval of any settlement from the Civil Division.

When negotiating a settlement with the government, defendants should keep in mind whether they are negotiating with the Civil Division or with the U.S. Attorney, and, if with the U.S. Attorney, whether the settlement must also be approved by the Civil Division. If approval is required by the Civil Division, the process may take longer, and the parties may be constrained by the fact that the government attorneys will need to adhere more strictly to Civil Division policies, such as model language for the settlement agreement. In qui tam cases in which the government has not intervened, the government will review the financial and nonfinancial terms of each settlement proposed by a relator and defendant, as well as related issues (e.g., settlement of a retaliation claim), and decide whether to accept it.[11]

1. Approval Process within the Department of Justice

The amount of alleged single damages determines the DOJ level at which a proposed settlement must be reviewed and approved before it can be finalized. Settlements of cases handled by the Civil Division's Commercial Litigation Branch usually must be approved by the Assistant Attorney General (AAG) for the Civil Division. The AAG's approval authority may be delegated to a Deputy Assistant Attorney General (DAAG) within the Civil Division. Settlement in cases handled by the USAO often may be approved by the U.S. Attorney unless the case was handled on a "supervised" basis, in which case the settlement will require Civil Division approval. "Supervised" cases are those that exceed the U.S. Attorney authorized amount of $10 million in single damages, but are being litigated by that office.[12] Within the Civil Division, the lead attorney on the case ordinarily prepares a memorandum that summarizes the key facts, the applicable law, various settlement considerations, and the view of the affected agency. The agency's recommendation usually comes from the General Counsel's Office, unless the agency's FCA settlement authority lies with the Inspector General's Office. If a Civil Division attorney prepares the settlement authority memorandum, they will also state the view of the USAO on the proposed settlement.

---

10. Justice Manual, 28 C.F.R. §§ 0.160–172, Appendix to Subpart Y.

11. The statute provides that a qui tam action cannot be dismissed without the consent of the Attorney General. 31 U.S.C. § 3730(b)(1).

12. Justice Manual, 28 C.F.R. §§ 0.160–172, Appendix to Subpart Y.

2. DOJ and the Agency/Contracting Office

Although the contracting officer lacks authority to settle fraud claims, they have authority under the Contract Disputes Act (CDA) to settle breach of contract claims. When, during its fraud investigation, DOJ has determined that there is a related breach of contract that does not involve fraud, it may be willing to resolve the breach as part of the FCA settlement. DOJ will involve the contracting officer as necessary.

C. Ability to Pay Considerations

Unlike many creditors, the government is not in need of immediate cash and, when justified by the defendant's financial status, is often willing to agree to a three- to five-year (or, in rare cases, even longer) payment period. In September 2020, DOJ issued guidance on its approach to "ability to pay" settlements.[13] Note, however, that if the Criminal Division is seeking restitution or fines relating to the same misconduct, the Civil Division must coordinate with the Criminal Division with regard to how much the defendant is paying in civil settlement and how much in criminal restitution or fines, as well as with regard to the timing of payment.

If the defendant seeks to reduce the amount of a settlement on the basis of its financial condition, the Civil Division or the USAO will require that the defendant, using DOJ forms, supply extensive financial data under penalty of perjury. This data will be analyzed either by financial analysts within the Civil Division or, increasingly, by financial analysts employed by or under contract with the USAO. In addition, DOJ may require that the defendant make its financial officers available to DOJ.

Points of negotiation can include the total settlement amount, the timing and amount of installment payments, and, sometimes, the form and amount of security for payment, such as a personal guarantee. DOJ typically insists on the payment of interest on the principal settlement amount, which usually runs from the date of a "handshake" on the terms of an agreement until the payment date. It is the present value of the settlement that will be approved. The settlement agreement will contain a standard provision to protect DOJ in the event of a bankruptcy filing, and may seek security, guarantees, or, on occasion, a "pocket judgment" (to be filed in the event of a default).

---

13. Mem. from Ethan Davis Acting Asst. Att. General Assessing an Entities Assertion of an Inability to Pay (Sept. 4, 2020), https://www.justice.gov/civil/page/file/1313361/download.

D. The "Yates Memo"

On September 9, 2015, then-Deputy Attorney General Sally Quillian Yates released a memorandum entitled "Individual Accountability for Corporate Wrongdoing" that sets forth principles to guide DOJ attorneys in seeking to hold accountable the individuals who perpetrated the wrongdoing.[14] The memo expressly applies to both civil and criminal cases. The Yates Memo, to the extent followed, has a significant impact on the FCA settlement process.

First, the Yates Memo shifts incentives for settlements away from financial recovery from the corporate entity and toward the deterrence achieved by holding individuals accountable. Deputy Attorney General Yates herself, in remarks delivered September 10, 2015, acknowledged that requiring corporations to supply complete cooperation as to individuals could result in fewer and smaller corporate settlements.[15]

Second, the Yates Memo heightens the role of "cooperation credit" in FCA settlements. Historically, cooperation credit in civil cases has played a less-structured role than in criminal cases where the degree of cooperation impacts the sentencing guideline range. However, in theory at least, cooperation credit will now be recognized in civil cases as well under guidance issued by DOJ on May 7, 2019, and subsequently incorporated into the Justice Manual.[16]

During a September 10, 2015, speech at New York University that addressed her memorandum ("Yates Remarks"), Yates explained that, "if a company wants any credit for cooperation, it must identify all individuals involved in the wrongdoing, regardless of their position, status or seniority in the company and provide all relevant facts about their misconduct."[17] Yates characterized this "all or nothing approach" as a "substantial shift from our prior practice."[18] Further, the Yates Memo provides that corporate cases "should not [be resolved] . . . without a clear

---

14. Mem. from Sally Quillian Yates, Deputy Atty. Gen. on Individual Accountability for Corporate Wrongdoing (Sept. 9, 2015), https://www.justice.gov/archives/dag/file/769036/download ("Yates Memo"). These principles are reflected in the Justice Manual, Chapter 9-28.000 *et seq.*

15. "Only time will tell. But if that's what happens, so be it. Our mission here is not to recover the largest amount of money from the greatest number of corporations; our job is to seek accountability from those who break our laws and victimize our citizens. It's the only way to truly deter corporate wrongdoing." Sally Quillian Yates, Deputy Atty. Gen. at N.Y. Univ. (Sept. 10, 2015), https://www.justice.gov/opa/speech/deputy-attorney-general-sally-quillian-yates-delivers-remarks-new-york-university-school ("Yates Remarks").

16. DOJ, *Justice Manual*, 4-4.112, https://www.justice.gov/jm/jm-4-4000-commercial-litigation#4-4.112 (last updated May 2019).

17. Yates Remarks, *supra* note 15, at 2.

18. *Id.*

plan to resolve related individual cases" before the statute of limitations expires and "memorialize any declinations as to individuals in such cases."[19] In meeting this requirement, DOJ might impose a requirement to cooperate in investigating and disclosing the role of individuals in the wrongdoing as a condition of its willingness to settle.

Lastly, the fourth principle of the Yates Memo is that DOJ should not provide releases to individuals as part of a settlement of corporate wrongdoing "absent extraordinary circumstances."[20] If this principle is implemented, DOJ can be expected to review the role of individuals without providing releases to them during the corporate settlement process. If warranted, DOJ may then pursue civil actions against those individuals who were behind the wrongdoing.

Since issuance, the Yates Memo has not been consistently followed. DOJ has made back-and-forth policy shifts on the question of whether a corporation seeking cooperation credit must disclose information on every single individual involved in the wrongdoing. In November 2018, DOJ, through a speech by the then-Deputy Attorney General Rod Rosenstein, reversed the prior "all or nothing" policy, and announced that to be eligible to receive cooperation credit, companies must provide relevant information about "all individuals substantially involved in or responsible for the misconduct."[21] This was seen as a relaxation of the Yates Memo in the interest of incentivizing cooperation.

Then, in March 2022, Attorney General Merrick Garland reverted to the "all or nothing" policy, announcing that to receive cooperation credit under the Yates Memo, companies must provide information about all individuals involved in the relevant misconduct, regardless of the degree of involvement, status, or seniority. Garland noted that the Biden administration intended to increase its prosecution of corporate misconduct, and that DOJ's "first priority in corporate criminal cases is to prosecute the individuals who commit and profit from corporate malfeasance."[22]

Given this directive, the settlement process has become more complicated, drawn out, and expensive, as corporate defendants grapple with the impact of the policy permitting further investigation of individuals. Simultaneous representation

---

19. Yates Memo, *supra* note 14, at 6.

20. *Id.* at 5.

21. DOJ, *Deputy Attorney General Rod J. Rosenstein Delivers Remarks at the American Conference Institute's 35th International Conference on the Foreign Corrupt Practices Act* (Nov. 29, 2018), https://www.justice.gov/opa/speech/deputy-attorney-general-rod-j-rosenstein-delivers-remarks-american-conference-institute-0.

22. DOJ, *Attorney General Merrick B. Garland Delivers Remarks to the ABA Institute on White Collar Crime* (Mar. 3, 2022), https://www.justice.gov/opa/speech/attorney-general-merrick-b-garland-delivers-remarks-aba-institute-white-collar-crime.

of a corporate defendant and key individuals can readily result in conflicts requiring the retention of separate counsel to represent individuals. The ability of corporate counsel to uncover all relevant facts can be undercut by the need or desire, in the interest of fairness, to warn individuals in the company of their possible exposure before interviewing them or taking statements.

E. Factors DOJ Tends Not to Consider in Settlement Negotiations

DOJ generally does not consider as a mitigating factor any defendant disclosures: (1) to the agency mandated by the government program's enabling statute or rules; or (2) in response to compulsory process such as an FCA Civil Investigative Demand. Indeed, statements in a mandatory disclosure might be deemed admissions of a party opponent under Federal Rule of Evidence 801 (and thereby excluded from the rule against hearsay evidence) and could strengthen the government's litigation position. In addition, DOJ generally does not consider as a mitigating factor a compliance program that failed to detect and correct the wrongdoing. However, DOJ may consider as a mitigating factor a compliance system that identified the risk or issue at hand,[23] as well as fulsome voluntary disclosures pursuant to 31 U.S.C. § 3729(a)(2).

F. Scope of Settlement

1. Releases

The scope of the release is among DOJ's highest priorities in the negotiation of an FCA settlement and should be a top priority for a defendant as well. The amount to be paid in a settlement should not be agreed upon without knowing what is being received in exchange for the payment, including the definition of the covered conduct and scope of the release being provided by the government. In general, the scope of release will be negotiated concurrently with the amount of settlement.

A description of the conduct subject to the release (the so-called Covered Conduct), the causes of action being released, the time period covered by the release, and the persons being released are all critical terms subject to negotiation. The government generally will insist on a release limited to the conduct it believes it investigated and for which it is receiving a settlement payment. If there are some claims in the case for which the government is not obtaining a recovery, defendant's

23. A defendant might argue that its compliance system nonetheless met a reasonable standard of care and is relevant to the question of whether the company possessed the requisite scienter to violate the FCA. Such an argument, based on evidence demonstrating the sufficiency of the compliance system, might impact the government's litigation risk analysis.

counsel may seek a release that encompasses those claims in order to end the litigation and threat of future litigation by the government or a qui tam plaintiff. The relator may support a release that includes such claims to bolster their claim for attorney's fees for all of counsel's work in the case, regardless of whether the work was in support of a claim that led to a recovery.[24]

In addition, DOJ generally will release only those claims asserted under the FCA, the Program Fraud Civil Remedies Act,[25] the Civil Monetary Penalties Act,[26] and the common law of fraud, unjust enrichment, and payment by mistake. With the agency's concurrence, limited contract claims—such as those brought under the Truth in Negotiations Act[27] or the CDA[28]—also may be released. The government will carve out of the release any federal tax or criminal liability and will exclude any claims for administrative action, such as suspension or debarment, unless expressly covered in the release. It will also reserve claims for breach of the settlement agreement and will also insist that any release is rescinded should the company avoid its obligations under the settlement via bankruptcy.

The government's release will be restricted to those corporate entities that are parties to the agreement as well as, in many cases, corporate parents, subsidiaries, and affiliates, and other entities in the corporate ownership chain, providing that there is no ongoing investigation of the matter targeting any of these entities. The government will release individuals who were the target of the investigation and allegations and who are parties to the settlement, but will not otherwise release directors, officers, and employees of the released entities.

DOJ also may agree to issue a "cold comfort" letter that states that it is not aware of any pending investigations or plans to initiate an FCA suit against the settling defendants with respect to allegations dismissed without prejudice, and perhaps other allegations that were investigated but not settled. Sometimes the letter may also include individuals or entities not subject to the release in the settlement agreement. DOJ and USAOs have different approaches to these letters, which may also change as leadership changes. They may or may not include representations on behalf of offices outside of the issuing office.

---

24. *See, e.g.*, Perez-Sosa v. Garland, 22 F.4th 312, 324 (1st Cir. 2022) ("a court should award fees for all hours logged in connection with work that is 'useful and of a type ordinarily necessary' to secure the final result obtained from the litigation" (internal citations omitted)).

25. 31 U.S.C. §§ 3801–3812.

26. 42 U.S.C. §§ 1320a-7a.

27. 10 U.S.C. § 2306a.

28. 41 U.S.C. §§ 7101–7109.

2. Dismissal after Settlement

Generally, dismissals of FCA cases after settlement will be with prejudice to the United States as to the Covered Conduct. In qui tam cases in which the government has not intervened, the dismissal of the case following settlement will be with prejudice to the relator but may be without prejudice to the United States as to those claims for which the government is not receiving a recovery. In those instances, a defendant must consider the risk that the allegations might be successfully pursued by the government or another relator in the future. If the statute of limitations has run for the government, that risk is obviously very small.

G. Other Settlement Considerations

1. Nonnegotiable Terms

Because DOJ has certain required and/or nonnegotiable terms for FCA settlement agreements, these agreements have a measure of consistency, though at times, DOJ may allow some flexibility in these terms. Thus, it is important that defendants and relators understand these terms, and the extent to which they may be negotiable, before they agree to a resolution.

2. Nonmonetary Department of Justice Concerns

As discussed, most FCA settlements look similar and contain particular provisions required by the government. These include:

a. Press Release

DOJ will insist on the right to issue a press release and will refuse to negotiate its wording or even provide the defendant with a draft. It may agree to provide the defendant a copy of the final release and notification as it is issued.

b. Cost Clause

Whether or not a company reports its costs to the government (e.g., for purposes of government contracting), the DOJ requires that all agreements include a provision specifying that all costs, as defined in the FAR 31.205-47, incurred by a government contractor in defense of an FCA investigation and any related proceedings, shall be unallowable and shall not be borne by the government as a direct or indirect cost on government contracts. DOJ does not negotiate the language of this clause, which requires a separate accounting for the costs. If a separate accounting is particularly difficult, the government has agreed to the costs being estimated, provided that government personnel may audit that estimate. DOJ also may be willing to discuss in a separate document the extent of "corrective actions" the clause covers.

c. Tax Liability

As noted earlier, the government will not release tax liability in an FCA agreement. However, as required by law,[29] DOJ will include in every settlement agreement the amount of the payment that it considers to be "restitution." Prior to settlement, defendants should discuss with their tax advisors the implications of this provision. Further, defendants should discuss with DOJ the determination of the restitution amount, which, occasionally, defendants can convince DOJ to revise.

d. Cooperation and Admission of Liability

The government generally will not agree to include in settlements a statement describing the defendant's "cooperation" with the investigation but may include factual statements regarding voluntary disclosures or other such communications by the defendant to the government. Long-standing policy since 1986 is that DOJ will include in the standard settlement agreement a statement that the settlement does not represent an admission of liability.

However, the USAO for the Southern District of New York now routinely requires admitted Statements of Facts as part of their FCA settlement agreements, and USAOs in other districts in some circumstances seek or demand factual admissions. The USAOs generally are willing to discuss with the defendant the wording of these factual admissions. If this issue arises in settlement discussions, it can add considerable complexity, and occasionally roadblocks, to a settlement. It is consequently essential for a defendant to determine whether the USAO will require admissions, and, if so, to begin the process of negotiating the language.

e. Corrective Actions and Warranties

The government will not agree to release warranty provisions unless the settlement goes to a particular defect and then the release will cover claims under the warranty only as it applies to that defect. In addition, the government will reserve claims for any consequential and third-party damages. While DOJ's focus is on the amount of money to recover, the agency may be interested in steps to remedy defects in a product. In this case, a defendant needs to determine the agency's goals and the costs that corrective action will add to the settlement.

f. Administrative Remedies

Releases or no-action decisions regarding suspension or exclusion must be discussed directly with the agency. Some agencies conduct such negotiations simultaneously and include terms in the FCA settlement agreement, while other agencies insist on separate agreements or administrative proceedings.

29. Tax Cuts and Jobs Act of 2017 § 13306 (Pub. L. No. 115-97). *See* 26 U.S.C. § 6050X.

g. Criminal Responsibility
Any criminal responsibility must be resolved in a separate negotiation with the prosecutor and explicitly will not be released in the settlement agreement.

3. Process

a. Timing
Generally, after the government has largely completed its investigation, DOJ will meet with the defense to discuss the strengths and weaknesses of the case and give the defendant an opportunity to convince the DOJ to close the matter or, in the case of a qui tam action, decline intervention. DOJ guidelines promote the exploration of settlement prior to initiating litigation or intervening in a qui tam suit. If settlement negotiations are making progress, DOJ often is forthcoming with information the defendant needs to assess the settlement value of the case.

If the matter involves a qui tam action, settlement timing is often driven by the expiration date of the seal on the case. The defendant may want to resolve the case before there is media coverage upon the relator's complaint being unsealed, whether or not the government is intending to intervene. If the government is going to intervene and has told the defendant about that decision, the defendant may want to speed up settlement or get the government to extend the seal period so that a case will be unsealed and a settlement announced at the same time, in the same news cycle.

4. Implementation/Signing Agreement/Filing

In qui tam actions in which a settlement agreement is reached during the seal period, DOJ will intervene for purposes of settlement at the time of settlement, the parties will work on the settlement agreement terms using the DOJ settlement agreement template, and DOJ will file a notice of dismissal. In declined cases, a settlement between the defendant and the relator will be subject to DOJ approval, and time must be planned to allow for that process. The relator will approach DOJ with the settlement terms.

IV. Qui Tam Litigation: Relator's Rights and Role in Settlement

The relator's role and rights differ depending on whether DOJ has intervened in the case.

A. Settlement Process in a Qui Tam Case in Which the DOJ Has Intervened

DOJ manages settlement of qui tam cases in which it has intervened and does not usually include the relator's counsel in those settlement discussions. If the relator and their legal team have been actively involved in assisting DOJ in its investigation, DOJ will usually keep the relator's counsel abreast as to any settlement discussions.

If the government intervenes for the purpose of settlement and not litigation, the settlement amount and any other financial terms (e.g., payments over time, contingent payments) are core issues. If the relator believes the settlement amount is too small, the FCA provides the relator with the right to a hearing.[30]

B. Documentation

There may be multiple settlement documents that separately address (1) the FCA and any related claims of the government against the defendant; (2) the relator's claim against the government under 31 U.S.C. § 3730(d) for a share of the recovery; (3) the relator's claim against the defendant under 31 U.S.C. § 3730(d) for reasonable attorneys' fees and costs; and (4) any side letter requested by the defendant, such as the "cold comfort letter" referenced earlier. In some cases, if all the preceding claims have been successfully addressed in settlement discussions, the government may draft an omnibus agreement to cover all claims.

The government ordinarily presents the relator and the defendant with the first draft of an agreement that includes the agreed-upon payment amount(s) and scope of release along with the government's standard terms, and, in some cases, as noted earlier, a resolution of the relator's claims for a share of the recovery and a section in which the defendant and the relator can include language resolving relator's claims for attorneys' fees. Both the defendant and the relator will have an opportunity to negotiate changes to this draft. If settlement discussions have not resolved the relator's claim for a relator share or their claim for attorneys' fees, the settlement agreement ordinarily will reserve the unresolved claim(s), which will then be decided through subsequent discussions between the parties or by the court upon motion of the relator. In such instances, the notice and proposed order of dismissal should reserve the court's jurisdiction over the unresolved claim(s).[31]

---

30. *See* 31 U.S.C. § 3730(c)(2)(B) ("The Government may settle the action with the defendant notwithstanding the objections of the person initiating the action if the court determines, after a hearing, that the proposed settlement is fair, adequate, and reasonable under all the circumstances. Upon a showing of good cause, such hearing may be held in camera.").

31. Defendants sometimes challenge relator's entitlement to attorneys' fees on the ground that relator's suit is barred under the FCA's "public disclosure" provision, 31 U.S.C. § 3730(e)(4), or "first to file" provision, 31 U.S.C. § 3730(b)(5). *But see* United States *ex rel.* Bryant v. Cmty. Health Sys., 24 F.4th 1024 (6th Cir. 2022) (holding that multiple relators who filed separate qui tam suits concerning the same misconduct were entitled to attorney's fees from the defendant, because they were parties to the government's settlement agreement and received a share of the proceeds, either directly from the government or indirectly from another relator). *Cf.* United States *ex rel.* Lovell v. Athenahealth,

Whether or not there is agreement, or reservation, on the issues of relator's share and attorney's fees, the government will require relator to agree in the settlement document that the underlying qui tam FCA settlement is fair, adequate, and reasonable.

The government usually will require the defendant to release the government from any and all liability arising from the Covered Conduct or the government's investigation, prosecution, or settlement thereof. In addition, the government ordinarily will include in the settlement agreement a paragraph in which defendant releases the relator from any liability arising from the relator's qui tam claims, including, in particular, relator's investigation and prosecution of the claims.

C. Settlement Process in Declined Cases

When the government declines to intervene in a qui tam suit, it will issue a letter to the relator and the defendant. That letter provides limits on some of the terms and conditions that the government will approve if the relator and defendant settle the case. In a procurement fraud case, that letter will include a requirement that the settlement agreement contain the standard provisions of a government-defendant procurement fraud settlement agreement, including the non-allowability clause, tax neutrality, consequential damages limitation, and warranty exception. Relators may agree to keep the agreement confidential, but they may not bind the government in this respect.

When a declined case is nearing settlement, relator should update DOJ on the status. DOJ may take an active role in the settlement process to help bring it to fruition and to ensure that the settlement adequately serves the interests of the

---

Inc., 56 F.4th 152 (1st Cir. 2022) (relator not entitled to attorney fees unless they received a relator award from the government; receiving an award under a private sharing agreement among multiple relators is not sufficient). Due to these decisions, defendants must carefully consider prior to executing a settlement agreement involving multiple relators if they have adequately resolved all issues with all relators prior to settlement, or alternatively, if they had adequately explicitly reserved the ability to contest relators' entitlement to any award of attorneys' fees due to public disclosure, first to file, or other issues. And, relators paid an award under a sharing agreement but not awarded a share by the government may be able to bolster their attorneys' fee claim if they are a party to the settlement agreement between the government and defendants.

In addition, defendants commonly challenge the "reasonableness" of relator's fees by questioning, for example, hourly rates, the number of hours spent on specific tasks, the seniority of the attorney handling work that might have been handled by a more junior attorney, paralegal, or administrative assistant, and whether a specific task is compensable, such as research or document review in support for the Government's investigation during the seal period. With regard to the latter issue, *see* United States ex rel. Nichols v. Computer Scis. Corp., 499 F. Supp. 3d 32, 44 (S.D.N.Y. 2020) ("the FCA does not impose a categorical bar on a relator recovering attorneys' fees for work done assisting the Government during the seal period").

United States. Even if DOJ does not participate in the process, the relator must send the proposed settlement terms, along with the proposed notice of voluntary dismissal and the proposed order granting dismissal, to the government for review and approval. Relator should use the nonnegotiable terms in the standard DOJ settlement form, such as non-release of tax claims, because they will be required eventually for DOJ consent to the settlement.

1. The Government's Role in Settlement

While the government may stay out of the settlement negotiations in a declined case, at times its presence may assist one or both sides. In the first instance, it can serve to broker a settlement and may offer "reality testing" to help either side take a more realistic view of the case. For the relator, its presence may send a message to the defendant that it is reconsidering the intervention decision if the case does not settle. For the defendant, its presence can provide assurance that the settlement and the release will be approved. However, the government attorneys may have limited time and may elect not to assist or participate in the settlement negotiation. Relator needs to take the laboring oar to get the paperwork discussed earlier approved by DOJ. If DOJ has issues with the settlement, then the relator, defendant, and DOJ need to continue negotiating while the case proceeds through discovery, motion practice, or trial.

2. The Government's Concern over the Scope of the Release

While a defendant may enter into a broad release of any separate claims the relator may have against defendant, the government will object to a broad release as to the claims of the United States. The government will not consent to a dismissal with prejudice of a claim, or release a claim, unless it is receiving money on the claim through the settlement. If the defendant is only paying attorneys' fees or wrongful discharge damages to the relator, then the dismissal of the qui tam action must be without prejudice to the government.

3. Settlement of Retaliation Claims

The government cannot settle any claims the relator may have under 31 U.S.C. § 3730(h) for retaliatory actions against relator by the defendant—these claims belong exclusively to the relator. If the relator and the defendant resolve such claims prior to the settlement of the United States' claims, they may be included either in an omnibus settlement document between defendant, relator, and the government, or in a stand-alone settlement document between defendant and the relator.

In a declined case, the government will often carefully scrutinize a § 3730(h) settlement to make sure the defendant and relator are not improperly overvaluing the retaliation claim at the expense of the qui tam claims. There is an incentive for relator and defendant to do so. Relator will receive 100 percent of the recovery on their retaliation claim, but typically just 25 to 30 percent of the recovery on a declined qui tam claim. As a result, the relator may be agreeable to a lower total settlement amount if more money is allocated to their separate retaliation claim. The differing tax treatments of these amounts may also be a factor in the defendant's settlement analysis.

If relator's claims for retaliation are not resolved by the time the United States' claims have been resolved, they need to be reserved in the settlement agreement and in the proposed order of dismissal, just like relator's fees and share claims, as discussed earlier. The retaliation claim will proceed through discovery, motion practice, and trial, if not settled. DOJ does not have to approve relator's and defendant's later settlement of the retaliation claim. Any eventual settlement agreement of the retaliation claim need not be on forms used by DOJ.

D. Settlement of Partially Intervened Cases

If DOJ or a state intervenes in some but not all of the relator's qui tam action, DOJ may settle claims in which it has intervened while the relator pursues others past that settlement. The partial settlement should be treated just like any other settlement in an intervened case, with the relator reserving all unresolved claims in the settlement agreement. If the relator believes any of the intervened claims are being settled at a value that is unreasonably low, they may seek a hearing as provided in the FCA, as discussed earlier. If the relator reaches a settlement with defendant on any declined claims, DOJ will need to approve the settlement terms of those claims, as already described. For best results, the relator and DOJ should be in regular, coordinated contact while pursuing the declined and intervened claims.

V. Defendant's Role in the Settlement Process

A. Interaction with DOJ Leading to Settlement Discussions

In an intervened case, DOJ will usually make a presentation to the defendant showing what DOJ thinks is its case and its damages. DOJ will give defendant a chance to make a rebuttal presentation.

In making a presentation to DOJ, a defendant has an opportunity to address key points and provide its views. Such a presentation might (1) provide information about the defendant's conduct; (2) explain defendant's track record of performance and compliance; (3) address any concerns or questions DOJ has communicated to the defendant; (4) present the defendant's version of the facts and circumstances concerning the alleged conduct; (5) present the defendant's legal analysis; (6) discuss the challenges that the government or the relator will face in proving liability and damages, if the claims are based on an ambiguous statute, regulation, or contractual provision; (7) address affirmative defenses such as the statute of limitations or release and satisfaction; (8) provide information as to the credibility of witnesses; and/or (9) present other reasons DOJ should not intervene in the action.

Defendants should seek DOJ's agreement that the presentation will be covered under Rule 408 and Federal Rules of Criminal Procedure 11, if applicable, and should mark the presentation materials accordingly. However, DOJ will likely insist on maintaining the ability to share defendant's information and positions with the relator because the relator's assistance may be helpful or necessary. If it wishes to share such information with the relator, DOJ ordinarily will only do so if the relator first enters into a "common interest agreement" in which it agrees to confidential treatment of the information. If the defendant nonetheless balks at providing DOJ with a meaningful presentation because of relator's potential access to it, a simple confidentiality agreement between the defendant and the relator could end that concern. If the relator is a competitor, though, it may be important for the defendant to get DOJ to agree to restrictions on sharing.

B. Settlement Terms Defendants May Want to Negotiate with DOJ

1. No Admission and Recitals

Settlements typically contain a standard provision stating that the settlement agreement does not constitute an admission as to defendant's liability. Among other benefits to a defendant, such a provision should prevent a suspension and debarment official from considering the settlement agreement as an admission of liability in a suspension or debarment proceeding.

Moreover, regardless of whether the settlement agreement contains a "no admission of liability" provision, a defendant should be concerned about the recitals in the agreement that are not stated as a government allegation. Generally, recitals merely set forth certain facts of record that could be established through sources other than the settlement agreement, but the settlement agreement could constitute agreement as to the recitals even with a no-admissions clause as to liability.

Importantly, by acknowledging fault in an FCA settlement agreement, a government contractor could trigger a requirement to self-report the acknowledgment in the Federal Awardee Performance and Integrity Information System (FAPIIS). Offerors with more than $10 million in federal contracts and grants must report certain information in FAPIIS pursuant to FAR 52.209-7. Under FAR 52.209-7(c)(1)(iv), such an offeror must disclose whether in the last five years in connection with the award or performance by the offeror of a federal contract or grant, the offeror or any of its principals had, inter alia, a disposition of a civil proceeding "by consent or *compromise with an acknowledgment of fault by the Contractor if the proceeding could have led to any of the outcomes specified in . . . (c)(1)(ii) . . . of (FAR 52.209-7)*" (emphasis added). FAR 52.209-7(c)(1)(ii) defines these outcomes to include "[in] a civil proceeding, a finding of fault and liability that results in the payment of a monetary fine, penalty, reimbursement, restitution, or damages of $5000 of more."

Finally, in addition to a "no-admission" acknowledgment, the defendant may negotiate for a provision that specifies that the settlement agreement (or even drafts) cannot be admitted in any proceeding as evidence of guilt or fault.

2. Scope of Settlement

a. Covered Conduct

Just as DOJ seeks a narrow delineation of "Covered Conduct," and thus a narrow release, a defendant may try to negotiate to include in the Covered Conduct, and thus the release, as many as possible of the FCA allegations that have been investigated or alleged, whether by DOJ or by the relator.

b. Releases

Settlement of an FCA action will sometimes involve releases of not only FCA claims but also claims under other laws, such as the CDA, based on the same Covered Conduct. If an FCA case includes a claim for breach of contract, the court will likely have supplemental jurisdiction over the claim, and DOJ can act for the government in settling the FCA claims as well as the breach of contract claim. Where DOJ is investigating allegations that could constitute both an FCA violation and a breach of contract, and there is no FCA case on file, DOJ has control of the investigation and can enter into settlement discussions. However, the defendant should try to insist that the contracting officer sign off on a release related to the breach claim in order to avoid future contract disputes arising from the same conduct.

DOJ routinely releases defendant's parent, subsidiaries, and other entities in the corporate ownership chain, including them within the definition of the released "persons." Providing protection to such entities does not trigger the individual accountability concerns reflected in the Yates Memo. Though the government will not typically release defendant's officers, directors, and employees, defendants often try to ensure that releases by relators do include these persons, as well as all entities in the corporate ownership chain, in a reciprocal release provision.

A defendant should be attentive to preserving whatever indemnification rights it might have and not inadvertently waive or release indemnification claims. A defendant should also consider its own indemnification liability to existing and former officers, directors, and employees.

3. Tax-Related Issues

The tax treatment of payments under an FCA settlement agreement is an important financial consideration for defendants. Section 162(f) of the Internal Revenue Code provides that "any fine or similar penalty paid to a Government for the violation of any law" is not deductible as an ordinary and necessary business expense.[32] However, "compensatory damages . . . do not constitute a fine or penalty."[33] Thus, particularly where there is a lump sum settlement, the amount of the settlement payment that is "compensatory" is critical. Prior to December 22, 2017, no clear statutory guidance assisted FCA defendants in determining the portion of the settlement that was "compensatory" within the meaning of the tax code.

The Tax Cuts and Jobs Act of 2017 changed this landscape. Section 13306 of this Act prohibits deductions for settlements paid to the government (or at the direction of the government), except for amounts defendants can establish were paid as restitution or expended to come into compliance with the law and that are specifically identified as such in the court order or settlement agreement. Thus, for any settlements entered into on or after December 22, 2017 (the effective date of the law), FCA defendants may be precluded from taking deductions for FCA payments to the government unless the settlement agreement specifies the amount as restitution.

Accordingly, FCA settlement agreements contain a provision that explicitly states the amount of "restitution," based on the multipliers used by DOJ to calculate the settlement amount, which can be complex (e.g., half the settlement amount would be considered restitution if DOJ characterized the settlement as "double damages"). The IRS has issued guidance on deductibility of FCA settlement payments, as well, which defendant's tax counsel should consult.

4. Cost Clause

As noted, DOJ insists on a cost clause to prevent a contractor from seeking reimbursement from the government of attorneys' fees and other costs incurred in connection with the matter being settled.[34] The inclusion and language of the cost clause are not negotiable under DOJ's current policies. Government contractors settling FCA cases consequently lose any opportunity to recover their costs of investigating and defending the matter. If the case were not settled and the government contractor were to completely prevail, 80 percent of the contractor's reasonable costs could be included as allowable costs in the contractor's indirect rates

32. 26 U.S.C. § 162(f).
33. 26 C.F.R. § 1.162-21(b)(2).
34. *See* FAR 31.205-47.

allocated to contracts in accordance with their existing cost accounting practices. Allowable and properly allocated indirect costs may be reimbursable under cost contracts. The reasonable value of the "give-up" would include the existing and estimated future reimbursable costs, adjusted to account for litigation risk. In determining the amount it is willing to pay to settle the FCA action, a defendant might wish to consider the reasonable value of its abandoned right to seek reimbursement of these costs.

5. Where There Are Multiple Defendants

Negotiations among multiple defendants in the FCA context are similar to any negotiation among multiple defendants, with these added factors: defendants in FCA cases are jointly and severally liable and, on public policy grounds, may not be able to seek contribution or indemnification under the common law. However, the D.C. Circuit recently decided that under some circumstances an FCA defendant is entitled to offset damages by amounts the government or relator has received in settlement from other defendants involving the same claims.[35]

If multiple defendants enter into a FCA settlement agreement, the settlement agreement will specify the amount owed by each defendant. Particularly in a declined case, a relator might want to settle with one or more defendants and gain their voluntary cooperation with their case as well as using the proceeds of settlement to finance litigation against any remaining defendant(s). Each settlement agreement must be separately approved by DOJ, and the same guidelines discussed earlier should be considered.

VI. Certain Matters between Relator and Defendant

A. Relator's Claims for Reasonable Attorneys' Fees and Costs

The negotiations between relator and defendant over fees and costs often take place after an agreement to settle the underlying case. Relators' counsel may insist upon this approach to avoid being in a position of negotiating how much of the settlement will go to their fees at the same time they are negotiating how much of the settlement will go to the government and then to their client in the form of a relator award. In addition, this approach prevents defendants from asserting that relator's claim for fees and costs is standing in the way of settlement of the qui tam claims, and prevents relators from holding up a settlement due to unreasonable or intransigent demands for fees and costs. However, these issues are also often resolved

35. *See* United States v. Honeywell Int'l, 47 F.4th 805 (D.C. Cir. 2022) (establishing the pro tanto rule and reversing the district court's proportionality approach).

fully at the time of the settlement agreement, and defendants and relators often seek full closure at that time.

When a qui tam case generates proceeds either through judgment or a settlement, the statute awards the relator their "'reasonable' attorneys' fees and costs and expenses" that have been "necessarily incurred."[36] The attorneys' fees calculation generally involves the lodestar model followed under most fee-shifting statutes. The negotiation can include the reasonableness of the relator's counsel's hourly fee rate, the time spent as shown in the time records, and as compared to the rates and time expended by defense counsel. Defendants may raise objections to fees for specific relators in multi-relator cases based on arguments that only one relator is entitled to fees for each settlement allegation under the "first to file" rule or due to the "public disclosure" bar.[37] Defendants also may assert that relators are not entitled to any recovery of fees as to specific claims on which the government did not receive a settlement, and for time spent on activities that did not contribute to the assertion, development, or settlement of the allegations.

If no agreement is reached, the relator will move the court for an award of attorneys' fees and costs and expenses incurred. Relator will provide their attorneys' billing records for review by the court. If challenged by the defendant, the court will review the records for scope and analyze the hourly rates charged, sometimes in comparison to defense counsel's time and rates. Relator may submit one or more declarations as to the reasonableness of the hourly rates given counsel's experience, the complexity of the case, and the appropriate market rate for similar counsel in the court's jurisdiction. Relator may be allowed discovery as to the defendant's attorney's hourly rates and time spent defending the action.[38] Following filing and consideration of defendant's opposition and relator's reply, the court will determine the fee award to the relator.

Generally, in intervened cases, the government will not care about the attorneys' fees claim. Some relator's counsel will share a ballpark number for fees and expenses during the qui tam omnibus settlement negotiation so that the defendant has some estimate of its exposure. If the claim can be settled without more litigation, it will save the defendant having to pay for relator's fees expended in seeking fees; it has been held that the FCA awards "fees on fees" against the defendant, because the FCA seeks to encourage the relator's counsel to take on these

36. 31 U.S.C. § 3730(d)(1), (d)(2).

37. *See* FAR 31.205-47.

38. *See, e.g.*, United States *ex rel.* Kirchgessner v. James River Air Conditioning Co., U.S. Dist. LEXIS 215250 (E.D. Va. Dec. 3, 2018) (directing defendant "to file its entire billing file for this case, including hours, rates, and time entry descriptions for all attorneys on this case").

contingency fee cases with significant financial upside to counsel in a successful qui tam.[39] However, while a relator may recover attorneys' fees for negotiating settlement of the qui tam or litigating attorneys' fees, the relator may not be able to recover the fees and costs associated with obtaining a relator's share from DOJ. Because the defendant is not involved in the latter claim, some courts have held the defendant is not required to pay the fees incurred in resolving it.[40]

B. Relator's Retaliation Claim(s)

The negotiations between relator and defendant over any retaliation claim under § 3730(h) and any state statutory or common law claims for wrongful discharge typically involve a discussion of the applicable law and whether the facts support a finding that relator was the subject of retaliation. That question is determined based on the judicial precedent in the circuit in which the qui tam was filed and on any applicable state law. The extent to which the relator is entitled to damages (compensatory and/or punitive) is often a fact issue. State law claims may involve punitive damages, but the FCA retaliation claim does not. There is now a fairly extensive body of law on these issues.

VII. Global Settlements and Parallel Proceedings

A. Concerns of Government Contractor Defendant

Government contractors investigated or sued under the FCA may face potential criminal liability as well as suspension or debarment from doing business with the government under subpart 9.4 of the FAR and under the Non-Procurement Common Rules (NCR).[41] To resolve these issues alongside FCA civil liability, the defendant will need to negotiate with DOJ's criminal prosecutors and the suspension and debarment authorities at the program agency; the latter may insist upon a corporate integrity agreement.

DOJ may be willing to agree that the FCA settlement is contingent upon resolving the administrative and/or criminal matters within a set time limit to facilitate the global resolution that most defendants want. Relators usually have little role in the resolution of criminal or agency aspects of the FCA action, but, by statute, relators get a share of any "alternative remedies" obtained by the government. The

39. *See, e.g.*, United States *ex rel.* Yasti v. Nagan Constr., No. 17 CIV. 7163 (AT), 2021 WL 1063437, at *7 (S.D.N.Y. Mar. 18, 2021).

40. *See, e.g.*, United States *ex rel.* Taxpayers Against Fraud v. Gen. Elec. Co., 41 F.3d 1032 (6th Cir. 1994).

41. 2 C.F.R. pt. 180.

meaning of the term "alternative remedies" as used in the FCA has been the subject of significant litigation. Relators may assert that the criminal or administrative resolution will involve payments to the government that amount to "alternative remedies" and are therefore subject to a relator share. The defendant and DOJ may seek, and the relator may challenge, any resolution of criminal, civil, or administrative issues.

1. Criminal Liability

To avoid any suggestion of undue pressure to settle a civil FCA case, the government typically insists that an FCA defendant facing potential criminal liability and seeking to resolve all allegations request a global resolution of both civil and criminal liability. Sometimes the civil and criminal negotiations can occur simultaneously, either in the same meeting or in separate discussions. While the government civil attorneys may not use the criminal process to leverage settlement of civil liability, the reverse is not the case. DOJ can use resolved criminal liability to support civil liability for that same fraud.[42] If a criminal prosecution obtains guilty pleas or verdicts against individuals and/or the corporate defendant, the relator and/or DOJ can obtain summary judgment on the FCA civil claims based on facts admitted in the pleas or deemed decided in the verdicts.

Given the difficulty of prevailing in the FCA action after criminal liability for the same misconduct has been established, a defendant who has been convicted or entered a plea should strongly consider settling the civil case. This may be all the more advisable when a defendant's resources have been depleted fighting the criminal case(s).

2. Administrative Remedies

A debarment can be based on a criminal conviction, a civil judgment involving fraud, or facts evincing a lack of business honesty and integrity. The issue for agency authorities is whether the government's interests are served by doing business with the contractor, as evidenced by the contractor's conduct and its "present responsibility."[43] The assessment of present responsibility, the remedies chosen, and the requirements for continued participation may vary dramatically from agency to agency. Agencies have various processes for making these decisions; some rely heavily on convictions or judgments, and others develop the facts and hold their own hearings.

---

42. 31 U.S.C. § 3731(e).

43. Causes for debarment and suspension are listed at 48 C.F.R. §§ 9.406-2 and 9.407-2, respectively.

Settlement of this issue when the agency has a serious concern about "present responsibility" may entail a separate agreement with the agency to include corrective actions, such as firing employees or ensuring that they have no further contact with government contracts. Agreements also may include terms for ongoing audit protections, education and training of corporate employees, and continuing reports to agency officials. They all, however, are influenced by the defendant's cooperation in resolving its outstanding civil liability. The timing of the settlement of these issues is critical—the defendant needs to know each element of a "global resolution" to determine whether the total package is worth accepting. Sometimes the civil settlement may be deferred until the administrative resolution has been concluded; sometimes the negotiations are simultaneous.

The relator is entitled to a share of any proceeds of an "alternate remedy," which, depending upon the circumstances, could include the proceeds of a criminal or administrative action. There is case law as to what constitutes an "administrative remedy" within the meaning of the FCA.[44] Because DOJ may not pay attention to relator's statutory interest in the proceeds of "alternative remedies," best practices require that relator monitor any criminal or administrative actions based on their allegations and, where supported by law, affirmatively seek a share of any remuneration paid by the defendant.

44. *See, e.g.*, United States *ex rel.* Westfall v. Medworx Compoundings, LLC, No. 3:15-CV-376-CWR-FKB, 2021 WL 863345, at *1 (S.D. Miss. Mar. 8, 2021) ("The plain language of the False Claims Act is very broad on this point, as it speaks to '*any* alternate remedy available to the Government.' This language is not limited to civil remedies alone. In addition, even if the statute does not contemplate relators participating in criminal prosecutions, the breadth of the statute casts doubt on whether the government may use the criminal restitution process as a means to avoid having relators share in its civil recoveries."); *see also* United States *ex rel.* Bledsoe v. Cnty. Health Sys., Inc, 342 F.3d 634 (6th Cir. 2003).

CHAPTER 14

Protecting the Company

DAVID F. DOWD[1]

I. Introduction

A False Claims Act (FCA) investigation or suit poses a number of practical risks and challenges for a company, beyond those presented by the litigation itself. The company needs to act with an awareness that, while an FCA matter proceeds, it will be interacting with a variety of different actors on the same or related topics, such as the corporate board, shareholders, media, employees, and the procuring agency suspension and debarment official (SDO). Statements and events in the FCA matter can influence interactions with those other actors, and vice versa; for example, shareholder suits sometimes have been brought in the wake of FCA settlements.[2] This chapter discusses issues that can arise in interactions with those other actors.

II. Interaction with the Suspension and Debarment Official (SDO)

A. Contact with the SDO

1. Unsealed Case

An agency SDO may become aware of an FCA case that has been initiated by the government or, in the case of an FCA qui tam action, an action that has been unsealed. The FAR provides that "adequate evidence" of a fraud in connection with obtaining, attempting to obtain, or performing a public contract or subcontract is a

1. David Dowd is a partner with the Potomac Law Group.

2. *See, e.g.*, *In re* Abbott Depakote Shareholder Derivative Litigation, No. 11 C 8114, 2013 U.S. Dist. LEXIS 78841 (N.D. Ill. 2013); May v. SmithKline Beecham Clinical Labs., Inc., 710 N.E.2d 460 (Ill. 1999).

basis for suspension.[3] Accordingly upon learning of an FCA lawsuit, the SDO may invite the defendant-company to present information to the SDO about the matter.

2. Sealed Case

As discussed elsewhere in this book, the government, prior to deciding whether to intervene in a qui tam action, will sometimes obtain a partial lift of the seal so that it can discuss the matter with the defendant-contractor. In such instances, the court ordinarily will lift the seal as to the contractor, but not as to other actors, such as other government agencies besides the Department of Justice (DOJ). When a matter remains under partial seal, it consequently may be difficult for the defendant-contractor to approach the SDO because it may be unclear what the defendant can share. The company needs to ascertain if the partial unsealing order permits a disclosure to the SDO and, if so, how it should be accomplished. If the matter otherwise remains under seal, it is likely that disclosure of the existence of, or allegations in, the qui tam would violate the seal, although disclosure of DOJ's investigation would not do so. To determine what may be disclosed to the SDO, the company may be well advised to consult with DOJ. Moreover, if disclosures are made to the SDO, the company may elect to inform DOJ of the nature of that disclosure or, at a minimum, advise DOJ that it has contacted the SDO about the matter. Often, an SDO will defer action on a matter while DOJ is investigating to avoid possible interference with the investigation.

B. Sharing Information with the SDO

1. Developments in FCA Litigation

Typically, so long as communications with the SDO do not violate a seal on the case, it is prudent to keep the SDO apprised of major milestones in the FCA matter, such as presentations to DOJ, the government's decision on intervention, and important court rulings, such as those on motions to dismiss and summary judgment. Although the SDO may defer any detailed discussion until the contractor has resolved the FCA matter with DOJ, it is prudent for the contractor to demonstrate its present responsibility by promptly and diligently providing such information to the SDO.

2. Responsibility and Corrective Actions

Information shared with the SDO potentially may differ from what a defendant might introduce or emphasize in litigation due to the different focus of an SDO meeting. For example, SDO presentations typically include the contractor's

3. *See* FAR 9.407-2.

assessment of how the problem at issue occurred and its report on what steps have been, or will be, taken to prevent its recurrence. In providing this assessment and report, it may be prudent for a contractor to acknowledge the full extent of a problem to assure the SDO that the company fully understands the cause, nature and magnitude of the underlying problem and is committed to overcoming it. Such statements might not necessarily aid the company's defense of any FCA allegations, but they might well support the contractor's position that it is presently responsible, and contractors (particularly those for whom the government is a major customer) may face a greater financial risk from a potential suspension or debarment than from FCA allegations. In addition, as noted earlier, the SDO may elect to defer any detailed responsibility presentation until after the FCA matter has been resolved with DOJ.

III. Relationship with the Board and Shareholders

A. Reporting to the Board Regarding Sealed Qui Tam Actions

In a sealed case, if DOJ permits the defendant to review the complaint after obtaining the court's partial unsealing, a company likely will want to share information with its board or a subset of the board and auditors. A company may consider contacting DOJ for guidance on whether the court's partial unsealing order will permit a limited disclosure to the board. Note, however, that DOJ may give limited (if any) guidance regarding what a company may do with the complaint, and a partial unsealing order may provide little direction. Indeed, DOJ may not provide the company with a copy of the partial unsealing order.

B. Publicly Traded Companies and SEC Filings

1. Engagement with Disclosure Counsel

A publicly traded company may need to address inquiries from auditors about an FCA matter made in connection with the auditors' preparation of the company's periodic filings under securities laws and Securities and Exchange Commission (SEC) regulations. Often, a company will use different counsel to handle SEC matters than the litigation counsel handling the FCA matter. With regard to outside counsel, public companies frequently rely on external disclosure counsel to satisfy security laws requirements. This arrangement may create challenges such as ensuring the timeliness and completeness of appropriate briefings for disclosure counsel. Companies also may have different in-house counsel managing litigation counsel (including FCA matters) than those managing securities concerns. This management approach requires careful coordination to ensure all of the relevant individuals are kept informed of material developments in the FCA matter.

2. Material Events

The initiation of a government or internal investigation into allegations of FCA violations, the uncovering of key facts in such an investigation, the filing or unsealing of an FCA lawsuit, and significant court rulings in FCA matters—these and other key developments in the course of an FCA matter all may constitute material events that should be disclosed to investors through SEC disclosures in the case of a publicly traded company (or otherwise in the case of a privately held entity). Thus, in light of the prospect of treble damages, penalties, and potential suspension or debarment, the mere existence of an FCA matter reasonably may be viewed as a material development that should be disclosed. Specific events that might be considered material, among others, include the partial unsealing of an FCA suit, the receipt of a DOJ civil investigative demand or Office of Inspector General subpoena, a government notice of intervention, court rulings on motions to dismiss and summary judgment, the initiation of settlement discussions, and the reaching of a settlement in principle. A company may want to consult with its disclosure counsel during a known government investigation or FCA matter to ensure any public disclosure requirements are satisfied.

3. Shareholder Suits

As already noted, company management may need to advise shareholders of the existence or progress of an FCA investigation or lawsuit. However, as a result of these disclosures, shareholders may file actions against the company, its management, or its board of directors seeking recovery of damages suffered by the shareholders as a result of the conduct at issue in the FCA matter. Moreover, such disclosures may have implications for any preexisting shareholder suit regarding such conduct.

IV. Dealing with the Media

Media inquiries are likely once news breaks that a company is being investigated or sued for a potential FCA violation. Some companies may decline to comment and reserve all public statements for SEC and court filings. In an effort to manage or mitigate damages to the company's reputation, however, some companies might be inclined to consider a public relations outreach or at least a response to media inquiries. What should the company consider in responding? The company should be forewarned that statements to the media may find their way into the hands of DOJ, the SEC, or the SDO, as well as appear in the litigation. A contractor will probably want to vet media statements with litigation and disclosure counsel so they are consistent with any disclosures or positions taken before the procuring agency and in SEC and court filings.

V. Dealing with Employees

An FCA matter typically will arise during the conduct of ongoing business operations. In such cases, the company may need to take some steps to inform employees of the circumstances and status of the matter, consistent with any unsealing order. More relevantly, the company may face the question whether it may or should provide information to the workforce regarding the underlying allegations or the remedial measures that have been or will be taken to address improper conduct.

A. Information and Rumor

Company employees can be expected to discuss allegations of wrongdoing that have come to light. Accordingly, a company may wish to consider what (if any) steps it should take to explain the matter to staff to mitigate the risk that inaccurate information is dispersed throughout the company (and possibly beyond). In doing so, the contractor should bear in mind that internal emails or notices to a broad group of employees pose concerns regarding waiver of privilege and may also have evidentiary ramifications.

Thus, a broadly shared communication likely would lose any protection it had under the attorney-client privilege or work product doctrine unless limited to employees with responsibility to handle or make decisions with regard to the FCA matter. Moreover, a company should assume that a broadly shared email or notice to employees will be shared outside the company and that employees receiving such communications will speculate regarding the basis for the matter under investigation and may share such speculation in emails or direct messages.

When providing notice to employees of an investigation or suit, it is therefore prudent to keep any email or other notice brief and to request that employees contact counsel or the company's ethics hotline with any questions or concerns. Although a company cannot eliminate the risk of speculation about the matters under investigation, encouraging the use of such reporting channels can mitigate this risk.

B. Relators in the Workforce

In the absence of a court order partially lifting the seal to permit disclosure of a qui tam action to the company, a company facing a government investigation under the FCA ordinarily will not know whether the government's investigation was prompted by a qui tam filing, and, if so, the identity of the relator(s). The company should assume that any statements it makes about the FCA matter within the company may end up—directly or indirectly—in the hands of a relator (and, in turn, the government), even in the absence of discovery and even if not responsive to a subpoena. In addition, the company should of course refrain from any actions that could be interpreted as retaliation against any known or suspected whistleblowers.

C. Corrective Action

FCA matters sometimes arise, at least, in part, due to systemic weaknesses or a lack of safeguards in a company's internal controls. In such circumstances, a prudent response may be to implement changes in processes or internal controls to guard against the risk of a recurrence of the problematic conduct. For example, a company may determine that the descriptions of labor categories or the means of documenting when personnel shift among categories needs to be revised to avoid concerns regarding labor mischarging. Or a company may determine that it needs to revise test procedures or stop shipment of goods.

Implementation of necessary corrective action may impact an FCA litigation and related proceedings. For example, implementation of fixes or process improvements may involve training with explanations as to the nature of the problem being addressed, and these explanations may be used against the company as admissions of the wrongful conduct. On the other hand, depending on the circumstances as to when management learned of the violations, prompt remedial measures may make it more challenging for plaintiffs to establish the requisite scienter in an FCA case and may help the contractor demonstrate its present responsibility to the SDO. Prompt remedial actions may also reduce the treble damages and penalties recoverable in the lawsuit.

CHAPTER 15

Protecting the Whistleblower

HAMSA MAHENDRANATHAN AND ELIZABETH SOLTAN[1]

This chapter discusses how attorneys can best protect their whistleblower clients from the risks they face in bringing a qui tam case.

I. Preserving a Relator's Right to Sue and Recover an Award

There are several considerations attorneys should raise during initial conversations with a potential whistleblower to ensure they preserve their right to bring a qui tam case and recover an award. Relator's share awards are important compensation for the professional, personal, and reputational harm whistleblowers suffer. As a result, it is critical to help would-be relators understand the risks implicated by severance negotiations, especially the impact of any purported release of qui tam claims. Counsel should also advise whistleblowers on potential bars to their qui tam claims to help them decide whether and when to file a False Claims Act (FCA) case and/or report the fraud in another forum.

A. Releases and Encumbrances

Whistleblowers often leave their employers close in time to when they contact qui tam counsel, either because they are forced out because they voiced opposition to the fraud, or because they resigned to avoid further involvement in the fraud. In connection with severance discussions, their employer may ask them to sign an agreement containing a nondisclosure or confidentiality provision or a release of claims. When advising a client about the impact of such an agreement on a contemplated or pending qui tam action, counsel should carefully research the applicable law in the relevant jurisdiction, because the law varies considerably between judicial districts and may evolve further following the publication of this chapter.

1. Hamsa Mahendranathan is a partner and Elizabeth Soltan is an associate with Constantine Cannon. The authors wish to acknowledge that Suzanne Durrell, Shelley Slade, and Rob Vogel provided substantive assistance to the authors with regard to the matters covered herein.

As a general rule, however, thanks to the strong public policy favoring those who report fraud to the government, the courts have held that a nondisclosure or confidentiality agreement will not prevent a whistleblower from bringing a qui tam case.[2] Moreover, if an individual signs a general or FCA-specific release before filing suit, and if the government had no knowledge of the fraud at the time, courts routinely allow the individual's qui tam case to proceed notwithstanding the prefiling release.[3] If the government was already aware of the fraud at the time the individual executed the release, however, a prefiling release may foreclose the individual from proceeding with a qui tam case.[4] Moreover, an individual who signs a prefiling, general, or FCA-specific release may bar themselves from pursuing a retaliation claim under 31 U.S.C. § 3730(h).[5]

With regard to a release signed by a relator *after* they have filed a qui tam action, the few courts that have addressed the issue have permitted such cases to proceed, with one court citing the FCA's requirement that a relator must obtain the consent of the United States and the court before they can dismiss a qui tam action, and another court pointing to the public interests that are furthered when a relator continues to have an incentive to cooperate with the government.[6]

Qui tam counsel who are consulted by a potential whistleblower before they have entered into severance discussions should make sure to warn the individual about the risks of threatening to bring a qui tam action during these negotiations. In one case decided under California law, a state court found that an employee's threat to file a qui tam action, made during settlement negotiations, amounted to extortion.[7] Moreover, tipping an employer off to the possibility of a

2. *See, e.g.*, United States *ex rel.* Ruhe v. Masimo Corp., 929 F. Supp. 2d 1033, 1039 (C.D. Cal. 2012); United States v. Cancer Treatment Ctrs. of Am., 350 F. Supp. 2d 765, 773 (N.D. Ill. 2004).

3. *See, e.g.*, United States *ex rel.* Ladas v. Exelis, Inc., 824 F.3d 16, 23 (2d Cir. 2016); United States *ex rel.* McNulty v. Reddy Ice Holdings, Inc., 835 F. Supp. 2d 341, 360 (E.D. Mich. 2011). United States *ex rel.* Class v. Bayada Home Health Care, Inc., No. CV 16-680, 2018 WL 4566157, at *5 (E.D. Pa. Sept. 24, 2018) (collecting decisions regarding enforceability of releases in FCA cases).

4. *See, e.g.*, United States *ex rel.* Hall v. Teledyne Wah Chang Albany, 104 F.3d 230, 233 (9th Cir. 1997), *as amended on denial of reh'g and reh'g en banc* (Mar. 19, 1997); United States *ex rel.* Ritchie v. Lockheed Martin Corp., 558 F.3d 1161, 1171 (10th Cir. 2009).

5. United States *ex rel.* Dillion v. St. Elizabeth Med. Ctr., Inc., No. 2:15-CV-13 (WOB-JGW), 2017 WL 3000662, at *4 (E.D. Ky. July 13, 2017); VanLandingham v. Grand Junction Reg'l Airport Auth., 46 F. Supp. 3d 1119, 1126 (D. Colo. 2014), *aff'd*, 603 F. App'x 657 (10th Cir. 2015).

6. *See, e.g.*, United States *ex rel.* Longhi v. Lithium Power Techs., Inc., 575 F.3d 458, 474 (5th Cir. 2009); United States *ex rel.* Scott v. Cancio, No. 8:10–cv–50–T–30TGW, 2011 WL 5975782 (M.D. Fla. Nov. 28, 2011); United States *ex rel.* Dillahunty v. Chromalloy Oklahoma, No. CIV-08-944-L, 2011 WL 227648 (W.D. Okla. Jan. 21, 2011); United States *ex rel.* Davis v. Lockheed Martin Corp., No. 4:09–CV–645–Y, 2010 WL 4607411 (N.D. Tex. Nov. 15, 2010); *see also* United States *ex rel.* El-Amin v. George Washington Univ., No. 95–2000 (JGP), 2007 WL 1302597 (D.D.C. May 2, 2007).

7. Stenehjem v. Sareen, 226 Cal. App. 4th 1405, 1423 (2014).

qui tam action during severance discussions could significantly undermine any future government investigation. Acting in reaction to the potential whistleblower's threat, the employer might destroy documents, threaten witnesses, or otherwise spoliate evidence relevant to the alleged FCA violations. Qui tam attorneys with no background in employment law can consider consulting or co-counsel arrangements with attorneys who specialize in employment matters to provide holistic advice to a whistleblower navigating these exit negotiations.

B. Jurisdictional and Nonjurisdictional Bars

1. Public Disclosure Bar

Because the public disclosure bar, discussed in Chapters 4 and 8, can foreclose a qui tam action, qui tam counsel should take care to investigate whether any facts about the fraud have been publicly disclosed. To start, counsel should ask their client whether they are aware of any public disclosures. Counsel should then follow up with a thorough and careful internet search to discern whether any of the whistleblower's allegations are in the public domain, such as disclosures in (1) federal court proceedings in which the United States is a party; (2) federal legislative or executive branch audit or investigative reports; (3) media reports; and (4) if the potential defendant is publicly traded, the portion of the company's SEC filings addressing legal actions and government investigations. This information, coupled with counsel's advice concerning whether the client can establish themselves as an "original source," will help the whistleblower decide whether to move forward with the qui tam with a realistic understanding of the chance of recovering an award—a critical decision in light of the professional and personal risk whistleblowers face.

If there is a risk that a court would conclude that the FCA violations have been publicly disclosed, and if the client did not provide information regarding the violations to the government prior to the public disclosure, counsel should work with the client to identify and voluntarily disclose to the government, before filing, any additional material information known to the client beyond that in the public disclosure to help establish the client as an "original source." In these circumstances, it is important to document in the complaint when and how the whistleblower disclosed the information to the government and provide the context for the disclosure to demonstrate that it was voluntary. The complaint and prefiling disclosure should detail all material facts known to the client, particularly nonpublic facts.

2. "First to File" Bar

Because the "first to file" bar, discussed in Chapters 4 and 8, also prevents a relator from pursuing an FCA case, prospective whistleblowers and their counsel should investigate whether there are signs that someone else has already brought a qui tam based on the same or similar information. To start, counsel should ask the whistleblower whether they know of any investigation or audit relating to the alleged FCA violations. Counsel should also conduct a thorough internet search to find evidence of lawsuits, enforcement actions, and Department of Justice (DOJ) press releases referencing the defendant. This search should include a review of the potential defendant's SEC filings to see if they reference lawsuits, subpoenas, or civil investigative demands (CIDs) relating to the alleged fraud. Qui tam counsel may also consider asking the U.S. Assistant Attorney responsible for affirmative civil actions in the district most likely to pursue the case whether the DOJ is already investigating the fraud or the company. Since qui tams are filed under seal, this inquiry often will fail to uncover an earlier-filed qui tam case that blocks the prospective client's case. Nonetheless, taking these steps may better position client and counsel to decide whether to pursue an action.

If the client files an FCA case and then learns of a previously filed, overlapping qui tam action, counsel should analyze whether their client has unique FCA claims that are not raised by the first-filed complaint. These unique claims can allow part of the client's FCA case to move forward, even if other parts are blocked by the previously filed case. Relators in competing FCA cases could negotiate a recovery-sharing agreement or agree in advance whether the later-filed case raises new allegations. Obviously, the relator in the first-filed case will have significant leverage in these negotiations, but the existence of unique claims in the later-filed case can counter that dynamic. In addition, counsel in overlapping cases can consider an arrangement in which counsel represent not only their original client but also the other qui tam plaintiff or plaintiffs. While client waivers of potential or actual conflicts may be advisable, and the scope of representation must be carefully thought through, this arrangement can augment the resources available to prove the relators' claims.

Finally, if any of the cases are resolved, counsel in later-filed cases should take steps to ensure that their client is a party to the settlement and that the release covers their client's unique claims. This may improve their client's ability to recover a relator share award and statutory fees.

II. Potential Counterclaims and Other Risks Arising from the Collection of Evidence

A. Collecting, Preserving, and Reviewing Evidence

It is not uncommon for FCA defendants to raise counterclaims against a whistleblower for inappropriately taking and/or disclosing confidential company information. In general, the public policy of encouraging whistleblowing protects those who support their qui tam allegations with *relevant* nonprivileged, company documents that their employer gave them access to for the performance of their job responsibilities.[8] Courts have allowed counterclaims against whistleblowers to proceed when they have found the whistleblower's document collection to be overbroad. For example, in *United States ex rel. Cafasso v. General Dynamics C4 Systems, Inc.*, the Ninth Circuit determined that the whistleblower's collection of 11 gigabytes of data replete with irrelevant information—including some trade secret, privileged, and otherwise protected information—was too "vast and indiscriminate" to warrant protection under the public policy exception.[9] Whistleblowers may risk criminal exposure under the Computer Fraud and Abuse Act (CFAA) if they intentionally access information from a protected computer or protected computer files without authorization,[10] or if they steal company documents or information from private desks or cabinets or other areas to which their employer has not provided them access.

A whistleblower's safest course of action is to limit their document collection to copies (not originals) of those nonprivileged documents (1) to which they had legitimate access in order to perform their job duties and (2) that are reasonably viewed as potentially relevant to the allegations in the FCA case. Counsel should be aware that their clients may be asked by their employers in connection with the termination of employment to return all company equipment, such as laptops, phones, tablets, and so on, and may even be required to certify that they have returned all such material. Counsel should do all possible to make sure that their clients comply with such obligations while, at the same time, preserving copies of relevant evidence without tipping off their employer of the prospect of a qui tam action. If faced with a counterclaim for taking documents during the litigation, counsel should consider requesting an evidentiary hearing at which their client can demonstrate the relevance of the documents to the allegations and challenge any defendant claims of attorney-client privilege or other protected status.

Whistleblowers, particularly in health care fraud cases, may also have documents or information that contain Protected Health Information (PHI) as defined in the Health Insurance Portability and Accountability Act (HIPAA). The whistleblower's use of such documents or information in connection with their lawsuit may be restricted by HIPAA if the whistleblower obtains the information as a result of their role with an entity covered by HIPAA, that is, a health plan, health care clearinghouse, health care provider, or, in some situations, a "business associate"

8. *See* United States *ex rel.* Cieszynski Lifewatch Servs., Inc., No. 13 CV 4052, 2016 WL 2771798, at *5 (N.D. Ill. May 13, 2016); United States *ex rel.* Ruhe v. Masimo Corp., 929 F. Supp. 2d 1033, 1039 (C.D. Cal. 2012).

9. 637 F.3d 1047, 1062 (9th Cir. 2011).

10. 18 U.S.C. § 1030(a)(2)(C); *see also* United States v. Nosal, 676 F.3d 854 (9th Cir. 2012) (distinguishing access restrictions from use restrictions within the meaning of the CFAA).

of one of the foregoing.[11] HIPAA allows covered entities to disclose PHI of another individual without the consent of that individual in several situations, including (1) to health oversight agencies[12] for health oversight activities, which, by definition, include civil investigations and actions necessary for the oversight of compliance with government program regulatory standards; and (2) to law enforcement for law enforcement activities when required by statute.[13] Nonetheless, relator's counsel may find it advisable to deidentify PHI—that is, redact any information that could be used to identify the patient[14]—before disclosing PHI to the government. Ordinarily, the government will not need the information to investigate the case, and, if they do need it, they can subpoena it from the relator or discuss another HIPAA-compliant disclosure method. As a best practice, and regardless of whether the relator is a HIPAA "covered entity," counsel should be careful not to disclose any PHI in the qui tam complaint or other documents filed on the public docket unless required to do so by court order.[15]

Another potential minefield relating to the development of evidence involves the surreptitious recording of conversations. Some state bar ethics rules prohibit attorneys from secretly recording a conversation, either directly or through an agent. These rules could implicate secret recordings by a client, and counsel should be mindful of their ethical obligations when counseling whistleblowers on this issue. If a client raises the possibility of making and using such a recording, counsel should educate the client on the lawfulness of these actions in the jurisdiction(s) involved. While federal law[16] and some states[17] allow the recording of a conversation with the consent of just one party, many other states[18] require that all parties to a conversation consent to its recording when there is an expectation of privacy. In some of these states, whistleblowers who violate these laws could even face felony

---

11. *See* 45 C.F.R. §§ 164.104, 164.302.

12. HIPAA defines a "health oversight agency" as "an agency or authority of the United States, a State, a territory, a political subdivision of a State or territory, or an Indian tribe, or a person or entity acting under a grant of authority from or contract with such public agency, including the employees or agents of such public agency or its contractors or persons or entities to whom it has granted authority, that is authorized by law to oversee the health care system (whether public or private) or government programs in which health information is necessary to determine eligibility or compliance, or to enforce civil rights laws for which health information is relevant." 45 C.F.R. § 164.501.

13. *See* 45 C.F.R. § 512(d) (disclosure to health oversight agencies for health oversight activities) and (f) (disclosure to law enforcement for a law enforcement purpose when required by statute).

14. *See* 45 C.F.R. § 164.514(a) and (b) (discussing the deidentification of PHI).

15. *See, e.g.*, 45 C.F.R. § 164.514(e) (permitting disclosure in judicial and administrative proceedings when certain conditions are met).

16. 18 U.S.C. § 2511(c).

17. *See, e.g.*, N.Y. Penal Laws § 250.00; Ga. Code § 16-11-66; Minn. Stat. § 626A.02.

18. *See, e.g.*, 18 Pa. Cons. Stat. § 5704; Mass. Gen. Laws Ch. 272, § 99.

charges.[19] If the parties to the communication are located in multiple states, multiple state laws may apply.

Importantly, if a whistleblower has recorded a conversation relating to their allegations, they may be required to disclose the recording (1) pursuant to their obligation to disclose substantially all "material evidence" in their disclosure statement; (2) in response to questions during a government interview; and/or (3) in response to defendant's discovery requests. This disclosure may have serious adverse consequences for the relator if the recording was made illegally. However, concealing or destroying an illegal recording likewise poses extremely serious risks if the fact of the recording comes to light, such as prosecution for obstruction of justice or spoilation of evidence, court sanctions, and, at a minimum, a loss of credibility with the government and the court. These risks weigh heavily in favor of thoroughly researching and counseling a client on the law relating to recorded conversations if the client shows an inclination to gather evidence in this way. Alternatively, prior to the client's making any recordings, counsel might contact law enforcement officials and ask them to authorize and oversee any recording the client might be in a position to make.

Another danger zone arises from documents and information protected by the defendant's or a third-party's attorney-client privilege. Qui tam counsel should take affirmative steps to avoid receiving or reviewing material of this nature and should ensure that neither the whistleblower nor counsel discloses such material to government counsel in writing or in conversation, as doing so could disqualify the government counsel from working on the case. If counsel learns that the defendant's or a third party's attorney-client privilege is potentially implicated in the relator's documents, counsel should consider engaging an independent, third-party law firm to review the documents, segregate the potentially privileged documents, and create a privilege log. Then, the third-party law firm can forward the nonprivileged materials to the whistleblower's qui tam and/or employment counsel.

Counsel will want to advise their clients to be very careful to preserve all evidence they have regarding the case, including privileged information, to avoid the risk of facing a spoliation claim by defendants.[20] The best protection against a spoliation claim is to scrupulously preserve relevant evidence, including—among other things—hardcopies, electronic documents, emails, texts, chat messages, recordings, and personal social media posts. While whistleblowers should be careful to preserve existing social media posts that are relevant to the case, they should

---

19. *See, e.g.*, Mass. Gen. Laws Ch. 272, § 99; Md. Code, Cts. & Jud. Proc. § 10-402.

20. Erhart v. BofI Holding, Inc., No. 15-CV-02287-BAS(NLS), 2016 WL 5110453, at *8 (S.D. Cal. Sept. 21, 2016); Burris v. JPMorgan Chase & Co., 566 F. Supp. 3d 995, 1018 (D. Ariz. 2021) *appeal docketed*, No. 21-16852 (9th Cir. Nov. 3, 2021).

be advised against making future posts about the case. Qui tam counsel may also consider using a third-party vendor to image thumb drives and external drives, laptops, phones, and any other devices that contain relevant discovery.

B. Criminal Exposure

Often whistleblowers learn about fraud on the job, sometimes because they were pressured or coerced into participating in some way. Consequently, some whistleblowers may be wary of bringing a qui tam case for fear of criminal prosecution. It is important to remember that the government is not incentivized to take criminal action against every person involved in a fraud. Doing so would discourage whistleblowing and other forms of cooperation. Nonetheless, whistleblowers who are concerned about criminal exposure should seek the guidance of criminal defense counsel, and qui tam attorneys should encourage their clients to do so. Criminal defense counsel may recommend seeking a "no target letter" or immunity agreement for the whistleblower and may want to represent the whistleblower at interviews with the government. Counsel should advise any whistleblower with significant involvement in the FCA violations that the FCA authorizes a court to reduce the relator share down to zero if the court finds that the relator planned and initiated the violations and requires the court to deny a reward if the relator is convicted of the misconduct.[21]

C. Navigating the Seal

Qui tam cases are filed under seal and remain sealed until the court decides to unseal the case.[22] As a result, the case typically remains a secret from the defendants, sometimes for years, until the court partially or fully unseals the case. During this seal period, the government investigates the allegations in the complaint and determines (1) whether it was already investigating this fraud; and (2) whether to intervene in the action. The seal protects the integrity of the government's investigation and protects the reputation of the defendant while the government is assessing the allegations.

It is important for whistleblowers to assiduously avoid breaching the seal in a qui tam case. Qui tam attorneys should counsel clients on this issue early and often and may wish to include warnings about the seal in the retainer agreement with the client. Putting the government's investigation at risk by violating the seal risks sanctions, including financial penalties, significant reduction in the relator's

21. 31 U.S.C. § 3730(d)(3).
22. *See* 31 U.S.C.A. § 3730(b)(2).

share, and even dismissal of the case.[23] There is some case law, however, holding that the FCA's seal requirement, 31 U.S.C. § 3730(b)(2), prohibits the relator from disclosing only the existence of the qui tam action and does not restrict disclosure of information concerning the alleged fraud.[24]

Protecting the seal can be especially tricky for whistleblowers who continue to work at the defendant after they have filed their qui tam action. The company may initiate an internal investigation and question the whistleblower about the fraud and whether they have reported it. Counsel should help their clients navigate these situations and practice how they will respond to questions in advance. Counsel will also want to strategize in advance about where they will draw the line and instruct their client not to answer. Asking for the government's advice in advance may be advisable.

Complying with the seal may also become challenging for relators involved in other legal matters. For example, the whistleblower may be called to testify under oath in a matter other than the qui tam action and face questioning about any other lawsuits in which they are involved. Or information relating to the qui tam action may be deemed an asset requiring disclosure in the relator's own prenuptial agreement, divorce, or personal bankruptcy, in a civil litigation that has resulted in a judgment against the client, or in a probate proceeding following their death. Counsel may consider seeking a partial seal lift in the qui tam action so that the client can comply with mandates in the other proceeding, while also seeking a protective order from the court overseeing the other proceeding to keep information about the qui tam from becoming public. As noted earlier, it may make sense for counsel to give the government advance notice of the issue and try to coordinate a strategy. Having the government's consent to a motion for partial lifting of the seal will be important.

Finally, if a client seeks litigation funding before a case is filed, the potential funder may expect updates during the seal period. Counsel should carefully research, analyze, and counsel the client on the impact of the seal on the client's ability to comply with such a request.

---

23. While a seal violation does not require the dismissal of a qui tam, courts have discretion to dismiss cases to sanction seal violations by relators. *See* State Farm Fire & Cas. Co. v. United States *ex rel.* Rigsby, 580 U.S. 26, 34 (2016) ("[E]ven if every seal violation does not mandate dismissal, that sanction remains a possible form of relief."); United States *ex rel.* Bibby v. Wells Fargo Home Mortg. Inc., 76 F. Supp. 3d 1399 (N.D. Ga. 2015) (imposing monetary sanctions).

24. *See* United States *ex rel.* Betteroads Asphalt, LLC v. R & F Asphalt Unlimited, Inc., 167 F. Supp. 3d 275, 278 (D.P.R. 2016).

III. Protecting Privilege

A. Risk of Attorney-Client Privilege Waiver

While attorneys will be intimately familiar with the ins and outs of attorney-client privilege, whistleblowers may not have the same level of familiarity. Qui tam counsel should advise whistleblowers early on about the risks of waiving the attorney-client privilege. For example, if a whistleblower insists on including a family member, work colleague, or friend in conversations with her counsel, the whistleblower generally will be deemed to have waived any attorney client privilege protecting those communications, opening the communications up to discovery in the lawsuit. Likewise, if a relator forwards to third parties communications between the relator and counsel, this could waive the privilege and subject those emails to discovery by defendants. Careful counseling at the outset of the representation will help whistleblowers avoid inadvertently waiving attorney-client privilege.

B. Common Interest Privilege

In FCA cases, communications between qui tam counsel and government counsel are typically protected by common interest privilege and, as a result, are not subject to discovery. There are, however, notable exceptions to this presumption. For example, there is a risk that the common interest privilege will not protect communications between the relator and the government prior to the filing of the disclosure statement.[25] There is also a risk that a court will require the production of some or all of the disclosure statement, even though it is attorney work product, if the defendant can successfully argue that it has a compelling need for the materials that outweighs the protection.[26] While the courts sometimes consider the strategic compilation of the facts and evidence in the disclosure statement to be protected opinion work product, discoverable only in rare and extraordinary circumstances, the underlying evidence—often contained in exhibits to the disclosure statement—is likely discoverable on its own. If this evidence is responsive to defendant's document requests, counsel might consider producing it without disclosing that the evidence was incorporated in the disclosure statement.

---

25. *See* United States v. Cameron-Ehlen Grp., Inc., No. 13-CV-3003 (WMW/DTS), 2019 WL 6875354 (D. Minn. Dec. 17, 2019).

26. United States *ex rel.* Bagley v. TRW, Inc., 212 F.R.D. 554, 566 (C.D. Cal. 2003).

IV. Professional and Personal Risks for Relator

Despite the FCA's retaliation protections, professional and personal risk is a fact of life for whistleblowers. While this risk cannot be eliminated completely, careful planning and frank discussions with counsel can be invaluable to a whistleblower embarking on this difficult path.

A. Risks to Career

For some individuals, the potential benefits of a qui tam case may be outweighed by the potential costs. For example, a potential whistleblower who is the sole source of support for a family and employable only within a single, specialized industry may not be willing to risk their job and reputation within that industry. Counsel should make sure to educate a potential whistleblower on the job and career risks of coming forward *before* the client takes that irreversible step. Counsel may wish to advise clients of other reporting avenues that don't pose the same level of risk, such as the Department of Defense Office of Inspector General Hot Line or another government-run, confidential reporting mechanism.

1. Filing Anonymously

If a client wishes to proceed with a qui tam case notwithstanding the potential damage to their financial well-being and career, they may nonetheless be interested in methods to mitigate that risk. One method available to a potential whistleblower who does not intend to proceed with their action in the event of government declination is to create a corporate entity—in a state that doesn't require the public recording of corporate owners or members—to serve as the relator in the case and draft the complaint in a way that does not identify the individual behind the allegations. Another method available to whistleblowers not inclined to proceed with a declined case is to file as a "John Doe" or "Jane Doe" relator.

Clients should be advised, however, that use of these methods will not necessarily prevent disclosure of their identity as the true whistleblower. Defense counsel may be able to discern their identity through analysis and investigation. Moreover, if the matter is settled, the defendants may require that the whistleblower behind the corporate entity or "John Doe" sign the settlement agreement, and a federal or state government in whose name the case was filed may name the whistleblower in their press release on the settlement. Finally, if a government plaintiff intervenes in and litigates the action, the whistleblower's identity inevitably will come out during the discovery process and might even be revealed in the government's complaint-in-intervention.

It should be noted that filing anonymously comes with its own risks. The courts and the government do not always look favorably on anonymous relators, and filing anonymously can raise other thorny legal issues, such as whether the anonymous person was the "first to file" the allegations in the lawsuit.[27]

2. Handling the Unsealing of the Case

Whether they have filed the case in their own name or anonymously, an employed whistleblower facing an imminent lifting of the seal should consider consulting with employment counsel before their employer learns of the qui tam. Employment counsel can advise whistleblowers on whether or how to stay with the company, how to document retaliation, how to respond to inquiries by the company, and how to negotiate severance agreements that protect the whistleblower's rights.

If a relator does not wish to continue working at the defendant following unsealing, they may be well advised to find new employment before the case is unsealed and their identity as a whistleblower is made known (or potentially discerned, if they have filed anonymously). If they do stay on, they may wish to inform their supervisors and colleagues of the unsealed case before they learn about it from the media. So that counsel can improve their odds of being able to alert their client to an imminent unsealing of the case, counsel should maintain regular contact with government counsel to learn about motions to extend the seal and intervention decisions and should research the history of the court with regard to government extension requests. Some district courts are known to grant the government no more than a certain length of time to investigate, and some judges hold the government's feet to the fire more than others. Because it will not always be possible to have advance notice of the unsealing, counsel should also closely monitor the docket so the client can be alerted as promptly as possible about the unsealing order.

B. Risks of Financial Hardship and Health Deterioration

Stepping forward as a whistleblower is a weighty decision. There is a high correlation between the filing of these cases and not only financial hardship but also divorce, mental illness, and other stress-related health problems, particularly for insiders to the fraud.[28] They may face workplace retaliation, ostracization, or gaslighting that makes them second guess their judgment regarding the fraud. They

27. *See, e.g.*, United States *ex rel.* Little v. Triumph Gear Sys., Inc., 870 F.3d 1242 (10th Cir. 2017).

28. As concluded by a New England Journal of Medicine analysis of the experiences of 26 whistleblowers who filed qui tam suits against pharmaceutical manufacturers, including 22 who were insiders to the fraud:

may struggle with guilt and feelings of disloyalty to their company or colleagues for bringing the fraud to light. They may be unable to find new work after being fired or resigning from employment. Compounding these difficulties, while a case is under seal, whistleblowers cannot tap into their normal support networks of family and friends to discuss the case. That makes sensitivity and support in the attorney-client relationship especially important, since an attorney may be the whistleblower's only listening ear.

Prior to filing suit, counsel should engage in an upfront conversation about these risks with the whistleblower. Whistleblowers may want to actively seek new friendships and professional relationships in anticipation of fallout in their existing circles. Counsel may wish to inform their clients about support groups and other resources that nonprofit, public interest groups, and others make available to help whistleblowers navigate the emotional and practical challenges of the experience.[29] In some circumstances, whistleblowers may be well advised to turn to mental health professionals for help. Counsel can inform them about the federal psychotherapist-patient privilege that covers communications with licensed psychiatrists, psychologists, and social workers.[30] Counsel can also reassure them that there is a privilege available in civil cases that protects communications between spouses that are intended to be confidential.

> The experience of being involved in troubling corporate behavior and a qui tam case had substantial and long-lasting effects for nearly all of the insiders, although no similar problems were reported by any of the four outsiders. Eighteen insiders (82%) reported being subjected to various pressures by the company in response to their complaints (Table 3). A common theme was that the decision to blow the whistle had "put their career on the line" (Relator 3). For at least eight insiders, the financial consequences were reportedly devastating. One said, "I just wasn't able to get a job. It went longer and longer. Then I lost — I had a rental house that my kids were [using to go] to school. I had to sell the house. Then I had to sell the personal home that I was in. I had my cars repossessed. I just went — financially I went under. Then once you're financially under? Then no help. Then it really gets difficult. I lost my 401[k]. I lost everything. Absolutely everything" (Relator 17). Financial difficulties often were associated with personal problems. Six relators (all insiders) reported divorces, severe marital strain, or other family conflicts during this time. Thirteen relators reported having stress-related health problems, including shingles, psoriasis, autoimmune disorders, panic attacks, asthma, insomnia, temporomandibular joint disorder, migraine headaches, and generalized anxiety

Aaron S. Kesselheim et al., *Whistle-Blowers' Experiences in Fraud Litigation Against Pharmaceutical Manufacturers*, 362(19) N. Engl. J. Med. 1836 (May 13, 2010).

29. Counsel should take into account and provide appropriate advice on the risks arising from participation in support groups, which include, among others, the client's breach of the court-ordered seal, waiver of the attorney-client privilege, and disclosures about the underlying facts case that turn other members of the group into witnesses and generate evidence that might be used against the relator.

30. Jaffee v. Redmond, 518 U.S. 1, 15 (1996).

TABLE OF CASES